Chefs
of the
Coast

RELATED TITLE BY JOHN E. BATCHELOR
Chefs of the Mountains: Restaurants & Recipes from Western North Carolina

JOHN F. BLAIR, PUBLISHER
WINSTON-SALEM, NORTH CAROLINA

Chefs of the Coast

RESTAURANTS & RECIPES FROM THE NORTH CAROLINA COAST

JOHN E. BATCHELOR

JOHN F. BLAIR,
PUBLISHER
1406 Plaza Drive
Winston-Salem, North Carolina 27103
www.blairpub.com

Library of Congress Cataloging-in-Publication Data

Batchelor, John E.
  Chefs of the coast : restaurants & recipes from the North Carolina coast / by John
E. Batchelor.
      pages   cm
  Includes index.
  ISBN 978-0-89587-639-3 (alk. paper) — ISBN 978-0-89587-640-9 (ebook) 1.
Cooks z North Carolina—Outer Banks—Biography. 2. Cooking—North Caroli-
na—Outer Banks. 3. Cooking (Seafood) 4. Restaurants—North Carolina—Outer
Banks. 5. Outer Banks (N.C.)—Description and travel. I. Title.
  TX649.A1B379 2015
  641.59756'1—dc23
                        2014046971

10 9 8 7 6 5 4 3 2 1

Page ii, clockwise from top left: Bryan Carithers of City Kitchen and Front Street Grill at Stillwater
  in Beaufort; Wes Stepp of Red Sky Café in Duck; Sam McGann of The Blue Point in Duck;
  Fabian Botta of The Ruddy Duck Tavern in Morehead City
Page iii, clockwise from top: Charles Park of Beaufort Grocery Company in Beaufort; Will Canny
  of Café Pamlico at the Inn on Pamlico Sound in Buxton; Gerry Fong of Persimmons Waterfront
  Restaurant in New Bern
Page vi, Herb-Grilled Shrimp with Black-eyed Pea Succotash from The Cedars Inn & Restaurant
  in Beaufort
Page x, Tuna Sashimi from Chilli Peppers Coastal Grill in Kill Devil Hills. Photo by Lori Douglas
  Photography

Cover Image: Shrimp and Scallops with Collard Green-Parmesan Risotto and Garlic Prawn Sauce
from The Cedars Inn & Restaurant in Beaufort. Photo by John E. Batchelor

For more information see:
johnebatchelor.com and johnbatchelordiningandtravel.blogspot.com

Printed in Korea

*For the men and women who farm
the land in North Carolina
and fish the state's waters and the ocean
along the Southern coast—
an endangered species*

The North Carolina Coast

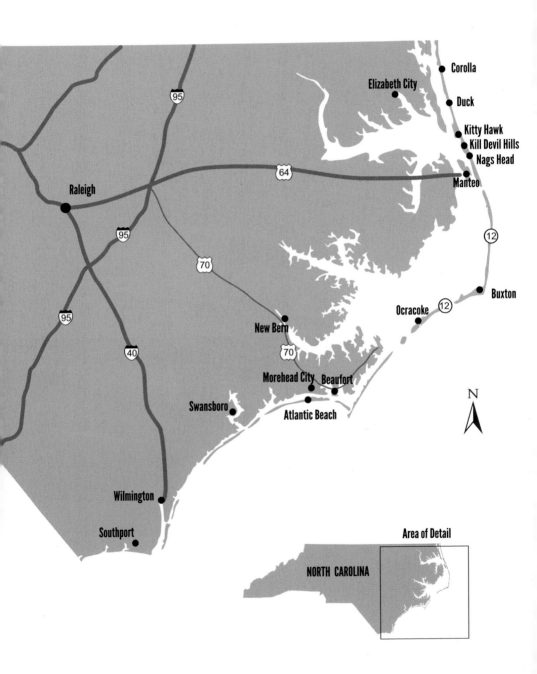

Contents

Preface

Chefs are the new rock stars.

Chefs are artists, contrasting colors and layering flavors. Chefs are chemists, juxtaposing ingredients and combining tastes. Chefs create shadings for the palate.

I admire what chefs do. I envy their knowledge and skills. This book is a tribute to their endeavors, and I thank them for sharing.

When I was researching and writing *Chefs of the Mountains*, this book's predecessor, I had two personal goals in mind. I wanted to cook like a chef on occasion, but avoid having to work as hard as a chef. The idea that other people might share similar goals led to the book.

After I finished, I realized I had written more than a cookbook. It was a travel guide for those occasions when people wanted to visit the mountains but not cook, and it was just a good read, thanks to the interesting personal histories I discovered about the chefs, the paths they followed into professional cooking, and the histories of some of the properties.

Those goals and features continue in *Chefs of the Coast*. Because of the location of these restaurants, many of the recipes are for seafood. That's good from my point of view, because I eat more seafood than any other protein. Chefs provided recipes for pork, beef, chicken, duck, and desserts as well. Most people won't want to eat fish every night.

The chefs themselves are fascinating people. They work long hours well into the night. I'm in bed before they get off work. One commented that he considers reality TV shows about chefs ludicrous, because they never show what it's really like—the amount of time it takes to break down a professional kitchen every night, the meticulousness that goes into cleaning. I've spent time in those kitchens, and I've seen what it takes.

I selected restaurants based on a combination of research, personal acquaintance, and recommendations from others. I wish to express appreciation to friends, friends of friends, readers of my restaurant columns in the *Greensboro News and Record*, and others who helped identify restaurants to be included. The editors at John F. Blair put me in touch with bookstores located on the coast and in port cities, and I sought their recommendations based on local knowledge. Bob Holmes contacted his friend, the eminent cookbook author Jean Anderson (www.jeanandersoncooks.com). She provided a list of her favorites and sent messages to some of her colleagues who had connections to the coast. Fran McCullough (cookbook author and editor and a James Beard Award winner), Patricia Bell (former travel editor of *Gourmet* magazine), Bill Smith (the chef at Crook's Corner in Chapel Hill), and Karl and Lois Taylor (former owners of

The Aerie Bed & Breakfast in New Bern) provided valuable recommendations. Published resources included the Distinguished Restaurants of North America (dirona.com) and North Carolina Department of Agriculture (ncagr.gov) websites, which helped identify restaurants that focus on locally caught seafood and locally grown agricultural products. I also studied the membership list of the Outer Banks Restaurant Association. I am grateful to that organization for inviting me to judge Taste of the Beach (www.obxtasteofthebeach.com), which helped me get acquainted with some restaurants I had not visited before. I also follow Liz Biro (www.lizbiro.com), dining guru of the Wilmington area and the southern coast of North Carolina. Restaurant spies Don King, Emily Ragsdale, and Laurel Maultsby (of *Focus on the Coast* magazine) provided valuable advice as well.

A large proportion of the selections were based on my own writing. I spend quite a bit of time on the coast. I have also been a judge for the Best Dish North Carolina and Fire on the Dock chefs' challenges (www.competitiondining.com).

Information contained in the chef and restaurant profiles came primarily from interviews with chefs, restaurant managers, and owners, research utilizing restaurant websites, plus newspaper and magazine articles about the chefs and restaurants. After I prepared the chef and restaurant profiles, I sent them to chefs, owners, and/or managers for their input and fact checking. I used the same procedure, where relevant, in preparing the sidebars.

Two criticisms of *Chefs of the Mountains* rang true. A few reviewers complained that most of the restaurants featured were fairly expensive. And some readers complained about a few recipes that were too long and complicated, although most were manageable for home cooks. I kept these issues in mind when I selected restaurants for *Chefs of the Coast*, seeking out a reasonable number of mid-priced and inexpensive establishments, in addition to the nicer places. I asked chefs to keep recipes reasonably simple. And when I transcribed their recipes, I tried to ensure that I explained steps that, while routine for chefs, might require more detail for home cooks. I refined those instructions when I test-cooked the recipes. If there was a way to screw it up, I probably found it, so I provided instructions that will help readers avoid similar mistakes. In addition to ingredient lists and cooking instructions, the recipes contain presentation instructions, so you can make the dishes look as well as taste professional. The sidebars will help you locate the same ingredients the chefs use. Special thanks to my wife, Dale Batchelor, for sharing all these meals and checking my writing.

If you are visiting or reside on the North Carolina coast, I hope this book will help you make well-informed decisions about where to go out to eat. If you want to cook at the beach or after you get home, I hope these recipes will represent some of the best of your experiences. And I hope you enjoy reading about a lot of interesting people.

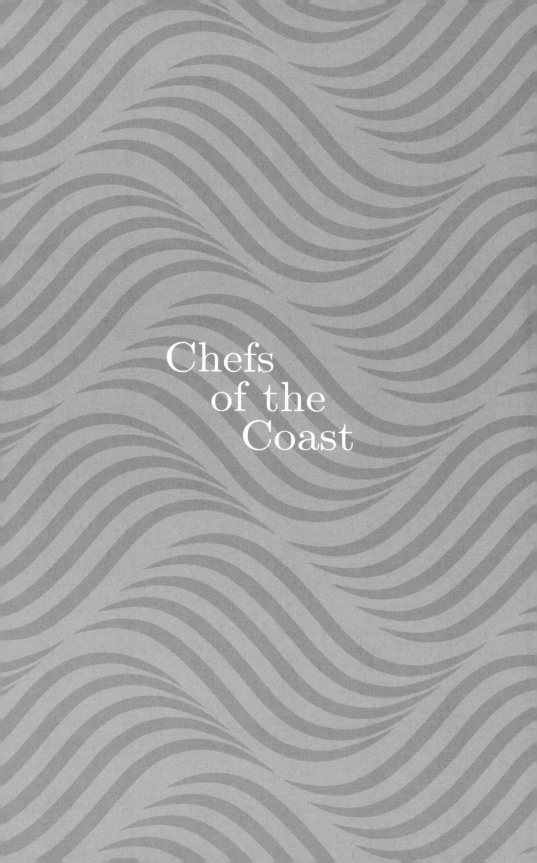

Chefs
of the
Coast

MONTERO'S RESTAURANT, BAR & CATERING

414 North McArthur Street

Elizabeth City, N.C. 27909

252-331-1067

monterosrestaurant.com

Andy and Karin Montero
PHOTO COURTESY OF MONTERO'S

The Chef

Andy Montero

Everybody knows that staying in school is the right thing to do. But for Andy Montero, dropping out proved the better course.

He was born and raised in Chesapeake, Virginia. His father, a surgeon, emigrated from the Philippines. Two of his brothers are also doctors; his other brother is a lawyer. Andy cooked at home while growing up, just for fun. One of his brothers helped him get a job at a local restaurant when he was 15, as a busboy/food runner. From that point, he knew he wanted to spend his life in restaurants. "I loved the environment, the pace, the people," he recalls.

He credits then-owner Patti Patillo and Chef B. J. Jackson at the Court House Café in Chesapeake for teaching him "how to be a good coworker and to enjoy what we do." That restaurant is still in operation after 28 years, and many of

Jackson's other kitchen employees have entered the restaurant business.

After graduating from high school, Andy went to Johnson & Wales in Norfolk. But he dropped out, over the strenuous opposition of his parents, and went to Italy, where he cooked for six months at Frasca Sull'Ambra and La Diga, near Florence. "The craziest thing for me was that there were no inspections or health codes that were enforced. We smoked and drank while working, went to a local store to buy most of our food. I was not allowed to do anything other than wash dishes until I could understand and speak enough Italian to communicate. This took about a month. I called home almost every day during that first month, often begging my parents to send me money for a ticket home. Of course, they wouldn't, since they knew it would get better. And it did. With the help of roommates who had gone through the same thing, I was able to start communicating, and then I was allowed to cook—mostly cold foods to start, later entrées and desserts."

When he came back to the United States, he worked in various food-related jobs for another six months before deciding to return to Johnson & Wales. There, he met Karin Strickland, who became his wife. Reflecting on that period, he observes, "Had I stayed in school, I would have graduated before she enrolled, and we never would have met."

The Monteros moved to Elizabeth City, Karin's home, in 1999. They now live three doors down from her parents in the neighborhood where she grew up. They have three daughters—Emma, Claire, and Anna—all of whom help out in the restaurant. The three are especially proficient at taste-testing cookies.

Chef Montero was proud to be invited back to Johnson & Wales to teach. He was an instructor there for three years, until the university moved to Charlotte. He teaches now as an adjunct instructor at the Culinary Institute of Virginia.

The family eats at the restaurant often. But "just recently, we have changed our eating habits—more fish, less starch," Andy says. "Pizza and taco nights are a big hit. We try to get out at least once a week to provide some support to another local restaurant. Sunday nights are almost always family dinner night with my in-laws—a home-cooked meal and fresh desserts. It's the highlight of my week!"

The Restaurant

Montero's Restaurant, Bar & Catering

Andy Montero started out in Elizabeth City as "the Muffin Man," selling "Texas-sized" muffins door to door at local businesses. He continued for the five years it took to buy and remodel the old home that is now Montero's. Muffins not only provided an income, they created an opportunity to meet hundreds of people and tell them about "what we were doing and letting them taste the quality of the product." In homage to that period, Montero's has always included muffins in its bread baskets. "I still get called 'the Muffin Man' by my old regulars," Andy says. "I am proud to say they are now restaurant regulars!"

Montero's opened in 2005. Andy and Karin try to maintain a sense of family among the restaurant's 45 employees. Many have been working at Montero's for six to eight years, and seven have been with the restaurant since it opened. Of nine cooks, six started at Montero's as dishwashers and moved up through the ranks. Restaurant personnel share a family meal each day and take occasional trips or share a cookout together several times a year.

"I grew up watching my mother and father devote time, energy, and money to the local community, to the medical profession, and to family and countrymen back home. That made a great impression on me, and we try to run our business the same way. We try to stay involved, take responsibility for our community, and help return support to our employees and to the customers who have supported us in our restaurant."

The former home that is now Montero's was built in 1904. "It was not even on the market. The previous owners are now good friends, and they dine with us often. They cried a little the first few times they came in."

The restaurant houses two banquet rooms, one large bar/dining room, and four smaller dining rooms. The two-acre site includes mature shrubs and trees planted by the original owners. The parking lot was previously a horse pasture. Andy and Karin held their wedding ceremony there, three months after they purchased the property.

As far as his culinary style is concerned, Chef Montero remarks, "We always tell people that we specialize in not specializing. I worked for a few chefs that had a well-defined style, and I found that, over time, they often made themselves one-dimensional. We try to use as much local produce as we can throughout the year. Sometimes, that means we are offering greens for three straight weeks. But I think that it means more to our local farmers and customers that the product is local, fresh, and its consumption is not only healthier, it is helping out a neighbor. We buy produce almost exclusively from one local farmer, but we also take advantage of any opportunity to grab fresh goodies from our local market or from other nearby farms."

Andy is involved in community groups such as the Elizabeth City Tourism Board. He and Karin helped establish the SAFE Schools Fund (safeschoolsfund. org); they are, respectively, PTA president and treasurer at Central Elementary, their daughters' school.

Montero's was a finalist in Regis and Kelly's Hometown Grill-Off Contest in

2009. The restaurant has also received awards for its work with the local school system and has been named Business of the Year twice by the local chamber of commerce.

The Recipes

Shrimp with Andouille Sausage over Grits
Serves 4

Grits
3 cups grits
6 cups water or stock (chicken stock provides extra flavor)
2 cups shredded smoked Gouda cheese (or other cheese)

Prepare grits according to package instructions up to 1 hour in advance. If you cook them in advance, it may be necessary to thin them with more stock or water prior to plating. Stir cheese into hot grits just before serving.

Shrimp with Andouille Sausage
2 tablespoons vegetable oil
½ pound Andouille sausage, sliced in half and cut into ¼-inch half-moon slices
1½ pounds large shrimp, peeled and deveined
kosher salt and pepper to taste
¼ cup yellow onion, diced small
1 tablespoon minced garlic
2 cups sliced mushrooms
1 cup roasted red peppers, chopped rough (you can buy roasted red peppers, sometimes called pimentos, or roast your own and peel away the charred skin)
½ cup dry white wine
1¼ cups shrimp or vegetable stock
3 tablespoons unsalted butter, cut into cubes

Using a large nonstick skillet over medium-high heat, add oil and sear sausage, creating a nice crispy texture on the pieces. (Determine from package if sausage has been precooked. Cook according to package directions if not.) Season shrimp with salt and pepper. Add shrimp to hot pan and sauté until slightly pink but not cooked through. Add

Shrimp with Andouille Sausage over Grits
PHOTO COURTESY OF MONTERO'S

onions and garlic and cook for 1 minute. Add mushrooms and peppers and cook for 1 to 2 minutes until mushrooms start to soften. Deglaze with wine and reduce by ½. Add stock and simmer for 1 to 2 minutes until reduced by ¼. Remove from heat. Using a wooden spoon or a coated whisk, stir in butter cubes to incorporate. Remove shrimp from sauce and hold in a 150-degree oven.

PRESENTATION

Portion grits into bowls, heaping them into the center. Spoon sauce onto grits, distributing vegetables and liquid evenly. Divide shrimp into equal portions and place atop grits in a circular fashion for a nicer presentation, or just pile on top for a more casual look.

Gingered Salmon
Serves 4

4 4-ounce fresh salmon fillets
kosher salt and pepper to taste
2 tablespoons vegetable oil
2 teaspoons minced ginger
1 teaspoon minced garlic
¼ cup yellow onion, diced small

Gingered Salmon

1 cup sliced wild mushrooms
½ cup dry white wine
1 cup vegetable stock
¾ pound asparagus
3 tablespoons unsalted butter, cut into cubes

Lightly season fillets on all sides with salt and pepper. Using a large nonstick skillet over medium high-heat, add oil and sear fillets to an internal temperature of 145 to 150 degrees, yielding a slightly opaque center. Remove fillets from pan and hold in a 150-degree oven. In the same skillet over medium-high heat, add ginger, garlic, and onions and sauté until onions are slightly translucent. Add mushrooms and cook about 2 minutes until they begin to soften. Deglaze with wine and reduce by ½. Add stock and simmer for 2 to 3 minutes. Blanch asparagus by immersing in salted, boiling water for 30 to 90 seconds, depending on size and density; remove and submerge in ice water. Add asparagus to skillet, heat through, and remove from heat. Using a wooden spoon or a coated whisk, stir in cubes of butter to incorporate.

PRESENTATION

Place salmon on plates along with your favorite starch and vegetable. Remove asparagus from pan and place atop fillets. Spoon sauce on top of asparagus and salmon.

PREPARATION GUIDELINES

SEAFOOD PREPARATION

SCALLOPS   Rinse, repeatedly if necessary, to remove grit. Dry carefully with paper towels and let scallops sit on a paper towel, turning at least once, to remove moisture. If scallops are not completely dry, they will not brown properly. Remove the "foot"—the membrane that attaches scallop to shell. It is whiter, it looks different, and it is tough to the touch (and seriously tough to the bite!).

SHRIMP   Buy either large or jumbo shrimp that have been shelled and deveined. This costs a little more but is well worth the time it takes to shell and devein them yourself. Do not overcook shrimp. For the simplest preparation, lightly coat with olive oil (maybe lemon-infused), sauté or grill for 2 to 3 minutes per side, then check for doneness. Or bake at 400 degrees for 6 to 8 minutes. I consider boiling shrimp the least satisfactory way to cook them. But if you want strong flavor, albeit flavor mainly from the seasonings, use the recipe on the Old Bay container. Bring seasoned water mixture to a boil, remove from heat, then add shrimp. Do not return to heat. Let shrimp remain in hot water for 6 to 8 minutes.

CRABMEAT   Buy jumbo lump or lump crabmeat. The extra expense will pay off in flavor. Pick through the crabmeat to remove any shell fragments.

SHELLFISH   Always discard any shellfish that do not open when steamed.

PREPARATION PROTOCOLS

When adding hot ingredients to a blender, be careful. Add a little at a time, and do not fill close to the brim. Hold the lid down when you turn the blender on. Hot liquids will expand quickly, blowing off the top. My wife is still finding remnants in crevices along the ceiling from a recipe I prepared five years ago.

If a recipe calls for wine, use a wine that is good enough to drink. Never use so-called cooking wine. If the wine does not taste good when you sip it, whatever you make with it will not taste good either. French Chablis and American Chardonnay are interchangeable as ingredients in these recipes; use whichever you prefer. In general, red-wine blends yield better flavor in cooking than do single varietals. Wines for cooking do not have to be expensive. Consider, for example, Kirkland (the Costco house brand), Rex Goliath, Twisted, or numerous wines that come in boxes but have decent taste.

Unless a recipe specifies salted butter, use unsalted.

COOKING PROTOCOLS

OVEN TEMPERATURES   All temperatures in this book are in Fahrenheit. Preheat oven according to directions.

SAUTEEING OR FRYING   Do not crowd the pan. Leave at least 1 inch be-tween items.

GRILLING   Clean the grill with an oiled cloth before heating. In most cas-es, preheating the grill to high, then reducing the heat to medium as soon as you put on the fish, other seafood, pork, or beef will produce the best results, crusting the exterior without overcooking the interior. For meats, turn when the internal temperature reaches 100 degrees. For fish, turn at 90 degrees after checking the grilled side to make sure it is crusted prop-erly. Leave service side on heat longer, if necessary to develop crust.

METROPOLIS

520 Old Stoney Road

Corolla, N.C. 27927

252-453-6167

metropolisobx.com

Mark Anthony
PHOTO COURTESY OF METROPOLIS

The Chef

Mark Anthony

"Tons of cute girls and lots of good tips." That was all Mark Anthony needed to hear.

His best friend from high school was already living on the Outer Banks, managing a restaurant named Miriam's. He offered Mark a job as a waiter. Mark had just graduated from college and already had experience waiting tables, so he relocated from his home in Pittsburgh, Pennsylvania, in 1996. Mark describes the Outer Bank scene at the time: "The parking lots were all sand, and the wild horses had yet to be penned in, up north, past the end of Route 12. I fell in love with the lazy, rural beach vibe of Corolla."

After several years at Miriam's, Mark jumped at the opportunity to buy a half interest in Nicoletta's, a "cash-poor" Italian restaurant. "I, along with my girlfriend at the time, ran the front of the house. I learned my first managerial skills there and developed a fairly refined wine palate. Our partner was

Heather McDonald, a chef who had gone to culinary school. She did not have enough help in the kitchen, so I started assisting with prep. I would do *garde-manger* work, taking down Roma tomatoes, peppers, onions, and such. After a couple of years, I developed pretty good knife skills. I enjoyed working with a blade and would always try to cut things faster and more precisely. I liked the exhilarating feeling of being deep in the prep weeds as dinner service approached and the feeling of accomplishment once all the ponies had been ridden.

"I enjoyed the loud music, foul language, pranks, as well as the honest, hard work that I found in the kitchen. I would prep five or six days a week and then at 5 P.M. move into the dining room, where I would wait tables and help customers choose what were, in the late '90s, unfamiliar Italian wines. We received a *Wine Spectator* Award of Excellence for an exclusively Italian wine list each year after I came on board." At that point, Mark had been a waiter in upscale restaurants for 10 years.

"About this time, I made my first soup for service. It was cream of mushroom. I didn't hold back on the butter and cream, and I took my time thickening it. The result was like velvet, deeply flavored. The soup was good, but even better was the reaction from customers when they learned that I had made it. There was an instant, engaged connection, as if they felt I had made this soup just for them. I had no idea how important this soup would be, laying the foundation for the next chapter of my career.

"I continued making soups at Nicoletta's for the rest of my time there, seven years. I got better at creating depth of flavor, understanding ingredients and their potential. More importantly, I got better at talking about the soup when I was out front.

"We sold Nicoletta's, and I spent the next few years working for Mike Dianna, a friend who owns Mike Dianna's Grill Room. Matt Kristof was manager. My wine experience and knowledge grew as I managed the wine program there. With almost unlimited buying power, I became exposed to the real heavy hitters of California, France, and Australia."

Mark took a job as chef at a new restaurant, but it closed. He followed Matt Kristof to Metropolis, which Matt was managing by then. "We ran Metropolis for two years. At that point, it was considered mostly a bar, but we saw potential to become a real restaurant. The location was perfect, situated between two of the most affluent communities in Corolla. So we bought Metropolis in July 2007, and I took over the kitchen. Our food in those early years was much simpler. With no formal training, I did not know enough to create more complex dishes. What I did know was that having the chef out in the dining room, explaining the specials during dinner service, created a strong connection with customers. Tapas was just emerging, and having the chef as a guide in this new dining style set wary customers at ease. It was time to raise the bar."

The Restaurant

Metropolis

Mark continues his narration: "What we needed was more culinary firepower. We brought in 'Chopper,' a young chef we had worked with at Mike Dianna's. One name is all he needs. Slight and wiry, he communicates very well and is amazingly consistent. A graduate of Johnson & Wales in Charlotte, he provided me with knowledge that I was lacking. 'Little Ann' was the next piece of the puzzle. I had worked for her at Miriam's. She had experience in New York with Larry Forgione early in her career. But she had been in a terrible car accident that resulted in the closing of her restaurant. We had stayed in touch, and she was a customer at Metropolis in the early days. Ann talked to us about making desserts. Then she started doing more. Now, she also manages ordering and inventory, freeing me up to be creative. She is an organizational genius and one of my dearest friends.

"At this point, we had the team necessary to take the food up several notches. We started bringing in more exciting ingredients—wild Alaskan halibut, Columbia River king salmon, mushrooms from the Pacific Northwest, fresh truffles from Italy, France, and Oregon, boar, pork belly, and the king of proteins, foie gras. As a smallish restaurant in a seasonal resort town, it is absurd how much duck liver we sell. You know why? Because the chef just explained how he conceptualized the dish and how the acidity of the fried green tomato is a perfect foil to the richness of the foie gras.

"Seasonality and locality of produce now dictate what we do—fiddlehead ferns and wild ramps in early spring, local strawberries, followed by asparagus, which we call 'green gold.' I live among the farms on the mainland, and I have developed a particular relationship with a local farmer, Terri Sawyer at the Farm Market. I stop at her farm on the way to work, and she takes me out back and gives me stuff she picked that morning. We serve soup that is made within six hours after the asparagus comes out of the ground.

"Soup is still the cornerstone of our platform. In asparagus season, I'll make 80 quarts of soup a week. Asparagus season gives way to local watermelon, corn, and tomatoes. You know fall has arrived when collards are for sale on the side of the road. We are so lucky to live in a place of such beauty and have access to such amazing local produce and seafood.

"When conceptualizing dishes for the restaurant, I look to achieve balance in color, texture, and flavor. If it makes sense in my head, it usually resonates with customers. In the seven years since becoming chef of Metropolis, we have won and placed in a variety of local cooking competitions, and we have cultivated a loyal crowd of supportive followers."

The Recipes

Cream of Asparagus Soup with Hot Buttered Blue Crab, White Truffle Oil, and Garlic Breadcrumbs

Serves 6

Garlic Breadcrumbs
2 tablespoons extra-virgin olive oil
1 clove garlic, minced
½ cup panko breadcrumbs
kosher salt to taste

Heat olive oil on low temperature. Slowly sauté garlic until golden brown. Add breadcrumbs and stir until they are uniformly mixed into the oil and garlic. Sauté on low until breadcrumbs are golden brown, stirring often. Season with salt.

Soup
1½ pounds fresh asparagus
4 tablespoons unsalted butter, divided
2 tablespoons kosher salt
¼ cup all-purpose flour
3 cups light chicken stock
1 cup heavy cream
6 ounces fresh blue crabmeat
6 sprinkles of white truffle oil

Cut asparagus where solid green fades; discard ends. Cut asparagus into 1-inch pieces. In a medium pot, melt 2 tablespoons of the butter on low temperature. Add asparagus and salt, cover, and cook until asparagus is tender and has released its juice. Remove from heat, add flour,

Cream of Asparagus Soup with Hot Buttered Blue Crab, White Truffle Oil, and Garlic Breadcrumbs

PHOTO COURTESY OF METROPOLIS

and stir until well incorporated. Add stock and cream and cook on low until thickened. Blend until smooth, then pass through a fine strainer, discarding any fibrous mash. Return to low heat until plating.

PRESENTATION

Melt remaining 2 tablespoons butter on low. Add crabmeat and toss gently until warm. Season with kosher salt. Place 1 ounce hot buttered crabmeat in center of a shallow bowl and surround with hot asparagus cream. Top crabmeat with Garlic Breadcrumbs and drizzle soup with white truffle oil. Repeat for 5 remaining servings.

Tartare of Pepper-Crusted Yellowfin Tuna with Whole-Grain Mustard and Applewood Bacon Aioli, Chives, and Pumpernickel Toast

Serves 4

½ pound sashimi-grade yellowfin tuna
kosher salt to taste
2 tablespoons freshly ground pepper
1 tablespoon vegetable oil
2 tablespoons Hellmann's mayonnaise

Tartare of Pepper-Crusted Yellowfin Tuna with Whole-Grain Mustard and Applewood Bacon Aioli, Chives, and Pumpernickel Toast
Photo courtesy of Metropolis

1 tablespoon whole-grain mustard
1 teaspoon applewood bacon fat, rendered and strained, room temperature
1 tablespoon chopped fresh chives
4 slices dark pumpernickel bread
1 tablespoon extra-virgin olive oil

Dry tuna thoroughly on paper towels. Apply salt and then pepper to both sides. Heat oil in a flat pan and sear tuna for 10 seconds on each side. Move tuna onto paper towels and into refrigerator to cool. In a small bowl, mix mayonnaise, mustard, bacon fat, and chives. Cut pumpernickel slices into triangles and drizzle with olive oil and salt. Toast on a baking sheet in a 250-degree oven until crunchy. Remove tuna from refrigerator and cut into ¼-inch cubes. Toss tuna with mayonnaise mixture in a bowl. Fill four 8-ounce ramekins with tuna and mayonnaise mixture. Invert and tap on plates to release.

PRESENTATION
Serve with pumpernickel toast on the side.

THE
BLUE POINT

1240 Duck Road

Duck, N.C. 27949

252-261-8090

thebluepoint.com

Chef Sam McGann
PHOTO PROVIDED BY
THE BLUE POINT

The Chef

Sam McGann

Sam McGann has always considered himself a gentleman. His mother, of the "First Families of Virginia," taught him Southern values and traditions that centered on good manners. "The table meant a lot to our family," Sam says. "She entertained quite a bit. We spent a lot of time at the beach, we trapped crabs, and I learned to pick crabs. We ate fried trout, spoon bread, watermelon, cantaloupe, Virginia ham, oysters, soft-shell crabs—all those things we were proud of locally then, that are now front and center in the culinary world. So my work as a chef grows out of that sense of heritage. I did not grow up hunting, I was more a city kid, but we did a lot of fishing—flounder, spots, and other saltwater fish."

Although art was his first love, Sam graduated from Lynchburg College with a degree in business, deciding it would provide him a better way to make a living. He played lacrosse and was involved in other athletics, which helped him develop a work ethic and understand teamwork. "If you play team sports as a kid, you understand the value of working together. I try to manage my kitchen that way."

He spent some time in a Norfolk restaurant bartending, waiting tables, doing some cooking, and serving as a management intern. Then he went off to see the world, traveling with friends on Eurail passes, following *Frommer's Europe on $35 a Day*. "We learned a lot of culture and history, and I became especially interested in foodways. We traveled in Italy, France, Britain, Greece, and Germany, experiencing local food in each country. I came back with a much different point of view. I learned how to navigate and speak a little of the languages and dine like the locals."

When he returned to Virginia, he answered an ad for a restaurant in Williamsburg, The Trellis. "It was a new style restaurant for the U.S., with a wood-fired grill, following a credo of 'New American' styles. They eschewed some of the classical sauces in favor of quick sauté, using higher temperatures, lots of nuts and vegetables." There, he spent almost two years under the tutelage of Marcel Desaulnier, a James Beard Award winner. "I was so impressed with the passion and pride and professionalism of the operation. The experience caused me to consider culinary school."

Sam was admitted to the two-year associate's program at Johnson & Wales in Providence, Rhode Island. He completed the entire program in only one year. When he had free time, he went to the ethnic neighborhoods in Providence, where markets offered food he had rarely experienced before, Italian and Portuguese especially.

He subsequently worked with a close friend, Todd Jurich, at Crawdaddy's in Virginia Beach, emulating the style of Louisiana chefs such as Paul Prudhomme, making jambalaya, gumbo, and étouffée and "having a wonderful time." Todd later opened Todd Jurich's Bistro. "We paid great attention to food coordinated with wine, and attentive service," Sam recalls.

The Restaurant

The Blue Point

The Blue Point overlooks Currituck Sound from the Waterfront Shops in Duck. Partners John Power and Chef Sam McGann consider it "the original Outer Banks farm-to-table restaurant." It has always maintained a focus on Southern cooking. Over the years, the kitchen's techniques have expanded to include brining, curing, pickling, smoking, and sausage making. The interior, elegant but not formal or stuffy, offers expansive views of the water.

Blue Point had its origins in a storm. John Power, a high-school friend and compatriot in the Norfolk–Virginia Beach restaurant scene, invited Sam to the Power family's cottage in Duck to look at a potential restaurant space. As gale-force winds blew across Currituck Sound and sleet began to fall, Sam tried to convince John that "he was nuts." But the next day, the skies cleared, the temperature climbed into the 60s, and Sam's perception grew brighter as well. A partnership was born, and The Blue Point opened with 50 seats and an oyster bar six months later, on July 15, 1989. The restaurant, with Sam at the stove and John at the front door, took off right away. The Blue Point became not only a destination for visitors but a favorite among locals.

While The Blue Point was always too small to accommodate everyone who wanted a seat, after 15 years, it was beyond its breaking point. Over the winter of 2006–7, John and Sam renovated and reinvented the restaurant in the same location, adding 2,000 square feet to the existing building. In 2013, they added an outdoor deck and bar by the water.

Chef McGann describes the food: "We cook everything from scratch. That is always a challenge on the beach, but we are determined to stick to it. We're open year-round. Business can go from 300 a week in winter to 3,000 a week in summer. But we still bake our own breads, make ice creams, sherbets, sorbets, jams, and jellies, as well as crackers and pickles. We brine and smoke pork chops, butts, and briskets, we make our own tasso ham, and we do it all within Southern traditions."

He travels extensively, constantly broadening his culinary horizons. He has studied at the Oriental Thai Cooking School in Bangkok, Thailand; the Perrier Jouet House in Champagne, France; and the Inn at Blackberry Farm in Walland, Tennessee.

Maintaining connections with local farms and seafood providers "takes an effort on both sides," Chef McGann observes. "We have to maintain a constant working relationship with farmers and fishermen, and they have to commit as much of their product as they can to us. It's an annual commitment, based on personal relationships. We get produce from Colin and Allie Grandy's farm in the town of Grandy. We serve peaches, cantaloupes, and watermelons in the restaurant within two days of picking. We also work with a family in Camden— Poor Boys Produce, run by Hunter and Susan Harris. We get crabs from Jay Ross in Stumpy Point on Pamlico Sound. A lot of fishing boats dock in Engelhard, and we get jumbo lump crabmeat, shrimp, and fish from them.

Sam's Facebook page features a chalkboard of current local providers. The restaurant also uses Sunburst Trout Farm in the North Carolina mountains (see the sidebar about Sunburst in *Chefs of the Mountains*), Anson Mills heirloom grains from South Carolina (www.ansonmills.com), Byrd Mill cornmeal grits from Virginia, S. Wallace Edwards & Sons country hams and sausage, and Benton's Smoky Mountains Country Hams cured bacon and ham from Tennessee.

Chef McGann is a James Beard Foundation member; he cooked at the James Beard House in May 1998. He is a supporter of the Southern Foodways Alliance and Outer Banks Catch. He gave the alumni address at the Johnson & Wales graduation in 2013, and a scholarship in his name supports a student from northeastern North Carolina or Tidewater Virginia every year.

Blue Point has been cited as one of the Outer Banks' most sophisticated restaurants by diverse publications including *Garden & Gun, Palate, Southern Living,* and *Gourmet* magazines.

The Recipes

She Crab "A la Minute"

Serves 6 to 8

CHEF'S NOTE "We are very fortunate to be in the crab capital of the world! I honestly believe that our Carolina blue crabs, in this case from Colington Island on Currituck Sound, to be the sweetest and firmest crabmeat that the Good Lord has blessed us with anywhere."

1 quart heavy cream
2 cups half-and-half
2 teaspoons Tabasco sauce
2 teaspoons Worcestershire sauce
¼ cup dry sherry, preferably Spanish
1 teaspoon kosher salt
½ cup fresh herbs (parsley, dill, tarragon, chervil), chopped coarse
female crab roe, if available
1 pound local jumbo lump blue crabmeat
¼ cup chives, cut gently
sprinkle of Old Bay seasoning for each serving

In a 2-quart heavy-bottomed pot, add cream, half-and-half, Tabasco, Worcestershire, and sherry. Bring to a simmer and cook for 1 to 2 min-

She Crab "A la Minute"
PHOTO BY CHEF SAM MCGANN

utes. Add salt. Taste and adjust. Add herbs and stir. Taste. Turn heat to very low. Add crabmeat and stir gently. Bring to a simmer. Remove from heat and add roe.

PRESENTATION

Divide soup evenly among warm soup bowls and garnish with chives and a good sprinkle of Old Bay.

Blue Point Pound Cake

Yields 1 cake

2 sticks salted butter, softened (Plugrá or similar recommended)
1 stick margarine, softened
3 cups sugar
5 large eggs
3 cups King Arthur unbleached cake flour
1½ teaspoons baking powder
½ teaspoon sea salt
1 cup half-and-half

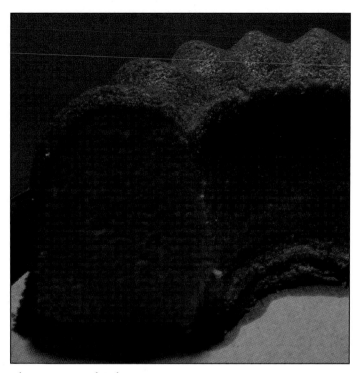

Blue Point Pound Cake
PHOTO PROVIDED BY THE BLUE POINT

1 teaspoon vanilla
1 teaspoon mace

Preheat oven to 350 degrees. Cream butter and margarine until light. Add sugar and cream. Add eggs 1 at a time, beating well after each. Sift flour, baking powder, and salt and add alternately with half-and-half and vanilla. Add mace. Bake in a greased and floured tube pan for 1 hour to 1 hour and 15 minutes until cake pulls away from side of pan; check after 1 hour. Cool 10 minutes and release from pan. Store covered at room temperature. Note: A heavier pan will cook cake faster and produce a deeper brown color on the exterior. This cake gets better after the first day and lasts about a week on a covered cake stand.

PRESENTATION
Serve slightly warmed with dollops of fresh whipped cream and seasonal fruit.

HOW TO FIND LOCAL SEAFOOD AND AGRICULTURAL PRODUCTS

This book includes sidebars on several seafood retailers, selected according to location, chef recommendation, and author familiarity. Use these sidebars to identify seafood markets located near you. When you read chef and restaurant profiles, note the markets the chefs use. Consider these as well. Some grocers set aside sections devoted to local produce.

The North Carolina Department of Agriculture and Consumer Services helps consumers identify seafood and agricultural products caught, grown, raised, and/or made in North Carolina and promotes their consumption. Use the websites described below to locate sources near you.

North Carolina Farm Fresh (ncfarmfresh.com/farmmarkets.asp) provides a directory of farms, farmers' markets, nurseries, and roadside stands that sell directly to consumers.

Got to Be NC Agriculture (gottobenc.com/find-nc-products) provides links to several search engines showing roadside vegetable stands, farmers' markets, seafood, aquaculture, and restaurants that focus on local ingredients. Savor NC, part of the "Got to Be NC" initiative, connects restaurants with farmers and identifies produce that chefs need.

Got to Be NC Seafood (gottobenc.com/find-nc-products/seafood-directory) and NC Catch (nccatch.org) are devoted to providing information about seafood caught or farmed in North Carolina, and to supporting the men and women engaged in seafood enterprises. NC Catch is subdivided into four divisions according to geography: Outer Banks Catch, Ocracoke Fresh, Carteret Catch, and Brunswick Catch. They educate the public about the importance of buying local seafood, including issues related to quality, freshness, health benefits, supporting local economies, continuing the state's commercial fishing heritage, and tourism. Look for the Outer Banks Catch, Ocracoke Fresh, Carteret Catch, and Brunswick Catch logos in restaurants and markets.

THE PAPER CANOE

1564 Duck Road

Duck, N.C. 27927

252-715-2220

papercanoeoobx.com

Marc Jean Berruet

PHOTO PROVIDED BY
MARC JEAN BERRUET

The Chef

Marc Jean Berruet

Marc Jean Berruet has quite a culinary pedigree. But he barely survived his apprenticeship.

He was born in Verdun, France, the son of a true French chef. When he was three, the family moved to Nantucket Island, Massachusetts, when his father became personal chef to Earl McAusland, owner/editor of *Gourmet* magazine. The Berruet family owned the Chanticleer restaurant on Nantucket for 38 years. During that time, the restaurant resided on many lists of the world's best. While growing up, Marc Jean returned to France every summer, where he stayed with his grandparents in the Loire Valley.

He recalls his early years on Nantucket: "When I was a young boy, the restaurant, especially the kitchen, became my domain, my playground, day care, babysitter, and best friend all in one. My father would set wooden wine crates upside down so I could reach the counter and have me chop parsley for hours—literally hours, because I was so slow and there was so much damn parsley. But he would kick my ass and tell me to move faster, and now I can chop parsley really fast!" By age 12, he was already cooking at a professional level.

"I knew the professional food industry was my path. That led me back to France for an apprenticeship, which, ironically, or maybe due to destiny, was at the same restaurant where my father had done his apprenticeship in the 1950s for the same chef/proprietor, Charles Barrier at Restaurant Charles Barrier in Tours, France, which Michelin awarded three stars. My father was an influential mentor. He is a master, a classically trained chef who has been leading kitchens for 60 years. My experiences staging in France laid the foundation of my skill set."

For formal schooling, Marc Jean attended the Fondation Escoffier culinary institute in Paris and Ecole Lenôtre in Versailles. He apprenticed at Le Lion d'Or in Ingrandes, France.

He describes the near-fatal accident he suffered during this time: "The building was old—not worn down but authentic, vintage old! Every morning, the apprentices had to walk about a mile to the coal room to get coal. We each lugged back several pounds of coal, where it was stacked and ignited in order to fire the oven and stovetop. The entire cooking line had a gravity-fed coal bin. There was a Frialator on the line that was the restaurant's only piece of electrical equipment—no convection ovens, no rotisseries, no mixers or blenders. The Frialator had cloth wires on the back that were somewhat frayed. One day, I grabbed a skimmer that was hanging from a copper water pipe. At one point, the pipe had been painted, but over the years the paint had been chipped off. When I grabbed the metal handle and went to pull the fry basket up at the same time, I was frozen in place. The chef had to hit me across the chest with a wooden stockpot paddle to free me. The inside of my entire forearm was blackened, burned from the inside out. The doctor told me that in a few more seconds I would have been killed. I was 14 years old at the time, living above the kitchen, working for room and board."

After his time as an apprentice, he cooked on the line at Le Toit de Passy in Paris, which also received three stars from Michelin.

Marc Jean moved to the Outer Banks in 2004, after his family sold the Chanticleer. "I enjoy living on the coast of eastern North Carolina for many reasons, one of which is the abundance of local resources, from land to sea. Being an avid fisherman, I find the sport to be world-class for certain species at the proper time of the year. I also love the beauty of the geography and terrain. The sense of community resonates with me. Despite the elongated landmass size, the Outer Banks has a small-town feel. Raising two boys of my own has created a great sense of comfort and security."

Chef Berruet owned The Pearl in Kill Devil Hills, then moved to Florida, where he owned L'Etoile Restaurant in Naples. But the Outer Banks lured him back. His career as a chef spans over 30 years.

At home, he will eat "anything that is honest," except for peanut butter. "Can't stand that stuff," he remarks. "Although seafood is my specialty and typically my favorite thing to eat, all food is fun, and I love to try new things and create new dishes. I love to use the grill at home."

Apart from cooking, Chef Berruet is an artist. He paints, sculpts, and carves duck decoys.

The Restaurant

The Paper Canoe

Tommy Karole, a UNC-Greensboro graduate, is originally from Ridgewood, New Jersey. He came to the Outer Banks for the first time in 1977 with a college buddy, then was lured back often by what he terms "this special place." In 1996, he opened his first restaurant, in Corolla. He has owned, operated, or consulted on eight restaurants. He learned about seafood when he worked as a fish grader in Kodiak, Alaska.

Karole is a big fan of the Grateful Dead. The group's song "Cosmic Charlie" refers to a paper canoe. Karole was trying to come up with a name for his new restaurant, so he Googled "paper canoe" and discovered *The Voyage of the Paper Canoe* by the intrepid explorer Nathaniel Bishop, about a journey in the 1870s from Quebec to Key West in a vessel of that description. Bishop touched shore along Currituck Sound right where the restaurant is located. The restaurant with the iconic name opened in 2011.

One of Chef Berruet's former employees introduced him to Tommy Karole. Berruet became executive chef at The Paper Canoe in 2013. The restaurant is casual, with a warm, friendly, inviting atmosphere. Its view of Currituck Sound is special.

Chef Berruet describes the food as "classic French cuisine with a creative twist. I like to use the best-quality ingredients, fresh, and keep it simple. Utilize quality ingredients from the beginning, because you can't make chicken soup from chicken shit."

One distinguishing feature of the kitchen is the wood-fired oven, used to bake pizzas, bread, desserts, duck, and some clay-pot specialties. Chef Berruet has established a network of local farmers and seafood providers who visit regularly.

The Recipe

Grilled Marinated Duck Breast Alexandre Dumas

Serves 4

CHEF'S NOTE "This recipe is from Alexandre Dumas, author of *The Three Musketeers* and *The Count of Monte Cristo*. Two sauce recipes are provided. Use whichever appeals to you. This recipe is intended for breast of duck only. If you have difficulty finding deboned duck breast, you may have to purchase a whole duck and remove the breast. You can always create another dish or meal with the legs and use the carcass for soup or stock. D'Artagnan [dartagnan.com] sells great duck products."

Duck Breast Marinade and Reduction Sauce

4 8- to 10-ounce duck breasts, deboned, skin on
2 bottles Cabernet or other red wine
pinch of nutmeg
⅛ teaspoon cumin
⅛ teaspoon coriander
½ teaspoon Herbes de Provence, ground fine
¼ teaspoon cinnamon
1 tablespoon black peppercorns in a sachet or cheesecloth
½ cup honey (orange clover blossom recommended)
⅛ teaspoon ginger
zest and juice of 1 lemon
zest and juice of 2 oranges
4 to 6 sprigs fresh thyme
4 cloves garlic, peeled and crushed
3 large shallots, peeled and julienned
2 laurel bay leaves
6 to 8 sprigs fresh parsley
2 tablespoons extra-virgin olive oil
¼ teaspoon sea salt
1 to 2 tablespoons butter
1 quart veal stock (chicken or duck stock may be substituted, but veal stock will give better results; it can be ordered online)
ground white pepper

Duck Breast Marinade and Reduction Sauce
PHOTO PROVIDED BY THE PAPER CANOE

Combine all ingredients except stock and pepper in a bowl and marinate duck for 12 hours. Remove duck from marinade. Reserve marinade to make sauce. Place duck in refrigerator until ready for cooking.

To make Reduction Sauce, strain marinade through a fine sieve into a thick-bottomed saucepan. Place on stove and bring to a boil. Reduce heat and simmer until reduced by ½; skim surface often, removing and discarding foam and other impurities. If using veal stock, add an amount equal to the reduced marinade (approximately 1 quart). If using chicken stock or duck stock, add 1½ times the volume. Bring combined liquids back to a boil, reduce heat to a simmer, and slowly reduce until sauce becomes viscous enough to coat the back of a spoon. The reduction process will require 1 hour or more of low and slow cooking. The goal is reduction (a concentration and intensifying of flavors), not evaporation (losing all the goodness into the atmosphere in the form of steam). Season to taste with sea salt and ground white pepper, plus a small amount of butter to finish and give a nice sheen to the sauce.

Roasted Red Bell Pepper Coulis

1 tablespoon olive oil
2 shallots, chopped small
2 sprigs fresh thyme, chopped
3 roasted red bell peppers (canned or store-bought will work), chopped small
1 cup Chablis or Chardonnay
½ cup chicken stock
1 cup heavy cream or whipping cream
½ tablespoon chopped garlic

1 teaspoon ground Herbes de Provence
salt and pepper to taste
2 drops lemon juice

In a heavy-bottomed saucepan, heat olive oil on medium heat. Sweat shallots and thyme until lightly browned. Add bell peppers, sweat for 5 minutes more, and add wine, stock, cream, garlic, and Herbes de Provence. Bring to a boil and simmer for 20 to 30 minutes. Remove from heat and purée in a blender until smooth. Season with salt and pepper and add lemon juice. This is a versatile sauce that can also be used on meat or fish.

Remove duck from marinade and either cook on a grill or sear in a skillet and finish in the oven for 15 minutes at 350 degrees. Either method will work fine; the grill will give more flavor but require more attention. Regardless of method, start with skin side down, get the skin crispy and thoroughly cooked, and turn over occasionally to cook the meat side also. As breasts cook, they will get very dark in color, looking almost as if they are burning. The honey in the marinade will cause them to caramelize and darken. This is normal. Duck is best served medium-rare. If it is too rare, it becomes unpalatable. If overcooked, it becomes dry. Whatever your preference, the key to any meat or fish protein is that, once it is cooked, it needs to rest a good 10 minutes before cutting. Otherwise, it will be dry and lose flavor.

PRESENTATION

Once duck breasts are well rested, slice as thin as possible on the bias and arrange neatly on plates. Cover with either Reduction Sauce or Roasted Red Pepper Coulis. Serve with wild rice and baby vegetables.

Grilled Marinated Duck Breast Alexandre Dumas with Roasted Red Bell Pepper Coulis
PHOTO PROVIDED BY THE PAPER CANOE

RED SKY CAFÉ

1197 Duck Road

Duck, N.C. 27949

252-261-8646

redskycafe.com

Wes Stepp
PHOTO BY SARAH KEENAN
CREATIVE DIMENSIONS

The Chef

Wes Stepp

Wes Stepp's passion for seafood and cooking began while he was working on the Outer Banks. He had a summer job at Carawan Seafood Company in Kitty Hawk, shelling shrimp and cleaning, scaling, and filleting fish. He subsequently paid his way through college by cooking in various restaurants.

After attending Marshall University in his native West Virginia, he returned to the Outer Banks to live permanently. He began working at Kelly's in 1988. "I started as the fry cook, eventually working up to head chef," he recalls. He held that position until he was able to buy his own restaurant in 2001. "Mike Kelly was definitely my mentor in the hospitality business. He set a tireless example for work ethic, and he really pushed us out of our comfort zones. We explored new foods and presentations. We were tested by huge volume and Mike's desire to offer the most cutting-edge coastal cuisine to his guests. I was also given the opportunity to explore my coastal cuisine creativity, which has set the stage for Red Sky and its catering business."

Wes's mantra is, "The first bite is taken with your eyes. Presentation is the key." He explains, "From the way food is stacked and dotted with sauces to the vessel it's served in, food should be presented in a way that catches the eye. Anything I do, from Southern barbecue to Pacific Rim to classical French, I want it to look good." He conducts seminars on presentation for other chefs.

He enjoys a challenge. "Two years ago, I was cooking at Taste of the Beach. A local resident from the Whalehead Club spotted me wearing a chef's jacket and camouflage pants and asked if I was a hunter. I am an avid outdoorsman, so we started talking about cooking game. From that conversation, a new tradition began at Whalehead, 'Mr. Knight's Wild Night.' We paired North Carolina wines with game, from boar and venison to rockfish and shrimp caught nearby. Even people who would never think about that stuff were eating game that night." The Whalehead Club's staff partnered with Wes for a second annual event. The event doubled in size and sold out immediately.

Wes is also a competitive bodybuilder. He refers to it as "body sculpting." He has worked out all his life, but in order to train for a competition, he had to learn to combine exercise with nutrition. "I didn't think I could eat the way a trainer does. The food doesn't look good, and it doesn't taste good. But I realized how well seafood fits the nutritional needs. So I created seafood dishes that are quick and easy, as well as healthy. If you eat these five to six times per day, you'll never get hungry, you'll enjoy the flavors, and you'll slim down." He dropped 25 pounds for the competition and has stayed close to his training weight since then.

Expanding the idea to the public, he created Tastefully Fit, a program that enables participants to eat well, lose fat, and retain muscle. He has worked with the Greenville Police Department on diet and conditioning, and he conducts seminars on how to jump-start a healthy lifestyle. "No products, just single-serving recipes designed to be cooked in the home," he says. "The key is food that is real, and as close as it can be to the way it appears in nature." Menus include seafood, lean beef, poultry, vegetables, and complex carbohydrates such as brown rice, sweet potatoes, and quinoa.

At home, Wes cooks for himself, especially when he is in training. "I cook things on Wednesdays and Sundays for the rest of the week. I have the fridge stocked with quick, healthy meals. It's easier and faster for me to eat at home than go to fast food. So I eat well, and I eat healthy. It's mostly seafood, really flavorful but really light."

The Restaurant

Red Sky Café

Red Sky Café is located across the street from the park in Duck, where outdoor concerts are regularly scheduled. The wide-ranging menu features traditional dishes as well as Thai- and French-influenced creations.

Chef Stepp describes Red Sky's concept: "I love food. But I never liked pretentiousness in restaurants, even when I enjoyed the food. Customers are not doing us a favor by coming in. The obligation is on us. So my concept was always classics twisted around, very fresh food coming in the door every day from local purveyors, in a casual atmosphere where you can just enjoy yourself. We also installed a wood-fired oven, which expands our capacity to be creative."

Red Sky uses several area providers, especially Etheridge Seafood in Wanchese. Many of the vegetables come from Wes's father's garden. In addition, "Mr. Malco in Currituck grows a lot of our produce. He sells strawberries to the public—just as you come across the Currituck bridge, look for a hand-painted sign. We get soft-shell crabs in season from Kitty Hawk."

The restaurant also serves salmon—which is, of course, not local. But it is a favorite not only of area residents but of tourists. And as a bonus, salmon can be prepared "Tastefully Fit." Chef Stepp adds, "I don't like farm-raised salmon if I can get wild, but when I can't get wild, I really like Scottish. It just tastes better, and I know it's sanitary. Salmon is recognizable—some people just don't want to take that leap of faith and order wahoo. Sometimes, people know a fish, but by another name—mahi versus dolphin, for example. Salmon doesn't have that problem. So we always have salmon on the menu."

Red Sky is both a lunch and dinner restaurant and a large catering operation. "I kept noticing that people around here don't have a family in a house," Chef Stepp explains. "They have three or four families in a house—a dozen or more people. So I started Chefs on Call. We prep ahead, bring everything we need, do cooking demos, and feed everyone at the vacation house. We cover everything from clambakes to sushi. It's like a night out for the family, but they never leave the house. Many of our extended families return each season, so we do a lot of repeat business. In May and June, weddings are popular on the Outer Banks, so we cater those parties, large and small, in various venues. In July and August, tourist season is in full swing, so we focus on the restaurant and Chefs on Call. In fall, the weather turns cooler, but it's still gorgeous. We return a lot of attention to catering and supporting other local events."

Chef Stepp is a frequent guest for cooking demonstrations on WAVY television in Hampton Roads, Virginia. He is on the board of directors of the Outer Banks Wedding Association. He conducts Tastefully Fit seminars for local municipal groups and police departments and has catered events for dignitaries, politicians, athletes, and celebrities such as the Carolina Panthers, *Wicked Tuna* cast members, Phil Collins, and others.

The Recipes

Scallops Casino

Serves 2

Guacamole
1 ripe avocado
1 tablespoon diced tomato
1 small onion, diced
kosher salt and cracked pepper to taste
½ teaspoon chopped cilantro
squeeze of fresh lime

Incorporate ingredients in a mixing bowl until mixture is smooth and consistent.

Scallops
olive oil
6 scallops
½ cup diced tomato
¼ cup diced Vidalia onion
¼ cup diced poblano pepper
crumbled bacon
1 tablespoon salted butter, softened

Scallops Casino
Photo by
Sarah Keenan Creative Dimensions

Heat olive oil in a hot sauté pan. Place scallops in pan for 2 to 3 minutes until brown. Flip scallops and add tomatoes, onions, peppers, and bacon. Add butter and swirl to incorporate.

PRESENTATION
Place each scallop on a dollop of guacamole. Finish with reduced tomato, bacon, and butter sauce.

Charred Tuna
PHOTO BY SARAH KEENAN CREATIVE DIMENSIONS

Charred Tuna
Serves 1

CHEF'S NOTE "This is a Tastefully Fit entrée."

Sauce
¼ cup honey
½ cup soy sauce
cornstarch
water

Place honey and soy sauce in a saucepan and bring to a simmer. Thicken with small amounts of cornstarch and water.

Wasabi Paste
2 tablespoons water
2 tablespoons wasabi powder

Slowly add water to powder until achieving desired consistency.

Tuna
olive oil
6-ounce fillet local yellowfin tuna
kosher salt and crushed pepper to taste

black and white sesame seeds
seaweed salad

Heat a cast-iron skillet and add olive oil. Sprinkle tuna with salt and pepper and encrust with sesame seeds. Sear 30 seconds on each side. Remove from pan and let rest. Slice very thin with an extremely sharp knife.

PRESENTATION
Place tuna on a plate and drizzle sauce over top. Place a small amount of seaweed salad and Wasabi Paste on plate.

Shrimp Scampi "Clean"
PHOTO BY SARAH KEENAN CREATIVE DIMENSIONS

Shrimp Scampi "Clean"
Serves 1

CHEF'S NOTE "This is a Tastefully Fit entrée."

olive oil spray
6 to 8 white domestic shrimp, tails and shells removed, deveined
¼ cup red peppers, sliced thin
⅓ cup mushrooms, sliced thin
2 tablespoons crushed garlic

1 tablespoon fresh basil
¼ cup seafood stock or chicken stock (99 percent fat-free)

Lightly heat a nonstick pan and spray with olive oil spray. Add shrimp and cook for 2 minutes. Add vegetables, garlic, basil, and stock. Simmer for 2 to 3 minutes.

PRESENTATION
Serve over brown rice and grilled summer corn. Garnish with lemon and a fresh basil sprig.

OUTER BANKS TASTE OF THE BEACH

Outer Banks Restaurant Association
P.O. Box 2283
Kill Devil Hills, N.C. 27948
obxtasteofthebeach.com

Outer Banks Taste of the Beach, one of the largest food and wine festivals in the South, is held in March. The Outer Banks Restaurant Association has been host since the early 1980s, expanding in 2008 to four days and multiple events. In 2010, *Coastal Living* named Taste of the Beach one of its top 10 seafood and wine festivals.

Each event is priced separately. Links on the website provide lists, organized by price or schedule. Meals run from around $20 up to $120 per person. Participants build their own schedules in advance from over 70 choices, attending as many or as few events as they wish. Ingredients are almost exclusively local, from seafood to seasonal vegetables from eastern North Carolina farms.

Breakfasts range from country-style bounty to seafood crepes, French toast, and broccoli and English cheddar breakfast casserole.

Lunch might follow a beer theme, with battered fish and chips. Or participants might enjoy multiple variations on oysters, a Latin theme, an American roots theme, or barbecued chicken, beef, ribs, brisket, or pork. Afternoon bus tours stop for tastings at an eastern North Carolina winery. Cooking classes and demonstrations of particular techniques appear frequently on the roster.

For evening meals, restaurants feature their specialties, often in multi-course dinners. Restaurant crawls, with samplings at each stop, are popular as well. Some of the dinners are elaborate, combined with wines for each course or with North Carolina distillers' whiskey tastings.

Celebrity guest chefs make frequent appearances. In 2014, an after-dinner "Meet the Chefs" reception party and Spanish cava celebration gave participants an opportunity to schmooze with chefs who had provided meals during the event.

The festival concludes on Sunday with the Beach Grand Tasting, when dozens of restaurants serve samplings and offer wine tastings. The day also brings the annual "TOB'y Awards"—Best Booth Presentation, Best in Show, Best Outer Banks Catch, and the two top awards, the Chef's Award and People's Choice Award.

Several lodging packages are available. Check the link on the website.

RUNDOWN CAFÉ

5218 North Virginia Dare Trail

Kitty Hawk, N.C. 27949

252-255-0026

rundowncafe.com

Michael Montiel
PHOTO PROVIDED BY MICHAEL MONTIEL

The Chef

Michael Montiel

Michael Montiel lives to travel, catch fish, and bring ideas that grow out of those activities to the menu at the Rundown Café.

He grew up in San Diego and started working in the hospitality industry at La Valencia, a 125-year-old La Jolla resort hotel, often rated the most romantic in Southern California. He eventually became bell captain.

He relocated to the Outer Banks in 1993, following his wife, who is from Nags Head. Restaurant work was not a specific career goal, but thanks to his experience in hotel service, waiting tables was a natural transition. "It was just the best way to make some money," he recalls. He took a job at the Rundown Café and became close friends with owner Will Thorp. Michael started following Will's circle, adding hunting and fishing to his lifetime love of surfing. He continued as a waiter at the Rundown for about five years.

"Will warned me I could not live a rock-star life on the Outer Banks without another level of investment, so I started in management," Michael says. "At some point, he started talking about wanting to do something else, and I was interested in owning a restaurant. But he said I could not even think about ownership if I could not cook at a commercial level. So I took a big drop in pay and stood beside him all day, every day, cooking on the line. We started with the basics—mother sauces, how to cook in huge quantities. It was about a two-year learning process. Once I did that, we decided I would work with him in the kitchen during the day. So I would come in at 6 A.M. and prep until two or three in the afternoon. Then I would go home, take a nap, return, and host and manage the floor until closing, usually around midnight. I maintained that schedule about five years.

"Around 2001, we began the transition for me to purchase the restaurant. During that time, the lease expired on the original Rundown property, so we moved about 100 yards up the road and started constructing a new building. I oversaw construction while Will still ran the old location. I took over full ownership during 2001–2, when the new property opened."

Michael's wife, Tamara, does the cooking at home. "She is a phenomenal cook," he reports. "The only thing I do is fire up the grill. We have a garden. We grow a lot of our own vegetables. We eat a lot of salads with grilled meat or seafood."

They are both surfers, kite surfers, and devoted anglers. "I think in terms of where would we want to go to eat on vacation, and that's what we try to convey to our customers," Michael says.

The Restaurant

Rundown Café

The name *Rundown Café* comes from a classic seafood and coconut soup that is made on Tortola in the Caribbean. Michael describes the origin: "Everybody identifies jerk seasonings with Jamaica, but most of our flavors and recipes actually reflect a stronger influence from Tortola. The phrase they use about the soup is, 'It run down so good!' "

"A family-friendly getaway with tropical style and surf motif" is the restaurant's stated theme. From the outside, the Rundown appears small. But it's a two-story structure, so the interior is larger than it seems. A koi pool flanks the entry. "Kids love to feed the fish," Michael observes. Upstairs, seating on the outdoor Hula Deck and most interior seating provide clear views of the ocean. The ambience is casual, the pricing moderate.

The restaurant operates at high volume. The staff serves over 250 pounds of beans a day, 150 pounds of rice, and 100 pounds of salsa. "When you're cooking on those levels, classical training is almost irrelevant," Michael says. "Culinary-school graduates have to learn the process all over. In our kitchen, I stir with a stainless-steel wand that looks like a canoe paddle, about five and a half feet long. We sell 450 pounds of fish a week. I trimmed it all myself until last year, when I started to develop tendonitis and had to let another guy help.

"I cook to my own palate," he says. "When I came to the Outer Banks in 1993, the majority of restaurants here had strong Caribbean influences, because that's where everybody traveled during the off-season. I came with West Coast flavors in mind. As a kid, when my friends and I wanted to drink and party, we went to Ensenada, Mexico. That's where the original fish tacos were invented, and that original recipe is the one we use. As I took creative control, I started adding to what Will had been doing so well all along, developing a wide range of island cuisine, bringing back things I enjoyed in Hawaii, Indonesia, Thailand, and the Pacific Rim."

Michael and Tamara grow vegetables and fruits themselves—figs, pears, Granny Smith apples, heirloom tomatoes, blueberries, and raspberries, for example. "We just love gardening," Michael remarks.

The restaurant has been written up extensively. "One time, I was on my way to Thailand. I picked up the Southwest Airlines magazine and saw a feature article about the Rundown Café. I had no idea it was being published. It was a great premonition for the trip. But I never framed it. I hardly ever keep articles about us. It's not the accolades that hang on the wall that matter. It's what last night's guests said. You are only as good as the last plate you served."

Michael is especially proud of a particular segment of his regular clientele: "A lot of chefs from other restaurants come here for a burger on their days off."

The Recipes

Grilled Salmon over Wilted Kale with Roasted Sweet Potatoes and BBQ Peaches
Serves 4

4 North Carolina peaches
brown sugar

Grilled Salmon over Wilted Kale with Roasted Sweet Potatoes and BBQ Peaches

light barbecue sauce
4 sweet potatoes
garlic-infused olive oil (or regular olive oil)
garlic powder
salt and pepper to taste
4 4- to 6-ounce pieces salmon
4 large handfuls baby kale
chopped spring onions

Peel, seed, and halve peaches. Roll in brown sugar and grill. Cut peaches into cubes and toss in barbecue sauce. Let sit in juices. Peel and cube sweet potatoes. Toss in oil and roast on a sheet pan dusted with garlic powder and salt and pepper. Preheat grill to high. Sprinkle salt and pepper on salmon. Place salmon on grill and immediately reduce heat to medium. Grill to an internal temperature of 135 degrees. Stir-fry or pan-toss kale and roasted sweet potatoes in additional oil long enough to wilt kale.

PRESENTATION

Mound wilted kale and sweet potatoes in center of plates. Top with salmon. Spoon on peaches. Garnish with spring onions.

Thai Ginger-Peanut Zoodles with Crushed Peanuts and Chopped Cilantro

Serves 4

2 scallions
1 bunch cilantro
1 tablespoon pickled ginger
1 tablespoon hoisin sauce
1 tablespoon seasoned rice wine vinegar
1 teaspoon crushed red pepper
1 tablespoon soy sauce
1 tablespoon sesame oil
1 tablespoon peanut butter
3 or 4 zucchini
2 or 3 red bell peppers
2 large carrots
4 tablespoons crushed peanuts

Thai Ginger-Peanut Zoodles
PHOTO PROVIDED BY MICHAEL MONTIEL

Mix in a blender or food processor scallions, cilantro, ginger, hoisin sauce, vinegar, red pepper, soy sauce, sesame oil, and peanut butter until mixture reaches a sauce consistency. Peel zucchini and julienne in a mandolin to make long noodles from outside rind; do not include the center with seeds. Julienne red peppers and carrots.

PRESENTATION

Toss vegetables in sauce and plate with additional chopped cilantro and crushed peanuts.

Thai Shellfish Hot Pot with Lo Mein Noodles

Serves 4

1 tablespoon grated fresh ginger
2 cloves garlic, minced

Thai Shellfish Hot Pot with Lo Mein Noodles
PHOTO PROVIDED BY MICHAEL MONTIEL

1 tablespoon sugar
1 tablespoon red curry powder
1 tablespoon olive oil
1 medium yellow onion, diced
1 red pepper, chopped
1 cup coconut milk
1 tablespoon fish sauce
2 cups lo mein noodles
½ cup sesame oil
8 mussels
8 clams
½ pound shrimp
16 pieces baby corn
1 cup chopped button mushrooms
1 cup shredded napa cabbage
2 spring onions, julienned
1 cup mung bean sprouts
8 wonton crisps

Sauté ginger and garlic with sugar and red curry in olive oil over medium heat until garlic is caramelized. Add onions and red peppers and continue to sauté for 3 to 4 minutes until onions are translucent. Add coconut milk and continue to simmer. Add fish sauce. Taste. Add more fish sauce if desired. Bring entire mixture to desired level of heat and flavor. This becomes the broth that determines the flavor and body of the dish. Cook noodles according to package directions. Rinse noodles, then toss them in sesame oil. Stir-fry or steam shellfish. Add baby corn, mushrooms, and cabbage. Add broth and heat carefully; high heat will separate the fats in the coconut milk.

PRESENTATION

Place noodles in deep bowls. Add broth mixture and top with shellfish. Finish with spring onions, bean sprouts, and wontons.

TRIO

3708 North Croatan Highway, Milepost 4.5
Kitty Hawk, N.C. 27949
252-261-0277
obxtrio.com

THE OWNERS: JOHN AND JENNIFER MINNICH, AND KENNY AND MELISSA HYMAN

They gave up lucrative professional careers in order to live on the Outer Banks and create the kind of life they wanted to live.

Kenny Hyman was an investment banker. He and his wife, Melissa, who was in securities investments, came from Richmond. Melissa grew up in Hawaii and loved the idea of living at the beach. Kenny was easily persuaded by the promise of beach living in a small community, combined with the perceived need for a good wine shop in the area. By 2003, Kenny and Melissa made the move and were operating Native Vine, a wine shop in Point Harbor. They wanted to expand.

Jennifer Minnich was a corporate attorney. John Minnich ran a management consulting firm. John's family had begun annual vacations to the Outer Banks in the 1970s. They built a vacation home in Duck in the late 1990s, around the time he and Jennifer met. John and Jennifer were mar-

John and Jennifer Minnich, Kenny and Melissa Hyman
PHOTO PROVIDED BY TRIO

ried in Duck, and it became their goal to live and raise a family there. John sold his company, and the Minnichs moved down from New Jersey in 2008.

John and Jennifer were customers at Native Vine and became friends with the Hymans. The couples began to discuss the possibility of becoming partners in a new venture. Things just seemed to fall into place. Kenny was the driving force behind the existing wine business. While he knew he wanted to include beer and cheese as part of the new operation, he did not have enough expertise in those areas. John (beer) and Jennifer (cheese) had the passion and knowledge to develop those elements.

"Outside of the obvious benefits of living at the beach, we really enjoy being a part of the tight-knit local community on the Outer Banks," Jennifer says. "Ten months out of the year, it's a small town that just happens to be on the beach. It's a great environment for our young children. We love it here and enjoy the laid-back pace of beach life."

THE CONCEPT

Trio is unique. It is a wine, beer, and cheese shop with retail space for wine and cheese accessories and unique glassware, plus small-plate food and cheese accompaniments. A long bar and seating area down one side provides tapas food service, well conceived to pair with wines and beers. Self-serve, automated wine stations dispense 24 exceptionally well-selected wines by the glass. On tap are a total of 24 craft beers, a number the owners believe to be the most on the northern Outer Banks; cask beer may also be available.

When Trio opened, all the owners tended bar at various times. They prepared food and took turns cleaning the bathrooms. They were surprised by their success. "As odd as it may sound, we never really planned to have a restaurant, but when we opened, it dawned on us that we had created one. Adding a full-time chef and kitchen manager has been a key step for us in making Trio an ongoing success," John observes.

"Out-of-town customers are always telling us they wish we were closer to home for them, even if they live in New York or D.C.," Kenny says. "We focus on offering people the opportunity to experience great wine, beer, and cheese, and then they can take some home with them. We do not offer a fine-dining menu, but flavor, freshness, and quality ingredients are as important to us as in any fine restaurant. The result is a range of cheese plates, small plates, salads, paninis, and desserts that, while casual, are inspired and creative."

John adds, "We are constantly rotating our offerings so that every day you can come in and try something new. Part of the reason we are able to do this is our large and diverse selection of retail items. A lot of restaurants now offer a limited retail selection, but we really have multiple businesses under one roof—restaurant, wine-tasting room, bar/taphouse, cheese shop, plus wine and beer retail outlet. We are also unique in that, if customers are interested, they can become more educated in what we are serving. Our staff is just as passionate about wine, beer, and cheese as we are. They are all knowledgeable in our offerings and are prepared to share that knowledge."

Trio is open year-round. "This allows us to attract and retain the kind of people to our staff that help deliver a consistently great experience for our guests," Kenny says. "As a way to further staff development, we have a Trio Book Club. This is an optional activity for staff. If they choose to participate, we buy a copy of the book for each of them—books on wine, beer, and/or cheese, of course, as well as customer service, pairing flavors, for example—and they commit to reading it and participating in discussion sessions on their own time, prior to the opening of the shop. All the staff chooses to participate. This is a reflection on the kind of people we have attracted."

Rob Robinson and Matthew Payne
PHOTO PROVIDED BY BAD BEAN

BAD BEAN BAJA GRILL

3105 North Croatan Highway

Milepost 5

Seagate North Shopping Center

Kill Devil Hills, N.C. 27948

252-261-1300

badbeanobx.com

BAD BEAN TAQUERIA

78 Sunset Boulevard

Timbuck II Shopping Center

Corolla, N.C. 27927

252-453-4380

badbeanobx.com

The Chefs

Rob Robinson and Matthew Payne

"Being out front, busing and waiting tables, made me realize that what I really wanted was to be in the back, with the knives and the flames."

When George "Rob" Robinson was able to make the move toward owning his own restaurant, he shifted from fine dining to casual food—but casual food conceived and prepared with knowledge and skills that grew out of a background that included some of the finest restaurants in the United States.

Rob grew up on Long Beach Island on the Jersey Shore but lived in other states as a teenager because of his father's job. "My earliest memories of cooking were trying to make breakfast for Mom and Dad. I was always trying to make the perfect omelet. It's one of those things in cooking—sometimes, the simplest things are the hardest to get right."

His first job in the business was in a pizza shop on the Jersey Shore. "I was immediately attracted to the colorful personalities and fast pace. The hook was set when I began spending summers on the Outer Banks toward the end of high school and during college, working with my uncle, who was a chef at Waves Edge Mesquite Grill [now closed]. I started in the dish pit, then moved on to the floor, busing and waiting tables. That's when I was drawn into the kitchen. I continued to cook in college and at a New Orleans bistro called Harry Bisset's. By then, I knew that's what I wanted to do."

After graduating from the University of Georgia with a degree in economics, he went to Johnson & Wales on the Vail, Colorado, campus. "But the real learning came after culinary school," Rob says. "I returned to the Outer Banks and quickly saw that I couldn't get what I was looking for, at least not at that time. Off to California I went, searching for the best chefs in the country, the best ingredients, and great waves. Surfing has created a deep connection with the ocean. It also goes hand in hand with the life of a chef, because it drives you to want to travel and experience new places and cultures, just as being a chef drives you to want to taste new flavors and ingredients.

"My first stop was at Aqua in downtown San Francisco, where Michael Mina was chef. This was my first experience with contemporary American-French cuisine. It was also my first taste of the incredible competition that goes on among line chefs. Each one wanted to move up and be the best. I went on to Pacific's Edge in Carmel, where the annual Masters of Food and Wine event was being held. It was amazing to meet some of the best chefs in the country and experience their food. One year, Charlie Trotter, Michel Richard, Mario Batali, Jean-Louis Palladin, and Thomas Keller were all there at once. I got to work with truffles that Jean-Louis handpicked in France.

"I met John Gerber, who had cooked at the French Laundry. He helped me get an interview there, and I felt honored when I was hired. Anthony Bourdain filmed one of the original *No Reservations* episodes while I was there, and I also met Julia Child. Among the many lessons I learned from my time at the French Laundry, a few really stand out: Respect the ingredients, focus on the flavors in those ingredients, and find the technique that brings those flavors out best. Don't put too many ingredients on the plate. A perfect example was the carrot soup. It was like a carrot sprang up and punched you in the face, but there were only two ingredients in it!

"I became friends with one of the pastry chefs, and when he decided to work at Todd Humphries's new venture, the Martini House in St. Helena, I was presented with the opportunity to learn something new. I had always been a line chef, and the opportunity to learn pastries would be a real benefit."

New opportunities began to present themselves. Rob returned to the Outer Banks in May 2002 as chef of the newly constructed Left Bank restaurant at the Sanderling Resort. He eventually opened his own restaurant, and when he decided to add a second location, he invited Matthew Payne to join him. "Matt and I have known each other for 10 years and have worked together for seven. It is truly a great experience as a chef-owner to have someone like Matt working with you to make a vision reality."

Matthew Payne was born in Newfield, New York. "Growing up in the Finger Lakes region, I was around fresh water a lot." He came to the Outer Banks in 2002 for his internship in culinary school. "I love being surrounded by the water. The Outer Banks has a great small-town feel, with a sense of pride that booms in the summer. I would never be able to live in a large city. I enjoy silence as a way to unwind after a long day."

He started cooking when he took a summer class in fifth grade. "I can still remember the Asian-glazed baked chicken wings we made," Matthew says. "I copied the recipe and took it home with me. My family was rooted in the farming fabric of my hometown. Picking corn at my uncle's farm, cleaning green beans for my mom to can for the winter, staring at a deer that my dad had killed as it hung upside down in our garage, watching Grandma pickle the watermelon rinds she took off our plates at family picnics—these remain clear memories. When I turned 16, I started in a short-order kitchen. After high school, I got a job at the Statler Hotel, part of Cornell University's Hotel Management School. After almost two years at the Statler, the executive chef, Craig Hartman, told me I had potential, and that I ought to think about culinary school. He recommended the Culinary Institute of America in Hyde Park, New York, his alma mater. I drove up, applied in person, and interviewed on the spot. A month later, I was accepted." He graduated with a bachelor's degree in culinary arts.

Matthew then took a banquet chef position at the Sanderling, where he worked under Chef Robinson. "That experience taught me planning and speed. Rob taught me how to push myself and hold myself to higher standards. I try to instill that ethic in every one of my cooks. After two years, I was offered the sous chef job at the Lifesaving Station.

"Cooking comes easy to me, but this was the first real job where I was introduced to managing a large staff. I left the Sanderling after almost five years and took a job at Blue Point in Duck, widely regarded as one of the best Outer Banks restaurants. I learned so much there about regional Southern food and methods from Chefs Dave McClary and Sam McGann."

Bad Bean was so popular that Chef Robinson decided to expand to a second location. "When a chef who has inspired you and has been a big influence has the confidence to hand you the keys and let you drive, you get excited," Chef Payne recalls.

The Restaurants

Bad Bean Baja Grill and Bad Bean Taqueria

Chef-owner Rob Robinson narrates the origin of his restaurants: "When I decided to break from fine dining, I wanted to explore Mexican cuisine, which I had enjoyed in California on my days off. Mexico has distinct regional foods, each with unique flavor, ingredients, and techniques. The culture is passionate and proud of its food. The thing that attracted me most about its cuisine was its simplicity, but intense flavors. That, in a nutshell, underlies the food at Baja Grill.

"I was frustrated by the disservice most Mexican restaurants do to this vibrant cuisine. Plates look the same and mostly taste the same, with a side of beans and rice. Menus are plastered with combinations of ingredients smothered with melted cheese and listed on menus by number. 'I'll have number 23.' Is that any way to order food? I wanted to take my background and apply it to these wonderful, true Mexican flavors and ingredients. The Tostones dish on our menu is a great reflection of blending my background and these new flavors—a smooth, rich black-bean purée, the mildly sweet flavor and texture of plantain, the tart richness of goat cheese, and the pungent flavor of truffle honey. France meets Mexico!"

In order to maintain freshness, ingredients are sourced nearby as much as possible. The Bad Bean chefs learned about O'Neal's Sea Harvest in Wanchese from another local chef. "Seeing local fish come off the boat and being cleaned right there, I loved it," Chef Payne says. "We also get soft-shell crabs from them during shedding season. I call my order in, and someone goes out to the crab shedders early in the morning, and they're in the restaurant by noon. Some of our cooks have small gardens, and they bring stuff in—fresh herbs, cherry tomatoes, peppers, cucumbers, and squashes. I love using them in daily specials. It also gives them great pride, seeing their gardening being used in a professional kitchen."

The Fish Tacos at the original Bad Bean in Corolla have been featured in *Coastal Living*, along with some of the restaurant's salsas. Bad Bean has won numerous local awards and chef's choice awards at Taste of the Beach. Several local publications and newspapers and magazines in Virginia have published articles praising Bad Bean.

The Recipes

Rockfish Ceviche
Serves 4

Rockfish Ceviche
Photo provided by Bad Bean

3 cups cold water
1 tablespoon kosher salt
1 cup ice
1 pound fresh rockfish, cut into bite-sized pieces (flounder may be substituted)
1 serrano or jalapeño pepper, diced small
1 small red onion, diced small (shallots may be substituted)
1 bunch cilantro, chopped
juice of 5 limes
zest of 1 lime
zest and juice of 1 orange
2 tablespoons olive oil
2 or 3 sweet potatoes, sliced ¼ inch thick, punched out in 1½-inch diameter discs
    with a ring mold (you will need 12 sweet potato disks)

Put water into a bowl. Dissolve salt in water. Add ice. Insert fish into cold water and let sit for 30 minutes. Strain off water. Make sure to remove any pieces of ice. Let fish sit in strainer for 5 minutes so excess water drains. Place remaining ingredients except for sweet potato disks in a bowl. Add fish, incorporate, and let sit for at least 1 hour in the refrigerator. Bring a pot of salted water to a boil, then reduce to a simmer. Cook sweet potato disks until fork-tender. Do not overcook! Strain sweet potato disks and run them under cold water to stop cooking.

PRESENTATION

Place 3 sweet potato disks on each plate. Spoon on the ceviche with a slotted spoon. Garnish with favorite herb or microgreens.

Tostones with Black Bean Purée, Goat Cheese, and Truffle Honey
Serves 5

1 cup dried black beans
1 small onion, diced small
2 cloves garlic, minced
2 tablespoons canola oil
1 teaspoon cumin
pinch of cinnamon
½ teaspoon Mexican oregano or 1 tablespoon fresh epazote
1 quart cold water
salt to taste
2 tablespoons cooking oil
3 green plantains
6 ounces goat cheese
truffle honey for drizzling
chopped cilantro

Soak beans overnight. Strain and let sit so water drains off. Sauté onions and garlic in canola oil over medium heat for about 5 minutes until translucent. Add cumin, cinnamon, and oregano and cook for 1 minute. Add beans to pot. Immediately add water. Bring to a boil, then reduce to a simmer. Cook until you can taste 5 beans in a row that are tender. Place 1 cup of cooked beans in a blender while still hot. Add ½ cup of cooking liquid from beans and turn blender on high; be careful

Tostones with Black Bean Purée, Goat Cheese, and Truffle Honey
PHOTO PROVIDED BY BAD BEAN

to hold lid on blender. Purée beans to the consistency of wet sand. Add more cooking liquid to achieve desired consistency. Season purée with salt.

Heat cooking oil. Cut each plantain into 5 pieces about 2 inches in length. Fry about 1 minute. Time will vary depending on how ripe plantains are. The greener the plantains, the longer cooking will take. Place fried plantain pieces between 2 pieces of wax paper and smash with a sauté pan to about ¼-inch thickness. When all the plantains are smashed into flat disks, fry them again until golden brown on the edges. Transfer onto a sheet tray lined with paper towels to drain excess oil. Season with salt while still hot.

PRESENTATION

Spoon about 2 tablespoons of Black Bean Purée onto 10-inch round or square plates and drag it across the plates with the tip of the spoon. Offset Tostones 3 in a row like poker chips onto purée. Sprinkle with goat cheese. Drizzle with truffle honey and garnish with cilantro.

Jim Douglas PHOTO BY LORI DOUGLAS PHOTOGRAPHY

CHILLI PEPPERS COASTAL GRILL

3001 North Croatan Highway

Kill Devil Hills, N.C. 27948

252-441-8081

chilli-peppers.com

The Proprietor

Jim Douglas

"When I opened up, not only did I not have any dollars, I didn't have any sense either."

Jim Douglas does not consider himself a chef. He is an owner who oversees the food served in his restaurant and helps develop the dishes. "I have learned most of my food knowledge by osmosis, working with very talented people who have had a lot more knowledge and training, and by experimenting with different ingredients from around the world."

Originally from Grand Rapids, Michigan, Jim started coming to the Outer Banks after college because of the great windsurfing. He got a job with Kitty Hawk Sports, teaching sailing and windsurfing. He settled here on a permanent basis over 25 years ago.

His mother was a great cook. "But being from Michigan, we ate a lot of meat and potatoes," he says. "We didn't have the fresh seafood that we have on the Outer Banks. It's really nice to get locally harvested seafood, from blue crabs to the best oysters and clams I have ever tasted, not to mention the great fishing, which allows us to have fresh fish all year."

He opened Chilli Peppers in 1993, when he was 30 years old. At the restaurant's core are the chili sauces Jim creates. Chilli Peppers has won several national awards for its products. The biggest was the grand prize at the Fiery Food Show in Albuquerque, New Mexico, at which the restaurant's creations competed against almost 500 products.

His favorite type of food is Asian. "I will cook anything, but I probably like cooking on the grill best. I love the foods of summer—fresh corn, heirloom tomatoes, fresh basil. . . . The list goes on."

The Restaurant

Chilli Peppers Coastal Grill

Chilli Peppers considers itself a "place for food and fun." An outside courtyard provides picnic tables for seating. Staff members tend an herb and vegetable garden "to produce the freshest homemade tastes."

Kelsey Thompson is the manager. She started out in theater but worked in a family-run Italian restaurant while she was in school. She performed on stage for a while but kept returning to the restaurant business. "When I was at work, it was like I had to put on a personal performance for every table," she says. "This seemed to go hand in hand with my theatrical skills. I started as hostess and worked my way into management. Chilli Peppers is the third restaurant that I have worked in and moved my way up. Each of these places gave me new tools to make the next experience better. I have now worked in restaurants 14 years and can honestly say I have found my home. Jim Douglas brought out a side of me that I have never seen. He allows me to be creative and welcomes the input that I give. We work off each other's strengths and weaknesses and continue to figure out how to make this the best restaurant it can be."

The food "has no geographical boundaries," according to Jim. It ranges from Tuna Sashimi (Asian) to Chimichurri Oysters (Argentinian) to Slow-Cooked Chicken Enchiladas (Mexican). The menu also offers traditional eastern North Carolina seafood preparations, along with a New England–style Steamer Pot and Southwestern-influenced creations that utilize Jim's chili sauces. Tapas specials usually grow out of Central and South American cuisines.

"We do a lot of fun things through the year," Jim says. "In the fall, we offer foods from around the world on Thursday nights, in tapas portions. We do a great Saturday and Sunday brunch during the summer, but just on Sunday in winter. On winter evenings, you can build your own pasta on Monday, then build your own pizza on Wednesday."

Jim's comment about Chilli Peppers' style could serve as a guide for all restaurant personnel: "We are in the hospitality business, as well as the food business. I really am afraid that lots of people have forgotten about being hospitable in general, and we really work at being the best in that regard.

"Chilli Peppers is always trying to expand the 'Flavors of the World' specials. We call the cuisine 'World Flavors,' and our menu really shows it. We have started serving fresh homemade beef jerky with some great sauces and hot salt. Nobody else does anything quite like this, and people really enjoy trying something that is new but not highfalutin."

Chilli Peppers has been recognized by the *Norfolk Virginian-Pilot* as serving the "Best Brunch on the Beach." Jim is perhaps best known as the originator of the iconic OBX logo, now synonymous with the Outer Banks.

The Recipes

Seafood Paella
Serves 6 to 8

2 cups rice
1 carrot
1 bunch celery
2 medium red peppers
2 medium green peppers
1 medium red onion
1 squash
1 zucchini
6 tablespoons olive oil, divided
2 cloves garlic, diced
½ teaspoon saffron
1 tablespoon chicken stock
1 tablespoon clam stock
2 quarts water

Seafood Paella

2 tablespoons cornstarch
salt and pepper to taste
1 pound shrimp, peeled and deveined
1 pound crab legs, separated
1½ pounds scallops
2 dozen clams

Cook rice according to package directions. Thinly chop or julienne all vegetables. Heat 3 tablespoons of the olive oil in a large pan on stovetop. Add garlic, carrots, celery, peppers, and onions. Sauté for 3 minutes. Add squash and zucchini. Sauté another 2 to 3 minutes. Add saffron, chicken stock, clam stock, and water and bring to a boil. Cover and reduce heat. Simmer for 10 to 15 minutes. Add cornstarch to thicken. Add salt and pepper. While sauce is simmering, heat remaining olive oil in a separate pan and sauté seafood until clams open.

PRESENTATION

Add sauce to seafood, mix, and serve over rice.

Shrimp Curry
Serves 6 to 8

2 cups rice
4 tablespoons olive oil, divided
2 cloves garlic, minced
13.5-ounce can coconut milk
2 teaspoons fish sauce
2 teaspoons brown sugar
1 teaspoon lime juice
1 quart heavy cream
4 tablespoons red curry paste
2 tablespoons cornstarch
¼ cup water
salt and pepper to taste
1 cup zucchini, chopped into ½-inch pieces
1 cup squash, chopped into ½-inch pieces
½ cup chopped red onion
½ cup broccoli, chopped into ½-inch pieces

Shrimp Curry
PHOTO BY LORI DOUGLAS PHOTOGRAPHY

1 cup red bell pepper, chopped into ½-inch pieces
1 cup green bell pepper, chopped into ½-inch pieces
1 cup carrots, chopped into ½-inch pieces
1 cup celery, chopped into ½-inch pieces
1 cup shredded cabbage
1½ pounds shrimp, peeled and deveined

Cook rice according to package directions. Heat 2 tablespoons of the olive oil over medium temperature. Sauté garlic for 30 seconds. Add coconut milk, fish sauce, brown sugar, lime juice, cream, and curry paste and finish with cornstarch and water to thicken. Add salt and pepper. In another pan, sauté vegetables in remaining olive oil until tender. Add shrimp and cook until shrimp are light pink. Add sauce to shrimp and vegetables.

PRESENTATION
Mound rice in center of bowls. Cover with shrimp and vegetable mix.

Tuna Sashimi
Serves 6

Chipotle Soy Mustard
1 tablespoon chipotle paste
2 tablespoons sesame oil
¼ cup soy sauce
1 tablespoon Dijon mustard
¼ cup olive oil

Blend ingredients until smooth. Set aside.

Wasabi Aioli
2 eggs, beaten
¼ cup rice vinegar
2 tablespoons wasabi paste
1 tablespoon lime juice
1 cup olive oil

Blend ingredients until smooth. Set aside.

Tuna Sashimi
PHOTO BY
LORI DOUGLAS
PHOTOGRAPHY

Noodles

8 ounces bean thread (cellophane) noodles
½ cup sweet Thai chili sauce
2 tablespoons sesame oil
2 tablespoons soy sauce
2 green onions, chopped
2 tablespoons chopped cilantro

Cook noodles according to package instructions. Add remaining ingredients and mix. Set aside.

Tuna

1½ pounds fresh yellowfin tuna
½ cup black and white sesame seeds
2 tablespoons olive oil
½ pound seaweed salad
½ pound pickled ginger slices
¼ cup wasabi paste

Crust tuna with sesame seeds. Heat olive oil in a skillet and quickly sear each side for about 30 seconds, making sure center is still red. Let rest a few minutes. Slice thin.

PRESENTATION

Plate noodles on serving dishes and fan tuna slices on top. Decoratively smear Wasabi Aioli and Chipotle Soy Mustard alongside tuna. Place seaweed salad, pickled ginger, and wasabi paste on plates as well.

THE COLINGTON CAFÉ

1029 Colington Road

Kill Devil Hills, N.C. 27948

252-480-1123

thecolingtoncafe.com

Carlen Pearl, Chef-Proprietor
PHOTO PROVIDED BY CARLEN PEARL

The Chefs

Carlen Pearl, Chef-Proprietor and Jeff Lane, Executive Chef

"When we first opened, we were so small, we didn't even have a waiting area," reports Carlen Pearl. "People just stayed in their cars in the parking lot. We would go out on the porch and holler, 'Blue Chevrolet, come on in!' "

Carlen and her husband, Ken, always wanted to have a restaurant. When they were finally able to put financing together, they figured they might serve 25 people for dinner. But within a few weeks, a rave review in an area publication brought in crowds, and they found themselves turning out over 100 dinners nightly. "It's just always been that way ever since," she recalls.

Carlen is from Virginia Beach, where her father, Kieran Sullivan, was stationed as a navy pilot. Her mother, Helene, was French. Helene was raised by her grandparents in France and Algeria. The family foresaw what was coming in Europe. Just before World War II, they sold all their possessions and moved to the United States. Helene became a navy nurse and met and married Carlen's father. Helene was the subject of several articles in the 1960s for her cooking and dinner parties in Virginia Beach. "We [four sisters] had to take off from school for at least two days every Christmas and help her bake cookies, pastries, cakes, and puff pastries for her parties," Carlen recalls. Her mother taught the girls to cook in the style of traditional French families, with influences from the Mediterranean and North Africa thrown in.

Carlen moved from Virginia Beach to North Carolina when she was in college about 40 years ago. "I have always loved the Outer Banks. I was studying to be a teacher and had a part-time job as a waitress." She taught school for a year but could not give up the dream of owning a restaurant. "When I was seven or eight, my father retired from the navy. We had eaten in this big house on the Eastern Shore, and I loved it so much, from then on I dreamed of having a restaurant in a house like that. So after we were married, my husband and I started trying to create a restaurant." They operated their first restaurant, which had only six or seven tables, for two seasons.

"I was driving by the house that is our present location, in a maritime forest. All our friends had always commented that it was the prettiest house in the area. The land itself is among the oldest deeded properties in Dare County. An oak tree in the front yard is estimated to be at least 400 years old. I wrote a letter to the owners and asked to be notified if they ever considered selling it. At first, they were insulted, but later they contacted us. We added a small kitchen and converted the laundry room into bathrooms. Everything else is original."

Although she and her husband had been operating a restaurant for years, Carlen decided to take a week's class at Le Cordon Bleu in Paris. "The experience caused an epiphany. I saw how they emphasized ingredients. I realized that was why people liked our food so much. We have always bought our food from friends and neighbors. We get produce from Riverview Farm in Columbia and George Wood's farm in Elizabeth City; our pork comes from Smithfield, Virginia; crabmeat is out of Lake Mattamuskeet; scallops come from Wanchese boats; shrimp from Pamlico Sound; tuna and mahi from Oregon Inlet; flounder from Albemarle Sound and from the ocean close by. Captains call us from their boats and tell us what they are bringing in. Colington is the soft-shell crab capital of the world. One time, my husband and I were eating in a restaurant in New York, and the waiter bragged that they were serving soft-shell crabs from Colington."

The Restaurant

The Colington Café

The small, picturesque Colington Café has about 75 seats. After Carlen injured her back and had to cut back on daily work in the kitchen, the restaurant brought in Jeff Lane as executive chef about 14 years ago. He is a hands-on chef, not only creating daily specials but doing a large share of the cooking every night. The regular menu retains Carlen's original recipes. Jeff worked at Joe's Sea Grill in Tidewater Virginia, then came to the Outer Banks to cook at the Sanderling Resort. Richie Buscemi joined the kitchen staff nine years ago from Chefs 505 in Greenville, North Carolina. In addition to cooking, he maintains an organic vegetable garden that helps supply the restaurant. James Joyce is the third member of the kitchen team. The trio prepares an average of over 200 meals per night, each cooked to order.

This is a true farm-to-table operation. Bread is the only thing in the restaurant that is not made from scratch in-house. The family tends an herb garden out back and grows heirloom tomatoes as well.

"We specialize in seafood, but our steaks are really popular, too," Carlen says. "We have a lot of filet mignon dishes on the menu. Several years ago, beef prices went sky-high for a while. Lots of places started bringing in Australian beef, but we stayed true to what we had always done, never cutting any corners or reducing quality.

"I just love making people happy with food and wine. I'm big on pairings. One big thing about this restaurant is people always say they feel like they are coming to someone's home. My husband always emphasizes staff, too. Most of our wait staff has been with us for 15 years or more. Our daughter, son, and son-in-law all work here, too. It would just break my heart if anyone ever left here unhappy."

In an article published about 10 years ago, *Southern Living* called The Colington Café the best restaurant for the best price on the Outer Banks. At least 75 percent of its summer customers are repeats from previous years—usually many years. For the last five years, the restaurant has received a Certificate of Excellence from TripAdvisor.com.

Tropical Salsa
Photo provided by Carlen Pearl

The Recipes

Tropical Salsa
Serves 8 to 10

CHEF CARLEN'S NOTE "The first time I ever left the restaurant for someone else to cook, I was so nervous, because I would order fresh seafood in the morning and decide on my special once I saw my seafood. Not knowing which would look best, I wanted to come up with a sauce that could go on shrimp, scallops, or fish. I was making a Mandarin Orange Cake. There was a fresh pineapple and lime in the window sill, and it was hot outside, so I wanted something refreshing and light. I started chopping, mixing together, and tasting. Voila! And the Tropical Salsa was born, and still remains one of the favorites on the menu. This salsa goes great on all seafood and even grilled chicken."

1 cup mandarin oranges, drained
1 cup crushed or fresh-cut pineapple
½ cup diced tomatoes
⅓ cup diced yellow bell pepper
⅓ cup diced red bell pepper

2 tablespoons diced purple onion
2 tablespoons lime juice
2 tablespoons orange juice
2 tablespoons rice wine vinegar
2 tablespoons chopped cilantro
½ teaspoon crushed pepper

Mix all ingredients together and let sit for 1 hour.

Filet de Mer
Serves 4

CHEF'S NOTE "My mother always said one of the hardest combinations was putting seafood and steak together in one dish. So that is why I worked on the Filet de Mer. It is subtle enough not to overpower either the fillet or the shrimp, but because the sauce depends on the juices of both, it marries them together. My mother was impressed."

2 tablespoons unsalted butter
4 tablespoons diced onion
salt and pepper to taste
4 6-ounce beef medallions
16 large shrimp, peeled and deveined
¼ cup cream sherry (good-quality wine, not cooking sherry)
3 tablespoons A1 sauce
2 tablespoons Worcestershire sauce
2 tablespoons Knorr demi-glace (or homemade veal demi-glace)
5 to 6 tablespoons heavy cream

Heat butter in a large sauté pan on medium. Add onions and cook for 1 minute. Salt and pepper medallions and add to hot pan, allowing space between each; do not crowd! For medium-rare, cook 3 minutes on each side; for medium, 4 minutes on each side. Remove fillets to an ovenproof dish. Add shrimp to hot pan and cook for 1 minute. Add sherry and light it, allowing it to cook down. Reduce by ½; this should take about 2 minutes. Add A1, Worcestershire, and demi-glace. Make sure all is blended. Bring to a simmer. Add cream. Simmer until thickened. Pour over medallions. Total cooking time is about 15 minutes.

Filet de Mer
Photo provided by Carlen Pearl

PRESENTATION

If serving a dinner party, you can cook fillets ahead and heat them to desired temperature as shrimp and sauce are cooking.

Berry Cobbler
Serves 6

CHEF'S NOTE "Chef Buscemi's three boys love to pick organic berries from Currituck. When the blackberries are plentiful in the spring, we do blackberry. When the blueberries come in, we do blueberries. When peaches are in, we do a blueberry-peach cobbler."

6 cups fresh or frozen blackberries, blueberries, or combination of both
¾ cup sugar, divided
1 cup plus 4 tablespoons all-purpose flour, divided
½ cup light brown sugar
¼ teaspoon salt

1 cup old-fashioned oats
1½ sticks cold unsalted butter, cut into 1-inch cubes
vanilla ice cream

Preheat oven to 350 degrees. Combine fruit with ¼ cup of the sugar and 4 tablespoons of the flour and place in individual ovenproof bowls or a 9-by-9-inch baking dish. Combine remaining flour, remaining sugar, brown sugar, salt, and oats. Add butter and mix at low speed or mix by hand until large crumbles form. Sprinkle evenly over fruit. Place bowls or baking dish on a sheet pan lined with foil. Bake for 45 minutes or until top is brown.

PRESENTATION

Serve warm with vanilla ice cream.

Berry Cobbler
PHOTO PROVIDED BY CARLEN PEARL

John Homcy

JK'S RESTAURANT

1106 South Croatan Highway

Kill Devil Hills, N.C. 27948

252-441-9555

jksrestaurant.com

The Chef

John Homcy

"There is just too much cute food around," thought J. K. Norfleet. He was an investment banker looking for something new and exciting. So he started a restaurant.

John Homcy met J. K. when J. K. was consulting for Steamers Raw Bar and Grill in Corolla, where John was cooking. John quickly became J. K.'s assistant, and J. K. gradually began serving as a mentor. "I owe a lot of my knowledge about food to J. K.," John remarks. He spent many days by J. K.'s side, learning his recipes.

John and his brother and co-owner, Matt, are New Jersey born and raised.

Their love for food started young. "Every town around us had a great pizza joint, a great deli, and a great Italian restaurant. I had the best food right outside my door," John recalls. He started cooking while he was still in high school and continued in restaurant kitchens part-time while attending Mary Washington College in Fredericksburg, Virginia. After a while, he realized that cooking had become his favorite thing to do.

He moved to the North Carolina coast because he wanted to live where "there were just not so many people. I love to fish, but I was also looking for an opportunity to get into a restaurant and learn the business. I knew that one day I wanted to own a restaurant."

At home, John cooks beef and fresh local seafood such as soft-shell crabs, cobia, tuna, and red drum. He also enjoys cooking fresh vegetables.

The Restaurant

JK's Restaurant

J. K. Norfleet started JK's Restaurant in 1984. All of the recipes came from his family. The original building burned in 1989. When the news got out, J. K. received calls from New York to Iowa from people asking if he would be interested in building a location there. He decided to sell the land instead. John and Matt Homcy became the owners in 1995. Guests took to the new ownership largely because the transition was hard to notice, since John had been working so long for J. K.

John Homcy stays true to J. K. Norfleet's vision, focusing on what he terms "straightforward cooking with fresh, high-quality ingredients. We believe we don't need flashy gimmicks to make our food better. What you see is what you get. Guests enjoy being able to view their orders from start to finish through a Plexiglas window overlooking the grill. JK's philosophy is to put the customer first through excellent service, in the raw product, and in the preparation of that product, and bring them to you with flavor and fair pricing."

JK's gets beef from the Midwest and buys only primal cuts. Its in-house butcher, Mac Magruder, has been cutting meat for over 50 years. When he started, a hacksaw was the standard implement butchers used. He has been with JK's since the restaurant opened. "Mac knows more about meat than we will ever know," says John Homcy. Beef is aged in-house for 30 days. Seafood comes fresh off the docks, sourced primarily through Etheridge Seafood in Wanchese. "They have great product that comes in daily on their boats," remarks John. The restaurant's chickens are raised free-range, without hormones or other chemicals.

Fresh vegetables are delivered from Small Bulman Farms in Weeksville through-out the week.

The kitchen cooks on a one-of-a-kind cast-iron grill fired with mesquite wood, which infuses the food with exceptional flavor. The grill was constructed by Kitty Hawk Iron & Steel.

JK's Cowboy Blend rub has become a favorite of patrons and retailers alike. It sells out frequently. It is used on all of JK's ribs and chicken dishes.

Our State magazine rated JK's one of the top five steakhouses in the state. *Vanity Fair* has published a feature article about the restaurant.

The Recipes

JK's Baby Back Ribs
Serves 1 or 2

¼ cup apple cider vinegar (½ cup for St. Louis ribs)
1 rack baby back pork ribs or 1 rack St. Louis–style pork ribs
JK's Cowboy Blend rub (available via jksrestaurant.com/cms/jks-store/)

Pour vinegar over ribs and rub in. Liberally sprinkle Cowboy Blend on both sides of ribs. Let sit for 2 to 3 hours. Grill baby back ribs from

JK's Baby Back Ribs
PHOTO PROVIDED BY JOHN HOMCY

start to finish over mesquite charcoal. The internal temperature should reach 160 degrees, but measuring temperature in ribs is difficult, so poke several places. Bake St. Louis–style ribs for 30 minutes at 350 degrees, then finish on grill.

JK's Baked Oyster Rockefeller
PHOTO PROVIDED BY JOHN HOMCY

JK's Baked Oyster Rockefeller
Serves 6

Spinach Walnut Pesto
½ pound spinach after cooking and processing (about 1 pound raw)
½ cup fresh parsley
⅓ cup Parmesan cheese, grated fine
¼ cup walnuts
2 anchovy fillets
1 tablespoon chopped garlic
½ tablespoon dried basil
½ tablespoon salt
sprinkle of fennel seed
sprinkle of ground fennel
½ cup olive oil

Blanch spinach and squeeze dry. Chop spinach in a food processor, then remove. Process all remaining ingredients except olive oil. Add spinach back in and process until mixed. Slowly add olive oil in a steady stream.

Oysters
25 oysters
¾ cup Parmesan cheese, grated fine

Preheat oven to 350 degrees. Shuck oysters and leave them on the half shell. Place 1 tablespoon Spinach Walnut Pesto on each oyster. Sprinkle a light coating of Parmesan on each oyster. Bake for 8 to 10 minutes and serve.

KILL DEVIL HILLS

Mako Mike's

MAKO MIKE'S

1630 South Croatan Highway
Milepost 7
Kill Devil Hills, N.C. 27948
252-480-1919
makomikes.com

The Chef

Fred Virgil

Fred Virgil came to the area 30 years ago with his wife, Diana, on vacation. They went back to West Virginia, sold their restaurant, and returned to the Outer Banks. They have never left.

Fred grew up on a farm south of Syracuse, New York. After high school, he started his education at a community college in Upstate New York. He washed dishes at Maples Restaurant in Pompey, south of Syracuse, while he was in school. He learned how to set up catering and began cutting meat. Fred says the owner, Andy Goodwater, was "a great guy. He taught me a lot." In another position, Fred learned to "break down beef" while working for John Morrell and Company, a meat-processing and transportation company. He prepared packages for stores and restaurants and loaded meat aboard tractor-trailers.

He transferred to SUNY Cortland, where he played soccer. While in Cortland, he waited tables and cut meat at the Rusty Nail, a small steakhouse. He then moved to West Virginia to attend Salem College (now Salem International University). He received an undergraduate degree in physical education and taught in Clarksburg. But he found that he liked working in restaurants better than teaching. He worked for about five years at Bridgeport Country Club, where he studied under a "great chef," Steve Creasey. "That's where I learned about fresh fish. He showed me how to handle it, keep it, sear it, and grill it. I still follow his rules."

Fred owned a bar/restaurant for about four years in Clarksburg after that. He met Diana there. He discovered that she liked fishing almost as much as he did. That was when they came to the Outer Banks.

He met another chef-mentor at Mako Mike's. "Mac Ritter was a walking encyclopedia regarding techniques and general food knowledge," Fred says. "He was from Elizabeth City, a culinary-school graduate who had worked in Europe. It was like he taught us something new every day. I learned more from him in a couple of years than in all of my previous life in the kitchen. Sauces, combinations of fruits and vegetables, soups—he was just a master."

Fred was sous chef at Mako Mike's for about six years and was promoted to executive chef when Mac left.

He reflects on work life at Mako Mike's: "In summer, we get people from all over the world who come here to work. I try to pick their brains and learn from their experiences, too. The best thing at this stage of my life [age 63] is watching the young kids work. You explain something, see a light come on, see what they put together, watch them run with an idea. It's great to see them grow. You teach them how to fillet a fresh fish, then just see how it becomes automatic. They go off to culinary school, then come back and work for me again.

"My wife cooks for me when I'm at home. My wife and two sons are all in food service. She is kitchen manager at the local elementary school. One son is a culinary-school graduate. He's the sous chef at Ruth's Chris in Wilmington. The other son is cooking pizza while he attends Cape Fear Community College, studying finance."

The Restaurant

Mako Mike's

Mako Mike's motto is "Let the Feeding Frenzy Begin." The restaurant is part of the Kelly Hospitality Group, named after Mike Kelly, who owns the three restaurants in the corporation. The Octopus Bar at Mako Mike's provides casual accommodations. The main dining room is decorated in rich blue and aqua and contrasted in beige and white. The accessories follow a shark theme.

In keeping with the theme, sautéed or deep-fried Mako Shark Bites are offered as an appetizer. Main courses include Angus beef, North Carolina seafood, chicken, and pork. More casual fare is on the menu, too: burgers, plus pizzas baked in a wood-burning oven. The pricing is especially attractive for dinner guests arriving before 5:30.

Chef Virgil remarks, "We have a base menu that we always offer. But we add to that often. We have to be versatile, because we have so many different types of customers. You have to keep them interested, and you have to challenge your staff, too. Most soups here are seafood-based, until winter, when we do some chili. A lot of the Italian influence on the menu comes from my wife, her mother, and their Italian family."

He considers Mako Mike's most distinctive feature to be its orientation toward families. "We can seat large groups of 20 or more. Locals come in, as well as tourists. We're open year-round. We have things children like to eat.

"Local connections here are huge. We get summer vegetables—zucchini, yellow squash—from a farmer in Edenton. Peaches, strawberries, and blueberries come from a farm in Currituck. Etheridge Seafood in Wanchese is our main fish and shellfish supplier. We get Gulf Stream fish from them. We get larger, offshore fish from a company in Newport News. We get them the day after they are caught."

Mako Mike's is a sponsor of Dine Out to Help Out, a fundraiser for the Food Bank of the Albemarle. It is also a strong supporter of Outer Banks Catch.

The Recipes

Crab and Artichoke Dip
Serves 4 to 6

2½ tablespoons butter, softened
1¼ pounds cream cheese, softened
2½ cups artichoke hearts, chopped fine
7 tablespoons Worcestershire sauce
¾ cup Dijon mustard
1 tablespoon pepper
1 tablespoon fresh garlic, chopped fine
2½ cups freshly grated Parmesan cheese
¼ cup chopped fresh parsley
1 pound lump blue crabmeat
pita wedges

Crab and Artichoke Dip

Preheat oven to 350 degrees. In a mixing bowl, blend butter, cream cheese, and artichokes until smooth. Add Worcestershire, Dijon, pepper, and garlic until blended. Mix in Parmesan and most of the parsley, reserving a little for garnish. Fold in crabmeat, being careful not to break up lumps. Bake in a shallow casserole dish for 10 to 15 minutes until warm and light brown on top.

PRESENTATION
Sprinkle with parsley and serve with fried or baked pita wedges.

Teriyaki-Glazed Gulf Stream Fish with Citrus Salsa
Serves 6

Teriyaki Sauce
½ cup fresh ginger, peeled, diced fine
¼ cup fresh garlic, peeled, diced fine
½ cup dry cocktail sherry
1 cup fresh orange juice
1 cup brown sugar
2 cups soy sauce
5 tablespoons cornstarch

Combine all ingredients in a 2-quart saucepan. Bring to a boil, stirring constantly. Lower heat and simmer for 5 minutes. Strain. Can be refrigerated for up to 1 week.

Teriyaki-Glazed Gulf Stream Fish with Citrus Salsa
Photo provided by Mako Mike's

Citrus Salsa

CHEF'S NOTE "Ingredients can be changed according to the season. Use what is fresh and ripe."

1 cup golden pineapple, diced medium
1 cup cantaloupe, diced medium
1 cup honeydew melon, diced medium
1 cup watermelon, seeded, diced medium
¼ cup chopped cilantro
½ cup red bell pepper, seeded, diced fine
zest and juice of 1 orange
zest and juice of 1 lime
¼ cup red onion, diced fine
1 teaspoon apple cider vinegar
salt and pepper to taste

Combine all ingredients in a mixing bowl. Keep chilled until ready to use.

Fish

salt and pepper to taste
6 4- to 6-ounce pieces firm-fleshed fish (grouper, mahi-mahi, or any other that is in season)

Salt and pepper each side of fish. Grill fish, starting with service side down. When internal temperature reaches 100 degrees, turn. Drizzle Teriyaki Sauce over top. Continue grilling until internal temperature reaches 135 degrees.

PRESENTATION

Drizzle more Teriyaki Sauce over top of fish. Scatter Citrus Salsa over fish.

OUTER BANKS BREWING STATION

600 South Croatan Highway

Milepost 8½

Kill Devil Hills, N.C. 27948

252-449-2739

obbrewing.com

Tony Duman
PHOTO PROVIDED BY
OUTER BANKS BREWING STATION

The Chef

Tony Duman

Tony Duman grew up in the latchkey kid era. "I came home and fixed whatever food was in the fridge for my brother and me," he recalls. "Until my senior year of high school, I wanted to become a marine biologist or an oceanographer. I took a catering class for an easy A. But my teacher saw how much I enjoyed cooking, and she urged me to enter an upcoming competition. I wound up winning a scholarship to the Art Institute of Atlanta culinary program."

He is from Portsmouth, Virginia. In 2002, his mother talked with the chef from the Currituck Club in Corolla. She told the chef that her son was about to graduate from culinary school. "He told me to come down and apply," Tony says. "I got the job in March 2003. I love the outdoor life and the fun, relaxed mindset of the Outer Banks. I love to just sit by the sound or ocean and feel the air, listen to the sounds, and zone out.

"Culinary school instilled the basics, but you really learn in the field. My style is a combination of my personal tastes, my maternal Boston Jewish palate, my paternal black Southern palate, and the ever-changing food culture that influences us all."

Tony worked at several places on the Outer Banks and in Atlanta. "I've taken something away from everywhere I've worked. You have to have your eyes and ears open at all times, then figure out what works best for you. I've seen things I didn't like, so I try not to fall into those patterns, and I've seen things I've put in my pocket for later use." He considers his strongest influences to be Asian or Latin, "but I don't want to get stuck in ruts."

On his own, Tony eats everything. "I was raised to try any food at least once. So there's not much I don't like. Pork belly tacos from Bad Bean (see pages 48-53), good fried chicken, home-smoked ribs or pulled pork North Carolina-style, pho, tamales, Indian food, Thai curry pork, green papaya salad—it really just depends on my mood. If I have time to put a butt on for a few hours for some barbecue, I will, or I'll grill a couple of steaks, make pasta, bacon and eggs for dinner, make a nice salad with grilled chicken, or maybe chicken saltimbocca."

The Restaurant

Outer Banks Brewing Station

The Outer Banks Brewing Station grew out of friendships formed in the Peace Corps.

Eric Reece graduated from Boston University with a degree in applied physiology. Aubrey Davis received his degree in mechanical engineering with a specialty in rural water generation from North Carolina State. They met during their Peace Corps training. When they were working in Thailand, they became acquainted with Christina Mackenzie. The restaurant's website contains a narrative of some of the trio's adventures.

When they completed their terms in 1993, they pursued different career paths but stayed in touch. Reece went to work in pharmaceuticals for Bayer Biologicals in Berkeley, California. Davis joined the National Park Service. Mackenzie earned her baking certificate at the California Culinary Institute in Berkeley.

Reece subsequently became enamored with Bison Brewing, a brewpub near his residence in Berkeley, one of the pioneers in the genre. The brew master there was Scott Meyer. Reece was so fascinated with beer making that he took a massive pay cut and went to work with Meyer.

While growing up, Davis had spent summers at his grandparents' house on the Outer Banks. He remembers his grandparents talking about meeting Orville and Wilbur Wright in 1902. He played around with home brewing when working for the park service. Davis and Reece began talking about starting a brewpub on the North Carolina coast. During 1997–98, a partnership of family and friends bought land. Volunteers organized by the Outer Banks Chamber of Commerce provided management assistance.

The Outer Banks Brewing Station opened in 2001, becoming one of the first brewpub restaurants in the state. The building, designed by architect Ben Cahoon, is an interpretation of a turn-of-the-20th-century lifesaving station; the bar represents a lifesaving boat, pointed toward the sea. Scott Meyer, who moved to North Carolina to become brew master, consulted in the design of the brewery.

By the time the Outer Banks Brewing Station opened, Christina Mackenzie and Eric Reese had married. Christina had developed a strong following for her work as pastry chef at Basnight's Lone Cedar Café (see pages 107-12), whose owner, Marc Basnight, gave her cupcakes to patrons, spawning her nickname, "Cupcake."

About five years after opening, the Outer Banks Brewing Station became the first wind-powered brewery in the United States, following the installation of a windmill on the premises. The restaurant was also the first business to produce wind power on the Outer Banks. That innovation brought recognition from *National Geographic* and other publications.

Tony Duman became executive chef in 2014 after several years as sous chef. He observes, "The brewery inspires me to use beer, malt, and hops in food. The owners allow freedom to experiment, so that keeps us fresh and different, because we aren't stuck in just burgers or Italian, Asian, or Latin." Regarding ingredients, Duman says that "the Outer Banks is a tight network, so we constantly connect with local farms and fishermen. Or they just pop in and introduce themselves and their product, and a partnership ensues."

Outer Banks Brewing Station beers have won numerous medals: bronze in 2002 in the Herb and Spice Beer category at the Great American Beer Festival; silver in 2010 in the Herb and Spice Beer or Chocolate category, bronze in 2012 in the German-Style Sour Ale category, and gold in 2014 in the German-Style Heller Bock/Maibock category at the World Beer Cup; and one gold and three bronzes in the Carolinas Championship of Beer in 2014. Reviews or features have appeared in *NC Boating Lifestyle, AAA Go, Our State*, the *Norfolk Virginian-Pilot*, the *Hampton Roads Growler*, and the Food Network's *Diners, Drive-Ins and*

Dives television show. The restaurant has taken several awards in Taste of the Beach. The team is extremely active in fundraising projects in support of local and national initiatives.

The Recipes

Caprese Salad with Blueberry Basil Vinaigrette

Serves 4

Caprese Salad with Blueberry Basil Vinaigrette

Blueberry Basil Vinaigrette

1 cup fresh blueberries
juice of ½ lime
½ cup chopped basil
¼ cup balsamic vinegar
3 tablespoons honey
½ teaspoon salt
½ teaspoon pepper
2 teaspoons Dijon mustard
½ cup olive oil

Combine all ingredients except oil in a blender and blend well. Scrape down the sides. With the blender on low speed, add oil in a thin stream until all is mixed in, then blend on medium. If vinaigrette is a little thick, add 1 or 2 tablespoons of water. Keep refrigerated until ready to use. Serve at room temperature. Stir before pouring, as vinaigrette may thicken or separate.

Salad

8 cups salad greens mix
1 pound fresh mozzarella cheese, sliced ¼ inch
    thick
3 or 4 local heirloom tomatoes, sliced ¼ inch thick
¼ cup basil, sliced thin

Divide salad mix among 4 plates and top with alternating slices of mozzarella and tomato. Scatter basil on each salad.

PRESENTATION
Drizzle Blueberry Basil Vinaigrette over salads and serve immediately.

Seared Scallops over Pea, Corn, and Bacon Risotto
Serves 4

Risotto
2 tablespoons butter
1 shallot, minced
1 cup Arborio rice
½ cup white wine
salt and pepper to taste
4 cups chicken stock
2 tablespoons chopped parsley
¼ cup shelled green peas
¼ cup corn kernels
¼ cup chopped bacon
¼ cup grated Parmesan cheese

Seared Scallops over Pea, Corn, and Bacon Risotto
Photo provided by
Outer Banks Brewing Station

In a medium-sized heavy saucepan, melt butter on medium-low heat. Add shallots and sauté about 1 minute. Add dry rice and sauté about 2 minutes, mixing until well coated and translucent. Add wine and salt and pepper and mix well until absorbed into rice. Pour 1 cup stock into rice and mix until absorbed. Add another cup. Continue adding and stirring for 20 to 25 minutes until all broth is absorbed. Add parsley, peas, corn, bacon, and Parmesan and mix well.

Scallops

12 medium to large sea scallops (16 to 18 ounces total weight)
salt and freshly ground pepper to taste
1 tablespoon butter, divided

Season scallops with salt and pepper. Heat a medium-sized pan on high temperature. When pan is hot, melt ½ of the butter and place ½ of the scallops in the pan. Be careful not to overcrowd, and make sure pan is hot or scallops will not get that beautiful brown crust and color. Sear for 90 seconds (being careful not to move scallops) until bottoms form a nice caramel-colored crust. Turn and cook about 90 seconds until centers are slightly translucent; check by viewing from the side. Be careful not to overcook. Remove scallops from pan and set aside on a warm plate. Add remaining butter and cook remaining scallops.

PRESENTATION

Plate risotto first, then top with scallops.

Seared Tuna Fillet over Jasmine Rice and Snow Peas with Watermelon Salsa and Goat Cheese

Serves 4

Watermelon Salsa

2 cups watermelon, seeded and diced
½ medium red onion, diced
1 cup tomato, seeded and diced
¼ bunch cilantro, chopped
juice of 1 lime
1 teaspoon lime zest
1 teaspoon salt
freshly ground pepper to taste

Combine all ingredients in a mixing bowl and let marinate while you prepare rest of dish. This can sit overnight in the refrigerator.

Spice Blend

1 tablespoon coriander seeds

Seared Tuna Fillet over Jasmine Rice and Snow Peas with Watermelon Salsa and Goat Cheese

PHOTO BY OUTER BANKS BREWING STATION

½ teaspoon cayenne pepper
2 teaspoons black peppercorns
1 teaspoon salt

Grind all ingredients in a mini food processor or spice grinder until they are powdery. If you don't have the equipment, just buy the ground versions of each spice. Spread spice mixture evenly on a large plate.

Rice

2½ cups Thai jasmine rice
3 cups water

Place rice in a small saucepan. Cover with water, swirl, and pour water out 2 or 3 times. (This rids the rice of excess starch and broken rice, which makes the cooked rice mushy and sticky.) Add just enough water (approximately 3 cups) to cover top of rice by ½ inch. Cover with lid and place over medium to medium-high heat. Bring to a boil. Reduce heat to low. Simmer for about 10 minutes until water has completely evaporated. Turn off heat and allow rice to sit, covered, for at least 5 minutes. Serve hot or at room temperature.

Fish and Vegetables

4 6-ounce tuna fillets, cut about 1½ inches thick
3 tablespoons olive oil, divided
¾ pound snow peas
¼ pound carrots, shredded
½ medium red onion, sliced
salt and pepper to taste
1 cup crumbled goat cheese

Rinse fillets and pat dry. Place 1 side of each fillet into spice mixture. Shake off excess. In a 10-inch nonstick skillet, heat 1 tablespoon of the olive oil over high heat until almost smoking. Carefully place 2 fillets spiced side down into skillet. A spice crust should form within 1 minute. Using kitchen tongs, turn over fillets, lower heat to medium, and cook for 2 to 5 minutes to desired doneness. Repeat process with remaining fillets. Quickly rinse and wipe skillet dry. Heat remaining 2 tablespoons of olive oil over medium heat. Add snow peas, carrots, and onions. Stir to prevent burning. Add salt and pepper.

PRESENTATION

Spoon a mound of rice in center of each plate. Layer rice with vegetables, tuna, and Watermelon Salsa. Garnish with goat cheese and drizzle small amount of olive oil over top.

BRAD PRICE, PERSONAL CHEF

bradpriceart@gmail.com

PHOTO PROVIDED
BY BRAD PRICE

Brad Price was executive chef at the famed Elizabeth's in Duck before it was sold in the fall of 2014. He is now a personal chef. Chef Price will arrange a menu with you in advance, then come to your location and prepare the meal.

He came to the Outer Banks after high school to surf and just have fun. He never planned to stay and never thought of being a chef. But he worked nights in restaurants in order to free up his days for surfing and wound up with a career in the kitchen.

He started out washing dishes at the Rundown Café (see pages 38-44). His experiences there helped him develop an interest in professional cooking. "Mike Montiel was a waiter then. He owns the place now." In the winter, Brad cooked at the upscale Red Fox at the Snowshoe ski resort in West Virginia.

His decision to go to culinary school came at about age 25. He graduated in the mid-1990s from the Florida Culinary Institute. "Culinary school then was set up for adults who were converting to new careers, not people straight out of high school, the way it is now," Brad says. "The change to a younger clientele started a few years later. What has happened is a bunch of kids come out of school thinking they are really hot, but they have never actually worked in a restaurant. So they have to go through a lot of professional growth on the job. My generation went to culinary school after we had already learned something about the real world. More recently, culinary programs have gotten more serious, with more elaborate internships. The profession is really growing."

Habaneros *painting by Brad Price*
PHOTO PROVIDED BY BRAD PRICE

After culinary school, he cooked at Paletti's in Melbourne, Florida, a fine-dining Italian restaurant, then came back to the Outer Banks. He took over the kitchen at Elizabeth's in 1998.

Chef Price takes his cooking cues from wine pairings and the freshest and best ingredients he can find. "I don't study recipes or keep many recipes. I just look at the ingredients that are in front of me and determine what the most important flavor ought to be. I don't try to put 21 different tastes in one dish. The older I get, the simpler I get, as long as the ingredients are right. I pick from different styles and make up my own stuff. I don't sweat over authenticity, although I respect tradition. I'm going to put my own spin on it, no matter what."

When he's not cooking, he is an artist, with food a frequent theme. When he cooks at home, "it's a hamburger on a grill with a six-pack alongside. I am more of a simple eater. I don't need to glamorize things for myself after I have done that all week in a restaurant. On my day off, I'm a backyard kind of guy."

He worries a little when "people are scared to invite me over for dinner because I'm a chef. They are afraid I'm going to pick things apart. But I tell them if you invite me and cook for me, it will be the best I've ever had, because you cooked it for me and I did not have to do it!" He seldom goes to restaurants. "It's not because I'm critical of their food, it's because I don't want to watch other people work. I especially don't like restaurants with an open kitchen! I don't watch any cooking shows. I've never seen a food TV program."

FULL MOON CAFÉ & BREWERY

208 Queen Elizabeth Avenue

Manteo, N.C. 27954

252-473-6666

thefullmooncafe.com

Sharon Enoch
PHOTO BY JAMES ISRAEL SOUTHERN

The Chefs

Sharon Enoch, Chef-Owner and
Paul Charron, Brewer-Owner

"My spice rack is my palette, the incredible bounty of the Outer Banks is my canvas," remarks Sharon Enoch, reflecting on how she creates dishes for the menu at Full Moon Café.

She grew up in Baltimore in a family of nine children. Cooking for the crowd was required of the older kids. One of Sharon's fondest memories involves standing on a chair over the stove making homemade spaghetti sauce. On Sunday nights, her mom would break out the china, set a formal table in the dining room, and serve up international fare such as veal piccata, Hungarian beef stew, imperial crab, and eggplant Parmesan. She learned to consider a meal as more than just food. "It's an adventure that can take you to exotic places and enlarge your view of the world," she observes.

Paul Charron, a Manhattan native, met Sharon in college. They dated for years, married in 1988, and moved to the Outer Banks in 1989, when Paul landed a job as chief pilot for Kitty Hawk Aero Tours. "Moving here was like falling in love all over again. The sun, the sky, the stars, the ocean, the sounds, the storms, the smell of salt air—it all makes you feel so connected to the earth," he says.

Paul and Sharon have been married for 26 years and have three sons. They have jointly run the Full Moon Café for almost 20 years, making theirs a lifetime partnership both at home and at work. "And we still like each other, we still consider ourselves best friends," Sharon vows. Their sons have all worked at the café, learning the business from the ground up by starting out washing dishes and busing tables. Paul, the oldest and an aeronautical engineering student at North Carolina State, has racked up a decade of hard work at the ripe old age of 22. Aidan, who aspires to be a veterinarian, is currently working as the summer fry cook. "Keagan is chomping at the bit to join in the family business, but I am making him wait until he's 13," Sharon declares.

The Restaurant

Full Moon Café & Brewery

Sharon opened the café in 1995, determined to bring a "sense of food adventure" to the Outer Banks. "Basically, when we arrived here, the culinary scene boiled down to whether you wanted your seafood fried or broiled," she recalls. "I had traveled extensively after college and was determined to bring the lessons of culinary experimentation to my menu. I was also riding the explosive wave of the California ethos in cooking and the fusion of ethnic culture into cutting-edge American cuisine. All of a sudden, curry wasn't a spice used exclusively in Indian cuisine, fish could be topped with mango salsa, and pasta could be sauced with something other than marinara."

She introduced customers to ingredients and recipes almost unknown in the region at that time: Brie, portobello mushrooms, hummus, baba ganoush, balsamic vinegar, Mushroom Gorgonzola Soup, Shrimp Etouffée, Cajun Shrimp, Curried Chicken Salad. "I didn't invent this stuff, but I was one of the first in this area to stretch the parameters of the typical coastal cuisine menu. All these 'exotic' ingredients are mainstream now, but back then I was 'the crazy Yankee whose cookin' wouldn't take.' We have grown and evolved every year. I'm happy to say that I'm not on the cutting edge anymore, happy to realize that my style and the Outer Banks 'fried or broiled' have meshed into a peaceful detente."

Paul started home-brewing about 10 years ago. The couple decided three years back that his beer "obsession" had to be taken to the next level, so they launched the Lost Colony Brewery as an adjunct to the restaurant. Out of the smallest brewery on the East Coast, Paul and his brewer, Owen Sullivan, have managed to produce world-class ales that have landed eight medals at the World Beer Championships. The tiny operation has competed and placed against craft-industry giants.

In addition to serving nine ales brewed on the premises, Sharon tries to incorporate Paul's beers into the menu whenever possible. The Fish and Chips are dipped in Paul's beer batter, soups and sauces get a healthy dollop of craft ale, and the couple is currently developing an Imperial Stout Ice Cream Float that uses beer instead of root beer.

Avid participants in Outer Banks Catch, they are dedicated to sourcing ingredients locally and regionally. "Local blue crabs begin molting right around the first full moon in May, and soft-shells appear on the menu shortly after," Sharon says. "The Andouille sausage used in our Shrimp and Grits is produced within 30 minutes of our door, and locally grown Currituck produce is used whenever possible. We also recycle whatever we can, not just plastic and glass but any by-product we can find a use for. Paul uses the spent grains from brewing to feed a local herd of Black Angus cattle. It's a scream to watch them come running whenever they see his truck round the corner in the field. Tortilla chips that are too broken up to serve get parsed out to anyone we know who has chickens. Spent grains are also used to produce our very popular Brew Chews for dogs. Paul has rigged up a system to capture the condensation from our main air-conditioning unit, which he uses to water all the plants on our property and anything in the town within range of his hose. He estimates that he captures and reuses 14,000 gallons a year. We believe in hard work and integrity. Our passion for what we do keeps us moving forward."

The next phase of their operation will include an expansion of the brewery, so their craft beers can be distributed to other locations.

The restaurant has received praise from national newspapers. The *Washington Post* judged it "delightful and affordable," while the *New York Daily News* commented on the kitchen's "culinary magic."

The Recipes

Crab Dip
Serves 4

8 ounces cream cheese, softened
1 teaspoon horseradish
1 teaspoon Old Bay seasoning
1 tablespoon parsley
½ clove garlic
¼ to ½ cup half-and-half or whole milk
¼ pound lump crabmeat
sprinkle of Parmesan cheese
toasted pita wedges

Preheat oven to 350 degrees. Put first 5 ingredients in a food processor. Mix until blended. Drizzle half-and-half into mixture until a dip-like consistency is achieved. Put dip into an ovenproof ceramic dish. Top with crabmeat and sprinkle with Parmesan. Bake about 15 minutes until bubbling. (You can microwave the dip for 1½ minutes until bubbling to save time.)

Crab Dip

PRESENTATION
Serve with toasted pita wedges.

Icarus Pasta
PHOTO BY JAMES ISRAEL SOUTHERN

Icarus Pasta
Serves 2

4 to 8 ounces large pasta noodles such as penne or rotini
1 small onion, sliced thin
handful of grape or cherry tomatoes, halved
10 Kalamata olives, pitted and halved
1 tablespoon olive oil
12 large shrimp
½ teaspoon dried basil
½ teaspoon dried oregano
½ clove garlic, minced
generous handful of fresh spinach
1 cup half-and-half
½ cup feta cheese
salt and pepper to taste
toasted French bread

Cook pasta according to package directions. Sauté onions, tomatoes, and olives in olive oil in a large pan until onions are slightly caramelized. Add shrimp and cook for about 5 minutes until light pink with no gray remaining. Add basil, oregano, garlic, and spinach and cook until spinach is wilted. Mix in half-and-half and feta and reduce until a creamy consistency is reached. Add cooked pasta and mix until coated with sauce. Add salt and pepper. (Be careful about seasoning with salt. Both the feta and the olives are brined and already salty. Taste before adding salt.)

PRESENTATION

Place pasta in bowls and cover with rest of mixture. Serve with toasted French bread.

ORTEGA'Z

201 Sir Walter Street
Manteo, N.C. 27954
252-473-5911
ortegaz.com

Marcelo Ortega
PHOTO PROVIDED BY ORTEGA'Z

The Chef

Marcelo Ortega

Lisa Ortega loves owning a restaurant. "It's like throwing a party every night!" she says.

Marcelo Ortega was born in Santiago, Chile, grew up in New York, and moved to North Carolina with his family. He started working in a restaurant at about age 16. He dropped his paper route when he was offered a position busing tables at Annabelle's in Hickory, North Carolina. There, he worked for Ken Howerin. He eventually moved into the kitchen, where he cooked beside Ken for about 25 years. "He taught me everything," Marcelo says. "He was like a father figure. He was one of the groomsmen in my wedding."

Ken eventually left Annabelle's to work for a corporate chain, and Marcelo departed with him, moving to Charlotte. He enjoyed the fast pace and was fascinated with how so many complex tasks came together in a restaurant. He began to appreciate the skills and knowledge required for professional cooking. "The corporate structure provides excellent training regarding consistency and cost control," he says.

Marcelo moved to Manteo in 2001 to work for his older brother, Freddy, who had opened a restaurant, the Magnolia Grille (now closed). By then, he had developed a special appreciation for seafood. He wanted to make the local connection with seafood and produce, as well as to reconnect with family.

He met Lisa, who became his wife, in Manteo. Originally from California, she joined the Coast Guard after high school and was stationed at Cape May, New Jersey. That period taught her that cold weather was not for her, so she started looking for work in the South after completing her tour of duty. She fell into the restaurant business easily. With their shared experiences in the business, starting a restaurant was an obvious goal. "Owning our own restaurant provides freedom and creativity. It also allows us to spend time with family when we need to," Lisa explains.

Manteo "is the perfect place to raise children," she says. They have two daughters, Emma and Abigail, and a son, Alexander. Emma, their oldest, helps out in the restaurant from time to time. She loves the interaction with the public, having developed social skills well beyond her age.

The Restaurant

Ortega'z

The name *Ortega'z* is a play on words, combining the English possessive sound and punctuation with the owners' name. The property has quite a history. Malcolm and Susan Fearing bought it in 2007. When they began renovations, they discovered remnants of previous businesses. Members of the famous Midgett family had run an Esso gas station there in the 1930s and 1940s. It became Fernando's Ale House in the 1970s, decorated in part with boards removed from the owner's barn. The Green Dolphin Pub emerged in the 1980s. A scene from the television series *Matlock* starring Manteo resident Andy Griffith was filmed there.

Interior designer Alison Martin, the Fearings' daughter, assisted the Ortegas with the redesign that produced the current concept. They honored history by retaining the previous occupant's barn siding. Hurricane Irene flooded Manteo in 2011, but the families worked together to repair and reopen the building whose life spans over 70 years of local history.

As befits Chef Ortega's background, the menu at Ortega'z is organized around Latin American dishes. A wine bar occupies center stage beyond the entryway.

"We call the food 'southwestern fare with a coastal kick,' " Chef Ortega explains. "Infusion of local seafood is the main difference between our restaurant, compared to more traditional southwestern restaurants. We are huge into Outer Banks Catch. We stay true to buying local. If it's not 100 percent, it's close. The only variations depend on the season and the area fishing restrictions."

The restaurant buys seafood from O'Neal's Sea Harvest in Wanchese. "They do a lot of retail selling, too, but they are huge in restaurant connections. Owners and chefs have the opportunity to pick whatever they want. It's a real hands-on experience," Chef Ortega says. Vegetables are sourced from Coastal Farmers Co-op in Kitty Hawk and Somerset Farm in Edenton.

Marcelo believes that fate has played a hand in his life. "The restaurant gods looked at Lisa and me and paired us up, then matched us with the Fearing family, and it has been a real blessing to be able to combine our talents and create our own stamp on an idea that would be appreciated in the area. To be able to do that and raise three kids in such a wholesome setting is very fortunate. We can go to soccer games, recitals, or other activities for the kids but still operate the restaurant, too."

Ortega'z has been featured on the Food Network series *Diners, Drive-Ins and Dives*, with a celebrity appearance by Guy Fieri. "When that episode was shown, it really gave us a boost," Marcelo recalls.

The Recipe

Shrimp and Chorizo Alfredo with Roasted Poblano and Sun-Dried Tomato Pesto
Serves 2 or 3

Blackening Seasoning
⅛ teaspoon smoked paprika
¼ teaspoon oregano
¼ teaspoon thyme
⅛ teaspoon cayenne pepper
⅛ teaspoon white pepper

Combine all ingredients in a bowl.

Shrimp and Chorizo Alfredo with Roasted Poblano and Sun-Dried Tomato Pesto
PHOTO PROVIDED BY ORTEGA'Z

Roasted Poblano and Sun-Dried Tomato Pesto

½ cup poblano peppers, veins, skins, and seeds removed, roasted and chopped
    fine
¼ cup rehydrated sun-dried tomatoes
¼ cup pine nuts, roasted
¼ cup chopped cilantro
juice of 1 lime
¼ teaspoon Worcestershire sauce
⅓ cup Manchego cheese
½ cup extra-virgin olive oil

Combine all ingredients except olive oil in a food processor. Turn processor on low and slowly stream in oil to form a thick, pasty sauce.

Shrimp and Chorizo

2 tablespoons olive oil
2 4-ounce Spanish-style chorizo sausage links, cut into ¼-inch pieces

8 large shrimp, peeled and deveined, tails removed
8 grape tomatoes, halved
5 cremini mushrooms, quartered
¼ cup chicken stock
¾ cup heavy cream
1 pound penne pasta, cooked according to package directions
½ lime
2 tablespoons shredded Manchego cheese
½ cup fresh spinach leaves
1 tablespoon chopped cilantro

Add olive oil to a sauté pan over high heat. When oil is hot, add chorizo and cook for 3 minutes. Toss shrimp in ⅛ teaspoon Blackening Seasoning, then sear on 1 side. Flip shrimp and reduce heat to medium-high. Add Roasted Poblano and Sun-Dried Tomato Pesto and cook until pesto begins to break down. Add tomatoes and mushrooms. Cook 2 minutes and add chicken stock to deglaze pan. Once deglazed, add cream and sauté until mixture comes to a rolling boil. Add pasta and sauté about 2 minutes until pasta is hot and coated.

PRESENTATION
Transfer mixture to a large bowl and squeeze lime over the top. Garnish with Manchego, spinach leaves, and cilantro.

Alfredo R. Landazuri
PHOTO PROVIDED BY STRIPERS BAR & GRILLE

STRIPERS BAR & GRILLE

1100A South Bay Club Drive

Manteo, N.C. 27954

252-475-1021

stripersbarandgrille.com

The Chef

Alfredo R. Landazuri

Alfredo Landazuri has two passions in life: food and family. "In my family, it's like you either cook or you don't eat!" he says.

He was born in Lima, Peru, and moved to the Outer Banks in 2003, when he was 18, after completing training at the Cenfotur Culinary Institute in Lima. His mother had a friend who lived in Manteo and talked about how beautiful the town was. Alfredo had grown up on the coast of Peru, so he was accustomed to fresh local seafood, beautiful beaches, and good people. He finds Manteo a lot like his original home.

He started cooking with his grandmother, whom he describes as "my best friend," when he was 11. Everybody in his family cooks. His father specializes in Italian, while family members on his mother's side cook "amazing" Peruvian cuisine.

Alfredo became seriously interested in professional food service after arriving on the Outer Banks. "I went to cooking school because I wanted to be a good chef. But after I moved to the Outer Banks, I realized that I not only love cooking, I also love customer service."

He started out working at Basnight's Lone Cedar Café (see pages 107-12) in Nags Head as a dishwasher. "That place taught me about good local seafood, fresh ingredients, and a passion for food," he recalls. At the original Stripers Bar & Grille, he worked for Tom Lozupone, the general manager, as a cook. One year later, at age 22, Alfredo was promoted to kitchen manager. "I learned a lot from my good friend Tom and from the way he runs the business." Alfredo moved to the Sunfish Grill for two years as kitchen manager and general manager. There, he says, "I learned more about myself and how to work better with other people."

Jim Douglas, owner of the original Stripers property, decided to sell it in 2011. He told Edward Groce and Tom Groce about the property's availability. They owned a substantial amount of real estate in the Shallowbag Bay development, as well as Art FX, a printing company. They initiated the purchasing process and talked to Tom Lozupone, who by that time was chef at Clyde's of Gallery Place in Washington, D.C. Lozupone mentioned that he knew a well-trained, respected, passionate chef who would be perfect for the new restaurant. Within a few days, Chef Landazuri met with the Groce family at their business in Norfolk. On December 31, they handed over the keys "to the beginning of my new future. Stripers Bar & Grille was reopened with my passion, desire, and drive," Alfredo says. He purchased the rights to the name *Stripers* from Jim Douglas. "Why change it? It was already in the heart of Manteo."

At home, Alfredo's children love their father's spaghetti. For his own part, "I eat anything," Alfredo says. "But I definitely love good rice or dishes with pasta."

The Restaurant

Stripers Bar & Grille

Stripers occupies a three-story building in the corner of the Shallowbag Bay Marina. Every seat has a view of Roanoke Sound. The first floor features a steamer bar, an outdoor patio, and a screened porch. Boat slips are available for guests who want to tie up and have dinner. The second floor is the main dining area. The third floor has an outside deck, along with inside seating.

In the kitchen, Chef Landazuri insists first on a clean work station from every cook. Then he allows his passion for fresh local ingredients to emerge in the dishes he creates. "We use a lot of local seafood purchased from fish houses in Wanchese," he says. "We are members of Outer Banks Catch. It's all about local seafood and fresh produce."

He supplements the menu with specials that are often derived from Latin American cuisine. At Taste of the Beach, he has provided a culinary tour of South America, including some especially noteworthy empanadas. Stripers won the "People's Choice" award at Taste of the Beach in 2013 and 2014, in addition to honors for chowder and barbecue. At the March of Dimes Signature Chefs Auction in 2014, Stripers was named Best Decorated Station.

The Recipes

Lobster Bisque

Serves 4

¼ pound yellow onion
2 stalks celery
2 tablespoons garlic
4 tablespoons butter
¼ pound lobster meat, chopped fine
1 tablespoon lobster base
¾ quart heavy cream

Lobster Bisque
PHOTO PROVIDED BY STRIPERS BAR & GRILLE

6 ounces softened cream cheese, room temperature
1 teaspoon white pepper
¼ teaspoon cayenne pepper
oyster crackers
chopped parsley for garnish

Shred onion, celery, and garlic in a food processor. Melt butter in a medium saucepan and add vegetables. Cook on medium heat until soft. Add lobster, stir, and cook for 10 minutes. Add lobster base, cream, cream cheese, white pepper, and cayenne. Bring to a slow boil, stirring often to prevent scorching. Simmer for 5 minutes.

PRESENTATION

Serve in colorful bowls with oyster crackers and parsley.

Tuna Sashimi
Serves 4

Tuna
1 pound small-eye tuna loin, approximately 5 inches in diameter
¼ cup blackening spice blend

Remove as much white streak and gristle from tuna as possible. Roll tuna in blackening spice to cover entire loin. On a hot flat-topped grill or in a lightly oiled hot pan, sear tuna for 30 seconds on each side. Remove from heat, place on a room-temperature plate, and refrigerate immediately. Refrigerate in a covered container when cooled completely.

Sashimi Noodles
1 pack Asian noodles
1 cup sweet chili garlic sauce
¼ cup chopped cilantro
¼ cup toasted pecans

Cook noodles in boiling water according to package directions. Cool by immersing in cold water. Drain when noodles are cooled. Place noodles in a large mixing bowl and toss with remaining ingredients. Refrigerate in a covered container.

Tuna Sashimi
Photo provided by Stripers Bar & Grille

Chipotle Soy Mustard

¼ cup soy sauce
¼ cup Dijon mustard
1 teaspoon garlic
1 tablespoon canned chipotle peppers
¼ teaspoon kosher salt
½ cup blended oil

Place all ingredients except oil in a blender and blend on low. Slowly add oil. Blend until fully incorporated. Refrigerate in a covered container.

Wasabi Aioli

¼ cup wasabi powder
1½ tablespoons rice wine vinegar
¼ cup blended oil
1 cup mayonnaise

In a large mixing bowl, dissolve wasabi powder in vinegar. Add oil and mayonnaise. Blend until fully incorporated. Refrigerate in a covered container.

PRESENTATION

Pile noodles on 1 end of long platters. Run a squiggly line of Chipotle Soy Mustard from top of noodles down 1 side of platter and a line of Wasabi Aioli from top of noodles down other side of platter. Slice cold tuna to desired thickness and layer from noodles toward end of platters, on top of lines of mustard and aioli.

Shrimp and Grits

Shrimp and Grits
Serves 4

Shrimp
1 pound large local shrimp, shelled and deveined
½ cup diced garlic
10 tablespoons diced shallots
2 tablespoons chopped scallions
1 cup red bell pepper, diced ¼ inch
½ cup butter
¾ cup sherry wine
6 ounces country ham, diced ¼ inch
3¾ cups heavy cream
¼ tablespoon pepper
¼ tablespoon kosher salt

Sauté shrimp, garlic, shallots, scallions, and peppers in butter until soft. Deglaze pan with sherry and add ham. Cook for 1 minute. Add cream and allow sauce to reduce on medium-high heat. Add pepper and salt.

Stone-Ground Cheese Grits

1 pint heavy cream
1½ cups chicken stock
1 pint whole milk
1 cup white stone-ground grits
¼ cup shaved Parmesan cheese
salt and pepper to taste
clipped scallion greens

Place cream, stock, and milk in a stockpot and bring to a boil. While stirring, slowly add grits. Reduce heat to a slow boil, stirring constantly. Add Parmesan and salt and pepper. Let rest for 5 minutes.

PRESENTATION

Place grits in center of colorful bowls. Spoon shrimp mixture over top and garnish with clipped scallion greens.

Bud Gruninger
PHOTO BY VICTORIA MAWYER

BASNIGHT'S LONE CEDAR CAFÉ

7623 South Virginia Dare Trail
Nags Head/Manteo Causeway
Nags Head, N.C. 27959
252-441-5405
lonecedarcafe.com

The Chef

Bud Gruninger

Until Bud Gruninger competed, no chef representing a state outside the Gulf Coast had ever placed higher than third in the Great American Seafood Cook-Off in New Orleans (www.greatamericanseafoodcookoff.com).

Bud grew up in a hotel kitchen, working the pantry from age eight through 10. His grandfather owned the Spray Beach Inn on the Jersey Shore. Bud loved watching the old-time chefs work. He started cooking in his early teens. By the time he was 17, he was already a sous chef. As a teenager, he came to the Outer Banks often for surfing and fishing. When he graduated from high school, he enrolled at the Culinary Institute of America in Hyde Park, New York, graduating in 1981. He credits one particular instructor, Chef Boagna from the Italian Alps, as his strongest influence.

Because he already had years of restaurant experience, Bud was able to move into leadership positions as soon as he completed culinary school. He worked in New York; Philadelphia; Portland, Oregon; Sedona, Arizona; and Boulder, Colorado. "The diversity of foods in the United States is huge," he remarks. He learned different styles and worked with a wide range of ingredients, learning in particular to appreciate local produce.

In Philadelphia, he cooked in several Center City restaurants, including Wildflowers (a Chaine des Rotisseurs–honored restaurant), The Frog, and The Commissary (widely recognized for its innovative, fine-dining cafeteria food). He was offered a position at the esteemed Le Bec Fin. "But the pay was too low, and I owed too much to take it," he says. "Maybe I should have. It would have been a great experience."

After about eight years in the Colorado mountains, he simply missed the ocean too much. "At some point, I started trying to find a way back to the coast. I opened a little Italian restaurant in Manteo, Anna Livia's, named after my niece. She was named after a character in *Finnegan's Wake*. The Basnights were regular customers. This was about 18 years ago. They had decided to open a restaurant, and they hired me about two months before they even bought the property, so I was able to help design it. Then, in 2007, there was a disastrous fire, so a new restaurant had to be built. I helped design that, too."

The commissioner of agriculture's office selected Chef Gruninger to represent North Carolina in the Great American Seafood Cook-Off. "I was flabbergasted when I learned I had been chosen. I just went crazy enthusiastic. They put us on a bus to visit New Orleans restaurants. The first year, I did not place. I realized that they were after real food, representative of regional cuisine. So when I was selected a second year, in 2011, I prepared the sort of locally focused northeastern North Carolina food that we serve at the restaurant. I placed second, the highest ever from a non-Gulf state. That was my highlight of many competitions," he recalls.

Having grown up in the Northeast, he likes Italian food. "From my time in the West, I also like Mexican and other ethnic foods. If I'm not cooking at home, I try to go to those kinds of restaurants. The only thing I miss about living and working in a big city is real ethnic foods in ethnic neighborhoods."

The Restaurant

Basnight's Lone Cedar Café

The name *Basnight's Lone Cedar Café* reflects two elements of the restaurant's history.

The founder, Marc Basnight, is an important fixture in North Carolina's political history. He was a leader of the North Carolina Senate, representing the First District from 1984 to 2011. He was a champion for education, especially the university system. Among his many legislative accomplishments, visitors to the Outer Banks will notice one in particular: plastic bags, which caused long-term impairment of local waters and the seafood they nurture, have been banned from the area.

Lone Cedar is derived from a duck-hunting club of the same name located nearby over 100 years ago.

The restaurant seats about 375. Every table provides a view of Roanoke Sound, a function of Basnight's location on the causeway between Manteo and Nags Head. The 2,000-bottle wine cellar is maintained at a constant 55 degrees. The Osprey Lounge features live music. The Boat Wall was designed and painted by the Tillett sisters, cousins of the Basnight family. It depicts more than 100 Outer Banks fishing and charter boats dating back to the 1940s.

Local connections have always been a core element of the restaurant's operation. All of Basnight's seafood is caught in North Carolina waters. Fish are cleaned and dressed on the premises in an adjacent building. Vegetables are purchased from local farms. All-natural poultry and pork products come from North Carolina farms. The USDA Prime Angus Beef the restaurant serves is raised on all-natural vegetarian feed free of hormones and antibiotics. Beef is the only protein that may not come from North Carolina. "There are some in-state beef producers that meet our standards, but you have to buy a whole side, instead of just the cuts we want," Chef Gruninger explains. An herb garden is maintained on the property. Deep-fried selections use all-natural soybean oil with no cholesterol or trans fat.

Chef Gruninger was one of the founders of NC Catch. "About six years ago, we started the organization to support the local fishing industry and make people aware of differences between local and imported seafood. About 60 percent of the seafood that is eaten in the U.S. is imported. Imports are rarely inspected, and in some places sanitation practices are questionable. In many Asian shrimp ponds, for example, after they harvest the shrimp, they put tilapia in the ponds to eat the shrimp feces. They sell the tilapia to the U.S., where they are cooked and eaten, often in restaurants."

Basnight's lists its partner fishermen and farmers on the menu. Desserts are handmade daily by Pastry Chef Ron Kneasel, also a Culinary Institute of America graduate.

The Recipes

Pan-Blackened Red Drum with Black Bean and Corn Salsa
Serves 4

Black Bean and Corn Salsa
2 cups black beans, cooked and drained
2 cups sweet corn, cut off the cob and steamed for 2 minutes
juice of 1 fresh lime
½ cup chopped cilantro leaves
½ cup red bell pepper, diced small
½ cup onion, diced small
1 jalapeño pepper, diced fine
2 teaspoons salt
1 teaspoon crushed red pepper flakes

Prepare salsa ahead. Combine all ingredients and refrigerate for 24 hours.

Pan-Blackened Red Drum
½ cup paprika
¼ cup salt
1 tablespoon granulated garlic
1 tablespoon granulated onion
2 tablespoons pepper
1 tablespoon cayenne pepper
¼ cup vegetable oil
4 8-ounce red drum fillets

Combine spices and oil. Dredge fillets to coat both sides. Heat a cast-iron pan really hot. Add fillets. Sear for 3 minutes on each side.

Pan-Blackened Red Drum with Black Bean and Corn Salsa
PHOTO BY VICTORIA MAWYER

PRESENTATION

Place fillets in center of plates and top with Black Bean and Corn Salsa.

Pan-Seared Wahoo with Summer Succotash
Serves 4

Pan-Seared Wahoo

4 8-ounce wahoo steaks, deboned
kosher or sea salt and cracked pepper to taste
2 tablespoons olive oil

Heat a carbon steak pan very hot. Sprinkle fish with salt and pepper and olive oil. Place fish in pan and sear each side for approximately 2 minutes.

Summer Succotash

¼ cup butter
2 ears sweet corn, kernels cut off cobs
½ pound fresh okra, cut into ½-inch pieces
10 to 12 grape tomatoes
salt and pepper to taste
fresh chives

Heat a sauté pan. Add butter, corn, and okra and sauté for 2 to 3 minutes. Add grape tomatoes and salt and pepper.

PRESENTATION

Place vegetables in center of plates, top with wahoo, and garnish with chives.

Fried Calamari with Garlic, Red Pepper, and Basil
PHOTO BY
VICTORIA MAWYER

Fried Calamari with Garlic, Red Pepper, and Basil
Serves 6 to 8 as an appetizer or 4 to 6 as an entrée

2 pounds Loligo squid, cut into ½-inch pieces
¼ cup buttermilk
2½ cups self-rising flour
1 tablespoon kosher salt
1 teaspoon cracked pepper
canola oil for frying
2 cloves garlic, chopped
pinch of red pepper flakes
2 tablespoons chopped fresh basil
1 tablespoon extra-virgin olive oil
fresh basil

Place cleaned, cut squid in buttermilk and let soak for ½ hour. Remove. Combine flour, salt, and pepper. Dredge squid in flour mixture and fry in canola oil at 350 degrees for 1½ minutes. Combine garlic, red pepper, basil, and olive oil in a bowl. Add cooked squid and toss to coat.

PRESENTATION

Garnish with basil and serve.

AUSTIN FISH COMPANY

3711 South Croatan Highway, Milepost 12.5
Nags Head, N.C. 27959
252-441-7412
austinseafoodco.com

Jimmy Austin founded Austin Fish Company over 50 years ago. The shop has been operating in the same location under the same ownership since 1960.

A commercial fisherman before he opened the store, Jimmy built the business around connections with other fishermen. The Austin women— Jimmy's wife, Sandra; daughter, Debbie; granddaughter, Tiffany; and great-granddaughter, Elly—have been carrying on the family business since Jimmy passed away in 2010.

Austin Fish Company is both a retail seafood market and a casual seafood restaurant, with frying and steaming the main means of cooking. Picnic tables out front provide seating on the premises. Much of the business is takeout, from individual portions to large combinations that will feed an entire family. Fish sandwiches, barbecue, clam chowder, and shrimp and sausage gumbo round out the menu.

In the seafood market, refrigerated cases display a wide variety of whatever local fish is in season—mahi-mahi, grouper, snapper, tuna, flounder—as well as shrimp, crabs, and several varieties of clams. In order to accommodate whatever customers want, Austin's also sells seafood caught outside the area, such as king crab legs, salmon, and sea bass. Some items including bacon-wrapped scallops are partially prepared, to facilitate cooking at home.

Austin Fish Company was voted "Best Seafood Market on the Beach" in 2013 by readers of *Outer Banks Voice*.

CAFÉ LACHINE

5000 South Croatan Highway N1

Nags Head, N.C. 27959

252-715-2550

cafelachine.com

Johanna and Justin Lachine
PHOTO BY SARAH D'AMBRA PHOTOGRAPHY

The Chefs

Johanna and Justin Lachine

Justin Lachine learned firsthand how dangerous professional kitchens can be. "I was tempering chocolate and got burned by the steam. I dropped the full bowl, splashing the chef, covering him from head to toe in hot, dark chocolate, along with the French onion soup he had been working on. I wasn't sure I would still have a job after that, but he was forgiving."

Justin is from Alexandria, Virginia. He moved to the Outer Banks in 2008 to be sous chef at Aqua in Duck. He considers the scenery and landscape to be "like no other."

He started in restaurants at age 16, washing dishes and busing tables at the

Family Café, a small restaurant in Stafford, Virginia, owned by Gary Fishman, a graduate of the Culinary Institute of America. "He taught me all the fundamentals of cooking, and I eventually became his sous chef," Justin recalls.

When Gary sold the Family Café, Justin moved to Fredericksburg and worked at several restaurants there before deciding to move to Tampa, Florida. In Tampa, he made bagels, breads, and pastries at Sunshine Bakery and also worked at Le Bordeaux, a small French restaurant. "My main responsibilities there involved preparing salads and desserts. This was my first real baking experience, which was very exciting." Le Bordeaux was also the scene of the chocolate accident. "My experiences at Le Bordeaux made me realize that I wanted to learn more about the culinary world, so I applied to Johnson & Wales and moved to Virginia Beach." He graduated in 2001 from the Virginia Beach campus.

"For my internship, I worked in Maui, Hawaii, with Roy Yamaguchi at Roy's. In Maui, I really learned to appreciate fresh seafood. I think that was when I fell in love with the coast. I moved back to Fredericksburg and became the executive chef at Brock's Riverside Grill. Later, I took a position at Claiborne's, also in Fredericksburg, as sous chef. The man who owned Claiborne's also owned a Ruth's Chris in Richmond. He decided to open a Ruth's Chris in Virginia Beach. I was originally hired as sous chef, but before the Ruth's Chris opened, the chef he had hired decided to open his own restaurant, so I became the executive chef. On Mother's Day one year, we had over 600 reservations. But a storm knocked out the power, and we had to turn most of them away."

Justin met Johanna when he hired her as a line cook at Brock's Riverside Grill. She learned to cook from her father, using ingredients from their garden. Traveling throughout North America and Europe opened her eyes to new ideas and concepts.

Justin followed Johanna to Hyde Park, New York, when she enrolled at the Culinary Institute of America. While a student there, she helped organize and care for the institute's organic garden. After she graduated in 2008, she and Justin moved to the Outer Banks, where they both worked at Aqua, then got into wedding catering. "We worked for a company that catered over 100 weddings a year," Justin says. "Then, when we got the opportunity to open our café, we took it. We had been talking about opening our own place for years."

At home, Justin and Johanna like comfort food. "A moist roast chicken with mashed potatoes and gravy is a perfect meal. I love chocolate anything, especially a warm chocolate cake, preferably with a molten center!" Johanna says.

The Restaurant

Café Lachine

Café Lachine is a café in concept, not just in name. Homemade scones, muffins, and cinnamon buns are special attractions in the morning, in addition to traditional breakfast choices. Breakfast sandwiches remain popular through lunch, when soups, salads, and sandwiches are added to the menu.

"We want people to feel at home when they walk in the door," Justin says. "Our staff is very inviting, and our food is very comforting. We make everything from scratch, including soups, breads, and desserts."

In season, the restaurant buys produce from the farmers' market in Raleigh, as well as Somerset Farm in Edenton and Coastal Farmers Co-op. "We only use local seafood," Justin says. "It wouldn't make sense not to. Whalebone Seafood in Nags Head and O'Neal's in Wanchese are our favorite places to get seafood. We try to keep as many North Carolina products in our café as possible. We buy local pecans and honey from regular customers at the café."

Johanna considers Alice Waters of Chez Panisse to be one of her strongest influences. "I know the importance of using fresh ingredients and enhancing the natural flavors of food," she explains.

Justin describes his approach to creating dishes at Café Lachine: "I like the food to speak for itself. If you use fresh ingredients, they just need to be highlighted. I like my plates to be simple and straightforward, not confusing and muddled." He names Patrick O'Connell of the Inn at Little Washington as a particular inspiration, for blending the importance of both taste and presentation.

Café Lachine, a member of the Outer Banks Wedding Association and Outer Banks Catch, is also a popular resource for catering.

The Recipes

Cider-Brined Pork Tenderloin with Vanilla Whipped Sweet Potatoes
Serves 4

Cider Brine
1 tablespoon canola oil
2 cups apple cider

Cider-Brined Pork Tenderloin with Vanilla Whipped Sweet Potatoes

Photo by Sarah D'Ambra Photography

2 bay leaves
1 teaspoon red pepper flakes
2 tablespoons chopped garlic
¼ cup salt
¼ cup sugar
2 cups ice cubes
2 pork tenderloins, trimmed and cleaned of excess fat

Prepare Cider Brine ahead. Combine all ingredients except ice and pork in a medium-sized saucepan. Bring to a boil, then reduce heat and simmer for 5 to 10 minutes. Remove from heat and let sit for a few minutes. Add ice. When brine is cool, marinate tenderloins for 2 days.

Apple Butter Sauce

canola oil
½ small onion, peeled and sliced thin
1 cup white wine
2 bay leaves
½ teaspoon peppercorns
2 star anise
1 teaspoon whole allspice
1 stick cinnamon
2 cups apple juice
1½ cups apple butter
4 tablespoons unsalted butter

Prepare Apple Butter Sauce ahead. Coat bottom of a medium-sized saucepan with oil. Heat over medium. Add onions and sauté until translucent. Add wine, bay leaves, peppercorns, star anise, allspice, and cinnamon stick and reduce by ½. Add apple juice and reduce by ⅓. Add apple butter, bring to a simmer, and mix well. Add butter 1 tablespoon at a time until all is incorporated.

Vanilla Whipped Sweet Potatoes

3 sweet potatoes, peeled, cut medium-large
pinch of salt
2 teaspoons vanilla paste or extract
4 tablespoons unsalted butter
¼ cup honey
white pepper to taste
1 tablespoon canola oil

In a medium saucepan, add sweet potatoes, cover with cold water, and add salt. Bring to a boil, reduce heat slightly, and cook 20 minutes until tender. Drain potatoes and let sit for 5 minutes. Place potatoes in a large mixer with a whip attachment. Add vanilla, butter, and honey and mix until smooth. Season with salt and white pepper.

Preheat oven to 350 degrees. Remove pork from brine, pat dry with a paper towel, and season with salt and pepper. In a large sauté pan over medium-high heat, add canola oil. Place pork in pan and sear all sides until golden brown. Transfer to a baking sheet and bake for 10 to 15 minutes until desired doneness. Remove from oven and rest on a cutting board for 5 to 10 minutes.

PRESENTATION

Place a mound of sweet potatoes in the middle of each of 4 plates. Slice each pork loin into 8 slices and arrange 4 slices over each sweet potato mound. Finish with ¼ cup or more Apple Butter Sauce on each plate.

Ho-Ho Cake
PHOTO BY SARAH D'AMBRA PHOTOGRAPHY

Ho-Ho Cake
Yields 1 log

Cake
6 ounces bittersweet chocolate
cooking spray
7 eggs, separated
⅓ cup sugar, divided

Melt chocolate in a double boiler. Set aside. Preheat oven to 350 degrees. Line a half sheet tray with aluminum foil, lightly coat with cooking spray, and dust with sugar. Whip egg whites until firm, add ⅓ cup of the sugar, and whip until stiff peaks form. In a separate bowl, whip egg yolks with remaining ⅓ cup sugar until light in color. Slowly add chocolate to egg yolk mixture while mixing on low speed. In 3 stages, fold egg whites into chocolate-yolk mixture. Pour cake onto sheet tray and bake for 12 minutes.

Filling
1⅓ cups heavy cream
2 teaspoons vanilla extract
¼ cup sugar
10 ounces mascarpone cheese

Whip cream, vanilla, and sugar until soft peaks form. Add cheese and whip until stiff peaks form.

Ganache
1 cup heavy cream
6 ounces dark chocolate

In a small saucepan, heat cream until it starts to boil. Place chocolate in a metal bowl and pour hot cream over chocolate. Let sit until chocolate has melted, then combine with a whisk.

Spread filling over cooled cake, leaving 2 inches without filling on 1 long side of pan. Start rolling from the side that has filling to the edge. Wrap the log in the aluminum foil to hold it together. Twist at the ends. Refrigerate for at least 1 hour. Unwrap and cut in half. Place on a wire rack fitted in a pan.

PRESENTATION
Pour chocolate ganache over log to coat. Refrigerate until ready to serve. Slice with a hot knife.

Frank Whitford

KELLY'S OUTER BANKS RESTAURANT AND TAVERN

2316 South Croatan Highway

Nags Head, N.C. 27959

252-441-4116

kellysrestaurant.com

The Chef

Frank Whitford

In the third grade, Frank Whitford was in a play in which he was cast as a chef. "There was something about being in that uniform that I really liked. I told my parents then that I was going to become a chef. They laughed. Now, I have worked in the profession for over 20 years."

Frank was born in Greenville, North Carolina. He moved to the Outer Banks in the early '90s for the summer but ended up staying 10 years. "The best thing about living on the coast is being near the ocean. Nothing beats seeing the ocean first thing in the morning."

He started cooking around age seven. His father managed Cliff's Seafood Restaurant in Chocowinity, North Carolina, and sometimes took Frank to work with him. The chefs would let him bread shrimp or fish and taught him to make simple dishes. He graduated from Johnson & Wales in Charleston.

"I think the chefs I worked for early in my career influenced my style, especially Chef Lee Miller at Pamlico Jack's in Nags Head and Chef Michael Palumbo at the Carolina Inn in Chapel Hill," he says. "They always emphasized using local ingredients as much as possible and letting those flavors shine."

Frank was sous chef at Kelly's for 10 years, then moved to Charleston for a change. "But after five years, I knew I wanted to be back on the beach." While in Charleston, he cooked at the Coast Bar and Grill. "One of the things the chef, David Pell, always said was, 'Don't be afraid to try new things.' I think this helped me to expand my knowledge and try different techniques and flavor combinations."

As far as style goes, Frank says, "I believe in using the best ingredients you can find and letting their flavors shine. Keep it simple."

His favorite foods are soft-shell crabs and almost anything Italian. "When I cook at home, it is usually late at night, so I cook simple, flavorful foods. My 'always go to' is white bean and chorizo tacos."

The Restaurant

Kelly's Outer Banks Restaurant and Tavern

Mike Kelly opened Kelly's over 30 years ago. It has been one of the premier establishments on the Outer Banks since its birth. The walls in the entryway are covered with awards and letters of commendation from national publications and patrons.

Kelly's concept centers on fresh local ingredients served with Southern hospitality. Three different menus are provided, including one for children and another for light fare in the tavern. Seating is available from 4:30 until 10:00 P.M., so Kelly's is regarded as a particularly good choice for early or late-night dining. The restaurant closes only on Christmas Day.

Mike Kelly has worked hard to establish relationships with local farmers and fishermen. He believes it is important that the restaurant "not only get great local products, but also give back to the community in the form of maintaining long-term relationships."

Private dining rooms provide space for large parties. Kelly's offers extensive catering services off the premises as well. Sweet Potato Biscuits by the dozen, whole cheesecakes, and other desserts are sold for takeout or pickup.

Kelly's has been featured in *Gourmet* and *Bon Appétit* magazines and has also received recognition from *Wine Spectator*. Pastry Chef Becky Miller has won the Taste of the Beach Best Dessert award for five consecutive years. The restaurant actively participates in Outer Banks Catch.

The Recipes

Sweet Potato Biscuits
Yields 5 dozen

6 cups sweet potatoes, steamed or baked
¾ cup water
4 cups light brown sugar
6 cups Bisquick

Preheat oven to 350 degrees. Cool and peel potatoes. Mix together all ingredients. This mixture will be wetter than regular biscuit dough. Sprinkle surface of work area with flour and roll out dough to ½-inch thickness. Cut with a 2½-inch cutter. Bake for 14 to 16 minutes until light brown.

NOTE Becky Miller's Sweet Potato Biscuits have been honored in *Gourmet* magazine.

Pecan Chicken
Serves 2

1 bunch asparagus
2 cups rice
2 cups pecan pieces
2 cups flour, divided
3 eggs
½ cup milk
olive oil as needed
2 6-ounce boneless, skinless chicken breasts
¾ cup heavy cream
2 tablespoons Dijon mustard

Grill or steam asparagus. Keep warm. Cook rice according to package directions. Keep warm. Preheat oven to 350 degrees. Place pecan

Pecan Chicken

pieces in oven and toast for 3 to 5 minutes. Remove and let cool. Place 1 cup of the flour in a mixing bowl. Combine eggs and milk in another bowl and stir to combine. When pecans have cooled, add remaining 1 cup flour and pecans to food processor and pulse until combined. Place in a bowl. Dip each chicken breast in flour on both sides, then in egg wash, and finally in pecan flour. Place olive oil in an ovenproof sauté pan over medium heat. Add chicken and sauté for 1 to 2 minutes. Flip and cook for 2 more minutes. Remove chicken from pan and place on a baking sheet. Cook in oven for 5 to 6 minutes until cooked through. Meanwhile, place cream in a pan and bring to a boil. Add mustard and reduce until mixture coats the back of a spoon.

PRESENTATION

Place cooked rice in center of plates and lay asparagus on top. Add chicken and spoon mustard-cream sauce on top.

Carolina Bouillabaisse

Serves 4

3 cups white rice
¼ cup olive oil
1 stick unsalted butter
1 yellow onion, diced large
½ bunch celery, diced large
1 green bell pepper, diced large
1 red bell pepper, diced large
¼ cup chopped garlic
1 large pinch saffron
2 to 3 tablespoons Cajun spice

Carolina Bouillabaisse
PHOTO PROVIDED BY KELLY'S OUTER BANKS RESTAURANT AND TAVERN

1 teaspoon celery salt
½ cup white wine
12-ounce can clam juice
2 12-ounce cans Angela Mia diced tomatoes
¾ cup cornstarch
water as needed
20 clams
1 pound fish (salmon, swordfish, or tuna), cut into 1- to 2-ounce cubes
20 scallops
20 shrimp, peeled and deveined
crusty bread

Cook rice according to package directions. Keep warm. Heat oil and butter in a stockpot. Sauté vegetables over medium heat until soft. Add garlic, saffron, Cajun spice, and celery salt and sauté for 5 minutes. Add wine and stir frequently, cooking until reduced by ½. Add clam juice and tomatoes and bring to a boil. Combine cornstarch and water to the consistency of thin pancake batter. Stir in a small amount at a time until vegetables are suspended in broth. Add broth to a large sauté pan and bring to a boil. Add clams and cook for 2 to 3 minutes. Add fish and scallops and cook for 2 minutes. Add shrimp and cook 2 more minutes. If clams have not opened, continue to cook. Discard any clams that do not open after 2 more minutes.

PRESENTATION

Place rice in the middle of 4 bowls. Surround rice with 5 clams. Place 5 scallops between clams. Add 5 shrimp and some fish on top. Pour broth to fill halfway up bowls. Serve with crusty bread.

Ray Fiorello
PHOTO PROVIDED BY MULLIGAN'S RAW BAR & GRILLE

MULLIGAN'S RAW BAR & GRILLE

4005 South Croatan Highway

Nags Head, N.C. 27959

252-480-2000

mulligansobx.com

The Chef

Ray Fiorello

Ray Fiorello went to college to study journalism but shifted to culinary school after a professor warned his class, "You all want to be famous sportscasters, but most of you will wind up in the morgue, writing obituaries."

Ray is from Newark, New Jersey, and spent most of his adult life in the central part of that state. But he vacationed on the Outer Banks and always wanted to live in the area. He applied to one particular restaurant on the Outer Banks several times, because it was big and similar to places where he had worked, but it never responded. In 2012, he became determined to make the move, so he sent out dozens of résumés, got about 25 replies, scheduled some interviews, and returned home with two job offers, one from Mulligan's.

Most of his work had been in hotels and conference centers in New Jersey and New York. But he also worked with Mario Batali at Pó in Manhattan. "New York is a food mecca," he says. "New Jersey is weird, in that it really is the Garden State. For a long time, it was predominantly farmland, and a lot of it still is, but for a shorter season than the South. There's nothing like the produce that comes out of that state—seafood that is indigenous to those waters, a different strain of oysters versus the ones we get in the Chesapeake Bay and the South, for example. The water never warms as much up there as in the South, so the oysters are saltier, and they have a different flavor. You get fluke, huge bluefish, New Jersey blue-claw crabs, and a particular variety of clams. Down here, the season is longer, and you can get fresh foods if not year-round, then almost."

He has cooked for numerous celebrities including Bruce Springsteen, Jon Bon Jovi, Brian Williams, and Helen Hunt, mostly during a period when he was working in Sea Bright, New Jersey. It was close enough to the city to draw famous people. "They were regulars, so they were not hounded as celebrities. Sea Bright is a barrier island, like the Outer Banks, but smaller. Lots of boats dock in the area. Very picturesque."

Ray grew up in an Italian home. "Life revolved around the kitchen. My parents were good cooks, and we always sat down to Sunday dinner with family. I had jobs cooking by age 13 or 14." After deciding to pursue professional training in food service, he successfully applied to the Institute of Culinary Education in New York City, one of largest culinary programs in the area.

He was hired at Pó shortly after graduation. "But at that age, I had to live at home in order to be able to afford to buy a car." So he started looking into hotels in New Jersey. He took a position at a Clarion Hotel near home and was promoted to supervisor within a year or so. From there, he moved up to his first executive-chef position, at a Sheraton in Eatontown.

"In a large operation like that, you have to have weekly planning meetings to ensure staffing and other preparation for catering and other big events, as well as providing guest services," he says. "One time, when I looked over the reservations for the week, I noticed a block of rooms reserved for 'Rat Dog.' Nobody else recognized the name, but I knew that was the name of a band led by Bob Weir, a former member of the Grateful Dead. I went to the manager and asked if it would be okay to send something up to his room. The manager gave the okay. I knew Weir's favorite beer was Heineken, so I included a few. Late that night, this big, brawny-looking guy—security, I guess—comes into the kitchen and asks for the chef. He hands me some backstage passes. It was one of best things that ever happened in my life. Weir really appreciated the food we fixed for him. That's what this business is all about. Pleasing people."

After 20 years as a chef, Ray considers his style "an evolution. You grow as a chef, just as you grow as a person. Early on, you want to throw everything you know on the plate, and you think it's fantastic because it's so complicated, but really it's a pile of uncoordinated shit. Later, you learn to refine. What I do at Mulligan's is fusion. You take a little bit from anywhere that is interesting and create a diverse menu. Customers know a lot about food these days, so you need a menu that touches on different cuisines without getting sloppy. People relate to things they can see in their personal history. It's about memory, family, values, giving everybody kind of a warm and fuzzy feeling."

The main reason he lives on the Outer Banks, "in addition to getting out of the rat race in the North, is to take advantage of the things I love—fishing, boating, and being outdoors." His favorite food is Mexican. "I spent a short time in Baja, California. I learned to cook real Mexican. It's my passion."

The Restaurant

Mulligan's Raw Bar & Grille

Gus Zinovis began working in a bakery at age 14, first preparing food, then baking. At 16, he began a delivery route. After graduating from the University of Bridgeport in Connecticut, his home state, he and his roommate opened a pizza shop in Virginia Beach with the help of his roommate's father. They introduced innovations to the genre at the time—a salad bar, draft beer, and an upscale design. Their restaurant eventually grew to nine company-owned shops, plus 15 franchises. They sold out to a large local bakery owner in 1981. Gus retained four locations but gradually sold them off.

He purchased a summer home in Nags Head in 1985. He bought Mulligan's, which was then a dive bar with a great reputation among locals, and gradually transitioned it into a restaurant with the "Best Burgers on the Beach." He and partner Shannon Moody relocated to the current, much larger location in 2006. From the second-floor deck, diners have views of the ocean, historic Nags Head cottages, and Jockey's Ridge State Park.

Chef Fiorello explains his role: "My family and I had been customers at Mulligan's for years, when we were on vacation on the Outer Banks. It has 330 seats now, so it's pretty big. But the menu balances between one of best burgers you've ever had plus a passion for local seafood. Mulligan's is about seafood, above all. I have tried to narrow the focus a little bit since coming here as chef. It's better to do everything right, as opposed to letting a few things slip because you tried to do too many things.

"The restaurant has always been good. But I would like to think it's getting better and people have noticed. For example, a hurricane came through here in July 2014—the earliest storm like that ever. But the next day, we had the busiest day in the history of the restaurant. I also think the kitchen staff is seeing and taking pride in a higher level of quality and productivity."

Mulligan's connects with local farms and seafood providers. "The Outer Banks is a busy destination for tourists. But outside summer, it's small town and family. Gus has had a long-term relationship with several farmers in the area. We use Etheridge Seafood and Captain's Oysters—local guys who have been doing this for decades. Our oysters are shucked and delivered to the restaurant within a day of harvest. These guys were on the water all night. Sometimes, they've been fishing around the clock for days. The Beasley family, when they catch crabs, they bring them in. There's no formal order, we just know each other. A couple of farms nearby bring vegetables. In season, it's all local, all fresh."

In 2013, Mulligan's won "Best Overall Chili" and "Best Beef Chili" at Taste of the Beach. Chef Fiorello says, "It was cool, to be a Yankee and come down here and win a chili competition. That was just great." Then, in 2014, Mulligan's won the Chowder Cook-Off. This heretical chef now has his sights set on 2015: "We're gonna win the barbecue prize."

The Recipes

Asian Sea Scallop Ceviche
Serves 4

juice of 1 lemon
juice of 1 lime
juice of 1 orange
3 tablespoons rice wine vinegar
2 tablespoons sesame oil
1 teaspoon minced garlic
pinch of salt
pinch of crushed red pepper flakes
12 large North Carolina sea scallops
4 large sea scallop shells
8 tablespoons seaweed salad
1 tablespoon black sesame seeds

Combine juices, vinegar, oil, garlic, salt, and red pepper flakes. Slice

Asian Sea Scallop Ceviche
PHOTO BY MULLIGAN'S RAW BAR & GRILLE

scallops into medallions and arrange 3 in each shell. Drizzle with liquid. Top each serving with 2 tablespoons seaweed salad.

PRESENTATION
Garnish with black sesame seeds and serve.

Crab Salad Caprese
Serves 4

8 ounces lump crabmeat
¼ red onion, julienned thin
4 spears asparagus, cut into 1½-inch pieces
3 tablespoons extra-virgin olive oil
salt and pepper to taste
2 large beefsteak tomatoes
12 ounces fresh mozzarella cheese
½ cup balsamic reduction
4 basil leaves

Combine crab, red onions, asparagus, olive oil, and salt and pepper. Slice tomatoes and mozzarella into 16 slices each.

Crab Salad Caprese
PHOTO BY MULLIGAN'S RAW BAR & GRILLE

PRESENTATION

Arrange a pinwheel of alternating tomato and mozzarella slices on each of 4 plates. Place equal portions of salad on center of plates. Drizzle with balsamic reduction. Garnish each plate with a fresh basil leaf.

Grilled Tuna Oscar

Serves 4

Lemon Garlic Aioli

½ cup roasted garlic cloves
zest and juice of 2 fresh lemons
1 quart mayonnaise

Combine all ingredients. Using a large blender, purée until smooth and incorporated well. Put desired amount into a squeeze bottle for immediate use. Place remaining aioli in an airtight container. This will last 1 month if refrigerated and handled properly.

Grilled Tuna Oscar
PHOTO PROVIDED BY MULLIGAN'S RAW BAR & GRILLE

Tuna

4 cups white rice
20 asparagus spears
4 eggs, beaten
½ cup milk
4 5-ounce soft-shell crabs
2 cups seafood breading
enough oil to immerse crabs in a deep fryer
4 4- to 5-ounce pieces yellowfin tuna
salt and pepper to taste

Cook rice according to package directions. Keep warm. Grill asparagus on medium heat until scored on each side. Keep warm. Beat eggs and milk together to make an egg wash. Place each soft-shell crab in egg wash, then dredge in seafood breading. Deep-fry at 350 degrees until golden brown. Remove and keep warm. Season tuna with salt and pepper. Sear on high heat for about 30 seconds per side to rare or medium-rare. Remove from heat.

PRESENTATION

Scoop 1 cup rice onto each of 4 plates. Place grilled asparagus on top of rice. Place grilled tuna on top, followed by a soft-shell crab. Drizzle with about 2 tablespoons of Lemon Garlic Aioli.

NAGS HEAD

Kathryn M. Weih
PHOTO PROVIDED BY SUGAR CREEK SEAFOOD RESTAURANT

SUGAR CREEK SEAFOOD RESTAURANT

7340 South Virginia Dare Trail
Nags Head, N.C. 27959
252-441-4963
sugarcreekseafood.com

The Chef

Kathryn M. Weih

Kathryn Weih has worked in only three professional kitchens in her entire career. She got the job at Sugar Creek after a feisty exchange between her mother and the owner.

Born and raised in Manassas, Virginia, Kathryn was already fond of the Outer Banks. Her parents have a beach house there, and she has been vacationing on the North Carolina coast almost since birth. While working in a corporate setting in 2012, she asked her mother on a whim to take her résumé down to the cottage and distribute it when she went out to eat.

Her mother walked into Sugar Creek and asked to speak to the manager. A gentleman wearing shorts—in February—stood up and said, "Hi, I'm Ervin Bateman, the owner."

"My mom handed him my résumé," Kathryn recalls. His first questions were, "Is she willing to relocate, is she married, does she have kids, and does she have a place to live?"

"My mom answered, 'She is willing to move, she's not married, has no kids, and she already has a place to live.' Then she finished off by adding, 'She is a bit of an Irish woman, and like her mother, she has a temper.' "

Ervin replied, "I like feisty women." And so the relationship began.

Kathryn describes her progress toward becoming a chef: "I have always loved food. Once my mom got me off baby food and Vienna sausages, there was no stopping me. Even as a toddler, I was willing to try anything. When I was accepted into culinary school, people would say to my family, 'I didn't realize Katie liked to cook.' My parents' answer would always be, 'Well, she sure likes to eat.'

"I became interested in the culinary world while I was in middle school. My other career goals were running for president or being a marine biologist. But I dropped the latter when I realized I might have to be in the water with sharks. I had excelled in home economics and the culinary programs at Osbourn Park High School. So, in 1999, my senior year, I applied to the Culinary Institute of America in Hyde Park, New York, as well as Johnson & Wales in Norfolk, Virginia. I worked for Giant grocery in Manassas, doing prep in their salad bar and in the service deli preparing takeout foods, in order to get my required prior hours of experience. I received my acceptance to Johnson & Wales in August 1999 while vacationing on the Outer Banks. Just as I was preparing to pack for school, I got the call that I had been accepted at CIA, too. So I went north. In culinary school, I had a love for seafood butchery and cooking, as well as ethnic cuisines. My chef-teachers drove me more to love food and all aspects of cooking."

After graduating from CIA in September 2001, she was offered a position at the Hyatt Regency in Reston, Virginia, where she had completed her culinary-school externship. Her first day of work was September 11. It was also her last, since the hotel industry went "on hold" at that point, especially among properties around the nation's capital. She was rehired by Hyatt part-time before the 2001 holiday season and continued with the corporation for 10 years. "I learned from some great executive chefs. I worked all aspects of the hotel—breakfast, line cook, room service, supervisor chef, and sous chef, as well as banquet. I learned that with proper prep and creativity, anything is possible, from small, intimate parties to lavish weddings."

She took a short break from Hyatt to work in Sterling, Virginia, at Falcons Landing, a retirement community for upper-echelon military personnel. In March 2012, she started at Sugar Creek, where she was "thrown right into the mix, as soon as we opened for the season in March. Then Ervin told me, 'By the way, Taste of the Beach is in a week, and we've entered you in the chefs' competition. Good luck.'

"So I hit the ground running. I love the island, the camaraderie of the chefs that work here, and the chances I have to spread my wings. Among my peers, there is a great sense of support. We appreciate each other's skills, and we are our own biggest cheerleaders."

As far as Kathryn's personal tastes go, "my favorite dish is country-fried steak. But I never make it for myself. I ask my mom to fix it for me when she comes to visit. I would hardly ever cook for myself if it was up to me. I would just be eating a sandwich every night after work, or maybe a salad. Thank God for my fiancé! He makes dinner most nights for me. I occasionally cook for us on my days off or when family visits. I would much rather cook for a big crowd. My staff loves it when I invite them to dinner."

The Restaurant

Sugar Creek Seafood Restaurant

Ervin Bateman, a fifth-generation Outer Banker, purchased the property and renamed it Sugar Creek around 2008. He had been working there for over 20 years, almost since the place opened as RV's Restaurant. Sugar Creek is a family operation. Ervin's wife, Teresa, is a retired Currituck County principal and school administrator. She greets people at the front reception desk. Their son, Jonathan, works at the Sugar Shack Fresh Seafood Market next door.

The restaurant is located on the Nags Head–Manteo causeway, overlooking the bay. Water views are abundant from most tables.

Chef Weih reflects on her time at Sugar Creek: "It is a great feeling to have local ingredients as your canvas—picking fresh seafood every day from local fish houses, and vegetables coming from local farms. I love taking classic menu items and putting a new twist on them. I also love bringing things to the restaurant that some of my staff and patrons have never tried before. The hardest person to please is myself.

"I love that Sugar Creek combines Outer Banks history with the restaurants of my childhood. We have been strongly involved with supporting local seafood and such events as the Outer Banks Seafood Festival. Ties to the local community are strong. I am grateful that after three years, this girl from Manassas is being recognized for culinary accomplishments in a North Carolina seaside community."

Ervin Bateman works extensively in the community. He is a member of the Outer Banks Marathon Committee, a charter member of the Outer Banks

Running Club, a founding member of the Outer Banks Relief Foundation's board, a member of the town council of Kitty Hawk (as well as a past mayor pro tem), and a member of the board of the Dare County Visitors' Bureau.

Some staff members at Sugar Creek have been with the restaurant as long as, or even longer than, Ervin. The restaurant has expanded its catering operations recently.

The Recipes

Oyster Stew
Yields 1 gallon

1 whole leek, whites diced medium, greens sliced thin for garnish
4 cloves garlic, minced
1 small Vidalia onion, diced medium
¼ cup olive oil
3 Idaho potatoes, peeled and diced
2 quarts heavy cream
2 pints oysters and their liquor
1 tablespoon salt
1 tablespoon pepper
2 tablespoons hot sauce
crackers

Oyster Stew
Photo provided by
Sugar Creek Seafood
Restaurant

Sauté leeks, garlic, and onions in olive oil until tender. Add potatoes and cream. Bring to a simmer. Remove from heat and blend together either in pot with a hand-held immersion blender or in a standard blender. (Be careful. Hot mixtures tend to blow lids off machines, so cover and blend on slow.) Return mixture to pot and add oysters, salt, pepper, and hot sauce. Cook over low heat until edges of oysters begin to curl and mixture is hot but not boiling.

PRESENTATION

Serve with crackers and garnish with sliced greens from leeks.

Shrimp and Grits with Andouille Sausage

Serves 5

Grits

6 cups water
6 cups milk
2 teaspoons salt
1 teaspoon freshly ground white pepper
4 tablespoons butter, divided
1½ cups stone-ground white grits
8 ounces cream cheese
½ cup grated asiago cheese
1 cup shredded cheddar or pepper jack cheese

In a large saucepan over medium heat, combine water, milk, salt, pepper, and 2 tablespoons of the butter. Bring liquid to a gentle boil. Stir in grits. Cook for 1 hour and 15 minutes, stirring frequently. (Constant stirring will prevent grits from sticking. But if you don't stir often enough and they do stick, do not scrape them off bottom of pan, or they will taste burned.) If grits absorb all liquid, add some hot water to thin them. Remove pan from heat and stir in remaining butter and cheeses. Grits can be served immediately or prepared in advance and reheated. If preparing in advance, grease a pan with a teaspoon of butter. Pour grits into pan and reheat in a 400-degree oven for 15 minutes.

Shrimp and Grits with Andouille Sausage
PHOTO PROVIDED BY SUGAR CREEK SEAFOOD RESTAURANT

Shrimp and Sausage

2 tablespoons butter
2 cloves garlic, minced
1 green bell pepper, chopped
½ pound Andouille sausage, sliced
2 pounds uncooked large shrimp, peeled and deveined
¼ cup dry white wine
1 teaspoon Sriracha sauce
salt and pepper to taste
chopped chives

Heat a large sauté pan over medium heat. Melt butter and sauté garlic and peppers until tender and translucent. Add sausage. When sausage has cooked, add shrimp and sauté for about 2 minutes. Add wine and Sriracha. Bring to a boil, then simmer for about 5 minutes. Season with salt and pepper.

PRESENTATION
Serve over grits. Garnish with chives.

SUGAR SHACK
FRESH SEAFOOD MARKET

Nags Head–Manteo Causeway, Milepost 16.5

Nags Head, N.C. 27959

252-441-3888

sugarcreekseafood.com

Soon after Ervin and Teresa Bateman purchased the property that is now the Sugar Creek Seafood Restaurant, they decided to establish a year-round seafood market. They built the Sugar Shack next door. Manager Colleen Melvin worked at the Sugar Creek restaurant for about eight years before transferring to the Sugar Shack.

The market is primarily a source for local freshly caught fish and shell-fish. But lunch and dinner are available, too, with seating at four tables inside and picnic tables outside, weather permitting. Takeout is the other role of the Sugar Shack. Clam chowder, tuna and shrimp salads, spring rolls, fried calamari, various seafood sandwiches, conventional choices such as grilled chicken and barbecue, steamer buckets, grilled entrées, and fried "boats" are available to go. A unique creation is the Seafood Pizza. Moreover, the Sugar Shack offers deliveries in the "Shack Car," brightly painted with the market's logo.

Locally owned boats pull up to the dock at the Sugar Shack and deliver freshly caught fish on the spot. Other deliveries come from Wanchese, the area's commercial fishing capital. For customers who want something from outside the area, lobsters, salmon, and crab legs are available.

In addition to food, the Sugar Shack offers visitors Water Leisure Rentals, a service providing kayaks, paddleboats, canoes, and stand-up paddleboards.

CAFÉ PAMLICO AT THE INN ON PAMLICO SOUND

49684 N.C. 12

Buxton, N.C. 27920

innonpamlicosound.com

Will Canny
PHOTO BY JOHN BATCHELOR

The Chef

Will Canny

Will Canny, a native of the Swiss Alps, was working as a ski and snowboard instructor and living with "a bunch of chefs" when he realized that "they were skiing more, eating better, and making more money than I was." In subsequent conversations, they urged him to go to culinary school. He enrolled at Le Cordon Bleu in London and received a diploma by age 17.

He and the other chefs remained a pretty close group for about 12 years. He cooked at King's in Verbier in the Swiss Alps, a fine-dining establishment that has consistently earned high ratings from Gault Millau. When he and his fellow chefs were not working, they traveled in Europe.

The group is "awesome," in Will's words. "We're pretty tight-knit. All of us have been to cooking school. I am trying to get some of them to work with me at Pamlico. When I had to go back to Switzerland to visit my mother, some of them came over and ran the kitchen here for me." Among their restaurants are Aquavit in Stockholm and the Nevai Hotel in Verbier. Chef Canny was sous chef at the Nevai Hotel for four years before taking the Pamlico job.

The Inn on Pamlico Sound was never in his plans. He had come to the United States on a surfing trip but got stuck on the Outer Banks during Hurricane Irene. He made friends with one of the servers at Café Pamlico, who gave him a place to stay during the storm. So he worked a little while at Café Pamlico the year Hurricane Sandy came through, then went back to Switzerland. But owner Steve Nelson invited him to return as executive chef in 2014, after the former chef decided to leave.

Chef Canny prefers cooking classical cuisine. "But I like to make people think classical can still be modern," he says. "An excellent cut of beef with a Béarnaise sauce is a favorite, but I aim for doing it in just a little different way to make it special. Asian seafood—Sesame Tuna over Bok Choy with Soba Noodles, stir-fried—is a big seller for us."

He hardly ever cooks at home. "I eat at the restaurant all the time, especially since coming to the States. If I eat at home, I go for an easy, fresh lunch or a salad. I often eat vegetarian. But more often than anything else, for dinner, I try different dishes that we are considering for the menu."

The Inn and Restaurant

Café Pamlico at the Inn on Pamlico Sound

The Inn on Pamlico Sound is a waterfront property on Hatteras Island. According to its website, the inn "offers the services of a European boutique hotel, the amenities of a small resort, and the comfort and charm of a North Carolina coastal bed and breakfast." Some rooms face the sound. The Cape Hatteras Lighthouse, Cape Hatteras National Seashore, and several villages are located nearby. Spa services, which can be provided in the rooms, are available. Most entertainment centers on the ocean and the sound. In addition, an in-house library and a 14-seat home theater provide entertainment exclusively for guests. The inn is especially attractive as a location for weddings, whether small or large, as well as other catered events.

Café Pamlico, the restaurant at the inn, has long been known as a fine-dining restaurant for special occasions. Steve Nelson, owner of the inn and restaurant, describes himself as "a burned-out corporate refugee from a Manhattan corner office." He vows that "our mission at Café Pamlico is to provide a world-class dining experience through exceptional food, outstanding detail-oriented service, an inspired wine and cocktail program, and gracious, attentive Southern hospitality."

Chef Canny wants to maintain that appeal but create a place that is more accessible as well. "We are creating a bar menu that is more casual and lower-priced," he explains. His goal is to create a farm-to-plate restaurant. "Everything will be sourced within the county. We get fresh fish from three local fishermen, who bring us their best catch whenever they have something particularly good." The menu will change according to the season, reflecting whatever is fresh at the moment.

The Times of London has described the food and service at Café Pamlico as "fabulous." The property has earned positive reviews from *National Geographic Traveler* and *Taste of the South* magazines, as well as the *Charlotte Observer* and Fodor's.

The Recipes

Tuna Ceviche
Serves 4

CHEF'S NOTE "At the inn, we serve this in a martini glass with a couple of cilantro leaves on top, plus either wonton crisps or turmeric crisps."

Ceviche Sauce
1¼ cups soy sauce
¼ cup sesame oil
1 tablespoon Sriracha sauce
1¾ cups lime juice

Blend all ingredients together. Chill in refrigerator overnight.

Tuna
1 cup tuna, cut into ½-inch pieces
1¼ cups mango, cut into ½-inch pieces
1 tablespoon jalapeño pepper, diced small

Tuna Ceviche
PHOTO BY JOHN BATCHELOR

1 cup spring onions, diced small
1 tablespoon chopped cilantro

Combine all ingredients and add 6 tablespoons Ceviche Sauce. Refrigerate for about 15 minutes before serving.

Chocolate Cake
Yields 1 cake

2 cups unsalted butter
2¾ cups dark chocolate (Nestlé semisweet morsels recommended)
2½ cups egg whites (about 12 large eggs)
1¼ cups sugar
1⅓ cups flour
whipped cream
fresh berries

Preheat oven to 350 degrees. In a medium saucepan, melt butter and chocolate over medium heat. Blend, then let cool to room temperature. Beat egg whites until soft peaks form. Fold sugar into egg whites until fully incorporated. Fold flour into mixture until fully incorporated. Gently mix in blended chocolate and butter. Pour mixture into a greased cake pan and bake for about 8 minutes.

Chocolate Cake
PHOTO BY JOHN BATCHELOR

Presentation

Cut cake in half on the diagonal. Stand 2 slices upright for each serving and add dollops of whipped cream. Sprinkle fresh berries on plates to finish.

Back Porch Restaurant PHOTO COURTESY OF BACK PORCH RESTAURANT

BACK PORCH RESTAURANT

110 Back Road

Ocracoke, N.C. 27960

252-928-6401

backporchocracoke.com

The Chef

Daphne Bennink

Daphne Bennink is a New Yorker. From the time she was two years old, she vacationed on Ocracoke with her family, who owned a summer home on the island. She met her husband on Ocracoke and "kind of never left," she recalls.

She has worked in the food service industry most of her adult life. "I've always been attracted to the energy and camaraderie found in a restaurant kitchen," she says. Her parents are French and are both great cooks. She learned primarily from them and during periods when she lived in France, where she developed "a love and passion for both discovering and creating great food."

She considers some of the best food to be basic. "Many people don't think they can cook when they actually can. Great food is within anyone's reach—you just have to put yourself out there and go for it. My style is primarily French, but with many other influences from the amazing food all around me."

At home, Daphne loves to eat "whatever is seasonal and available to us on our little island."

The Restaurant

Back Porch Restaurant

The Back Porch takes its motto from the French Renaissance author Michel de Montaigne, known for balancing philosophy with personal anecdotes and observations from daily life. He once remarked, "The art of dining well is no slight art, the pleasure no slight pleasure."

The restaurant takes its name, in part, from the long screened-in porch where guests can enjoy the air and the ambience of Ocracoke.

The Back Porch is open only for dinner; a roadside stand, the Back Porch Lunchbox, provides takeout selections during the day. The menu focuses primarily on seafood, since "it is by far our most abundant local food and worthy of being front and center," Chef Bennink says. The staff takes pride in providing a great dining experience. "We have one of the bigger wine lists on the island, creative house-crafted cocktails, and an excellent, knowledgeable staff."

The menu is international in scope, mixing small plates with full entrées. First courses, or tapas samplings, might include Crab Beignets, Shrimp Empanadas, or Bacon-Wrapped Scallops. Among the main courses, a local seafood platter is always available, but more elaborate creations are on the menu as well: Fillet of Fish with Vietnamese Lime Sauce, Horseradish-Encrusted Wild Salmon with Remoulade Sauce, Shrimp Piccata, Bourbon Pecan Chicken, and Homemade Spaghetti with Meat Sauce, for example. Burgers, sandwiches, and other light fare are on the bar menu.

All seafood is sourced locally. "We work with both island fishermen and neighboring village fisheries to provide a wide range of the best local seafood possible," Chef Bennink says.

For the past three years, Chef Bennink has hosted a food-based radio show, during which she shares her love for good food and the concept that delicious food is within everyone's reach. Her cookbook, based on the Back Porch's menu, is available for purchase at the restaurant or by contacting her through the website.

*Bacon-Wrapped
Scallops with Red Wine–
Caramel Sauce*

The Recipes

Bacon-Wrapped Scallops with Red Wine–Caramel Sauce

Serves 4 as an appetizer

Red Wine–Caramel Sauce

1 cup red wine
1⅓ cups sugar
¼ cup water
1 tablespoon butter

Reduce wine by ½. Measure after reduction to ensure precise amount. Combine sugar and water in a pan and cook over high heat, stirring until sugar dissolves; do not stir after sugar dissolves. Continue to cook until pale golden in color. Remove caramel mixture from heat and carefully add wine. Mixture will sputter. This is normal. Return to medium heat and cook until caramel dissolves and mixture is uniform and viscous. Add butter. Cook and stir to dissolve.

Bacon-Wrapped Scallops

4 strips applewood smoked bacon
8 dry-packed sea scallops

Cut bacon in half and wrap each scallop with a half-strip of bacon. Pan-sauté scallops until bacon browns.

PRESENTATION

Drizzle scallops with Red Wine–Caramel Sauce and serve.

Flounder Meunière
Serves 2

2 medium flounder fillets (or other mild fillets)
plain flour seasoned with salt and pepper
3 generous tablespoons butter, divided
2 tablespoons white wine
juice of ½ lemon
½ cup Roma tomatoes, diced fine
1 to 2 teaspoons capers
freshly minced parsley

Flounder Meunière
PHOTO COURTESY OF
BACK PORCH RESTAURANT

Use a frying pan big enough to hold both fillets. Generously dredge fillets in seasoned flour. Heat pan over high heat (medium-high if electric). Melt 2 tablespoons of the butter in pan; do not brown. Add fillets skin side up and cook for 2 to 3 minutes, depending on thickness. Turn fillets to skin side down and cook another few minutes until done. Remove fillets to a platter. In the pan, add remaining butter, wine, lemon juice, tomatoes, and capers and cook, stirring to create sauce. The residual flour from fish and the liquids will come together to form the sauce, so don't skimp on the flour or extra wine if necessary to get a nice light sauce.

PRESENTATION

Spoon sauce over fillets, garnish with parsley, and serve.

OCRACOKE

Dajio   PHOTO BY JOHN BATCHELOR

DAJIO

305 Irvin Garrish Highway

Ocracoke, N.C. 27960

252-928-7119

dajiorestaurant.com

The Chef

Doug Eifert

"In the early '80s, the job market for BAs in political science was pretty slim. I started out as a bartender and then moved into management. One place I worked would hire big-shot chefs to come in and redo their menu and then let them go. I became the stop-gap chef until they brought in another one."

Doug Eifert has been cooking for about 25 years. He remarks that his "only prior interest in food was eating it." Originally from New Jersey, he has also lived in Pittsburgh; Cincinnati; Lexington, Kentucky; and Shawnee, Kansas. He and his wife, Judy, moved to the North Carolina coast in 2008. "I love the ocean and island life, although it can be inconvenient, with ferry access only [to Ocracoke].

Once you get past all the natural beauty, it's the people that make you want to stay. They are incredible."

He says he learned to cook "through a combination of self-teaching and some influences within restaurants. I like color and textural combinations. I like rustic interpretations. I used to like complex flavor combinations, but now I have moved toward simple, quality ingredients."

Doug likes to eat "most all foods, but I prefer comfort-type foods. I rarely cook at home, except in the off-season." He lives with his "amazing wife of 28 years in a tiny old house with a kitchen circa 1950." His son is pursuing a master's degree in architectural engineering.

The Restaurant

Dajio

The name *Dajio* is derived from "Doug and Judy in Ocracoke." Dajio blends two different concepts. "Inside, it's a converted old house, slightly upscale, particularly in the evening," Doug says. "Outside, we have a beautiful courtyard and an adjacent covered bar which could be considered a dive bar. I think we appeal to a wide cross section of folks.

"We are truly committed to fresh and local ingredients. I know that sounds cliché, but we work very hard on our sourcing and our scratch cooking. We serve many original dishes, and we maintain a backyard garden. We recently built an outdoor wood-fired brick oven, where we do scratch Neapolitan-style pizza."

Doug and Judy had a restaurant for 12 years in Lexington, Kentucky. "When it closed, I thought it would be a good idea to work for someone else. But I didn't enjoy it so much. After six years with little creative influence, we decided to do our own gig again. Our son went off to college, so we were able to move to Ocracoke, the place we had wanted to be for quite a while. We sold just about everything, cashed in our savings, and made a go of it. So far, so good."

They have made connections with local farms and seafood providers "mostly by word of mouth," according to Doug. "I hooked up with my fisherman right away. Then I got a shellfish guy out of Oriental. Veggies generally come from Swan Quarter or the backyard."

Yelp has named Dajio the number-one restaurant on the island, and it has consistently been first or second in the rankings for full-service restaurants on TripAdvisor. The restaurant has also been recognized by AAA and Urbanspoon.

Crab Macaroni and Cheese
PHOTO BY JOHN BATCHELOR

The Recipe

Crab Macaroni and Cheese
Serves 4

Gruyère Sauce
¼ cup chopped shallots
2 tablespoons clarified butter
¼ cup all-purpose flour
1 quart half-and-half
1 cup chicken broth
4 egg yolks
1 cup shredded Parmesan cheese
1 cup shredded Gruyère cheese
1 tablespoon chopped thyme
2 tablespoons Cajun seasoning

Sweat shallots in butter. Add flour and cook until mixture browns slightly and has a nutty aroma. Heat half-and-half and chicken broth in a saucepan until steaming but not boiling. Whip egg yolks. Stir a small amount of warm liquid into eggs, swirl, and repeat until combined. Add to flour mixture and cook on low heat. Stir in cheeses and seasonings until thickened. Keep heat low and stir constantly to keep eggs from scrambling.

Crab Macaroni

2 pounds pasta (trottole, cavatappi, and penne work well)
1 pound local jumbo lump crabmeat, picked
salt and pepper to taste
1 cup shredded Gruyère cheese
green onion, chopped small
red bell pepper, diced
2 tablespoons chopped flat-leaf parsley

Preheat oven to 425 degrees. Cook pasta according to package directions. Heat Gruyère Sauce in a medium saucepan. Stir in crabmeat gently, being careful not to break up lumps. Add hot cooked pasta and stir. Season with salt and pepper. Transfer to 4 ovenproof dishes. Top each dish with shredded Gruyère. Place in oven and bake until brown and bubbly.

PRESENTATION

Garnish with green onions, red peppers, and parsley. Serve with crusty bread and fresh garden salad.

THE CHELSEA

335 Middle Street

New Bern, N.C. 28560

252-637-5469

thechelsea.com

Shawn Hoveland
PHOTO BY JOHN BATCHELOR

The Chef

Shawn Hoveland

Shawn Hoveland grew up fantasizing about being a chef.

He shadowed his mother in the kitchen and cooked with his father on weekends. In between, he watched all the cooking shows available at the time—"from Martin Yan to Julia Child," he recalls. While in high school, he worked at the Annapolis Yacht Club as a busboy, prep cook, "and any odd-and-end spot I could get to learn something new."

A year before graduating from high school, he began working at the San Remo, widely regarded as the best restaurant in Annapolis at the time. But he confesses that "I lied about my experience. I got the job after the chef tested me on cleaning fish. I chuckled when I saw that was my test. I had cleaned fish from the time I was little, having grown up fishing on the Chesapeake Bay, so this was easy for me. The Sicilian bread chef, Sal, was no picnic to work for, though. He was much harder than Chef Ramsay on the *Hell's Kitchen* TV show. Chef Sal soon realized I was not a prep cook. But he could see that I loved cooking and would do anything to stay, so he helped me.

"Things looked great after working for Chef Sal for three years. Then he moved to Baltimore and invited me to come with him to his new restaurant. That was when I realized he liked me. But I was not ready to move that far from home. I received word from a friend that Dominic's of Georgetown was going to open a new restaurant in Annapolis. So I set out to get a job at Dominic's, cooking French food. I saw this as my moment to obtain some great learning. The chef at Dominic's was Chef Cloud. He started me off as saucier. I did not lie this time. I simply told him I had no idea what to do. But Chef Cloud was great. He just started teaching me. I was hooked by this time. I knew I was going to have a career in the kitchen, and I would be a chef someday.

"I had always intended to go to culinary school, but for one reason or another my formal education kept getting pushed farther away every year. I could not afford to take time off. I needed to work. So I made the decision to start working in a different style restaurant about every 18 months." One of the places he wound up was The Chelsea, under its original owners, in the early 1990s. But he found that New Bern was a difficult place to live for a single guy.

"I decided I needed to get my degree. So I moved to Charleston to attend Johnson & Wales University, but I never made it to school. I started working for Chef Steve Martin, a consultant who was revamping several restaurants in the Charleston area. He was working on master-chef certification. He told me the paper looks great in a résumé, but with my skills and knowledge I could do fine without them."

Life got better when Shawn married Carolyn, whom he met in Morehead City. His brother, Chris, who lived in New Bern, contacted him and told him they might have an opportunity to buy The Chelsea. They took over the restaurant in 2004.

The Restaurant

The Chelsea

The Chelsea celebrated its 20th anniversary in 2011. The historic structure was built in 1912 by pharmacist Caleb Bradham, the famed inventor of

Pepsi-Cola. A large mural pays homage to the Pepsi–New Bern link.

The conversion of the property into a restaurant respected its historic significance and preserved as much of the original structure as possible. The bar and casual-dining area on the first floor is situated under the original pressed-tin ceiling, on a carefully restored mosaic tile floor. An elevator provides transportation to the second floor's more formal dining room, which has high ceilings and transom windows. Large parties can be accommodated in a separate banquet section.

The restaurant is noted for its New American cuisine, which blends international influences with traditional Southern cooking. According to its website, The Chelsea features "the freshest seafood, center-cut beef, delightful pastas and salads to suit everyone." Chef Hoveland makes a Southern Egg Roll with pulled pork and braised collard greens. Roasted pork shank forms the foundation for the restaurant's Southern Osso Buco. The recipes below are always popular items on the menu.

The Recipes

Shrimp and Crab al Fresco
Serves 4 to 6

CHEF'S NOTE "This dish is named 'al Fresco' because it is light and garlicky and lemony. It reminds me of the outdoors."

Garlic-Lemon Butter
2¼ sticks butter, divided
¼ cup diced garlic
2 tablespoons lemon juice
pinch of crushed red pepper
1 teaspoon sea salt
zest of 2 lemons

Melt ¼ stick of the butter and keep remainder cold. Sauté garlic in melted butter until it turns light brown. Remove from heat and let cool. While butter and garlic are cooling, mix lemon juice, red pepper, salt, and cold butter in a large mixing bowl. Add cooled garlic-butter mixture and lemon zest. Combine.

Shrimp and Crab

1 pound jumbo or large shrimp, peeled and deveined
¾ cup diced tomatoes
6 tablespoons chiffonaded basil
4 tablespoons diced green onions
1 pound gemelli pasta, cooked according to package directions and drained
¾ pound jumbo lump crabmeat
kosher or coarse sea salt to taste
lemon juice to taste
shredded Parmesan cheese to taste

Sauté shrimp in Garlic-Lemon Butter for about 2 minutes until half cooked. Add tomatoes, basil, green onions, pasta, and crabmeat. Toss lightly. Try to avoid breaking up crab lumps. Taste. Season with salt and more lemon juice if desired. When hot, add Parmesan.

PRESENTATION

Ladle mixture into bowls and serve. Garlic-Lemon Butter will coat pasta and blend with shrimp and crab blend, but you may not use all of it; apply to taste.

Shrimp and Crab al Fresco
PHOTO BY JOHN BATCHELOR

Chorizo Cheesecake with Shrimp and Scallops in Lobster Cream Sauce
PHOTO BY JOHN BATCHELOR

Chorizo Cheesecake with Shrimp and Scallops in Lobster Cream Sauce
Serves 12

Chorizo Cheesecake
½ pound white onions, diced
1 teaspoon chopped garlic
1 tablespoon thyme
½ teaspoon paprika
½ cup all-purpose flour
1 pound chorizo sausage
1⅓ pounds cream cheese
1½ cups grated Parmesan cheese
4 eggs
¾ pound angel hair pasta, cooked according to package directions

Sauté sausage on 2 sides until it releases grease. Retain grease. Preheat oven to 250 degrees. Sweat onions in sausage grease. Add garlic and continue to sauté until onions begin to turn translucent. Add thyme and paprika. Add flour, stirring frequently. Continue to cook until flour turns light brown. Set aside and let cool.

Add sausage to cooked, cooled onion mix. Blend sausage-onion mixture with cream cheese, Parmesan, eggs, and pasta. Bake about 1½ hours until light brown on the surface. Let cool. Refrigerate if not serving promptly.

Cut cheesecake into 12 wedges. Place each piece on a metal pan and wrap in aluminum foil. Reheat at 500 degrees for 3 to 4 minutes just before serving.

Lobster Cream Sauce

1 quart heavy cream
¼ tablespoon chopped garlic
½ teaspoon kosher salt
¼ teaspoon white pepper
½ cup dry sherry
½ tablespoon sugar
1 cup lobster stock
½ teaspoon paprika
¼ cup cornstarch
2 tablespoons water

Combine all ingredients except cornstarch and water in a pot and bring to a boil. Reduce heat and simmer for 5 minutes. Mix cornstarch and water thoroughly. Add to lobster-cream mixture. Return to a low boil, then simmer until creamy in texture.

Shrimp and Scallops

3 or 4 medium scallops
8 large shrimp
2 tablespoons sliced mushrooms
2 tablespoons butter
2 tablespoons diced tomato
½ tablespoon green onions, chopped fine

Sauté scallops, shrimp, and mushrooms in butter for about 2 minutes; shrimp and scallops should be about half cooked. Add tomatoes, green onions, and 10 tablespoons of Lobster Cream Sauce.

PRESENTATION

After cheesecake is reheated, place it on center of plates and top with seafood mixture, allowing liquid and some shrimp and scallops to fall over sides onto plates.

PERSIMMONS WATERFRONT RESTAURANT

100 Pollock Street

New Bern, N.C. 28560

252-514-0033

persimmonsrestaurant.com

Gerry Fong
PHOTO BY JOHN BATCHELOR

The Chef

Gerry Fong

Gerry Fong grew up helping out in his parents' Chinese restaurants, Fong's, in Rockingham and Laurinburg, North Carolina. As a teenager, he hated the restaurant business. But in his mid-20s, he realized he had actually learned to cook, and that he missed the kitchen.

He says he started out "studying in the school of my dad's style. He taught me about flavor." Gerry was fortunate to have parents who took him to fine-dining restaurants in New York and other locations on family vacations, so he experienced high-quality dining early in life. He went to college at UNC-Wilmington, spent some time soul-searching in the Philippines, and returned home, where he put in a brief stint working on a hog farm. Then he followed his mother's advice and pursued professional training at the Culinary Institute of America in Hyde Park, New York.

After graduating, Gerry moved to California to take a position at the Ritz-Carlton in Half Moon Bay, where "Chef Brian Bistrong taught us to seek perfection. I try to take his motto with me everywhere: 'Perfection and integrity are the hallmarks of good cooking.' Every dish we serve must be something we would be proud to serve our parents!" Gerry came back to North Carolina and cooked at Ashten's in Southern Pines. "Chef Ashley Van Camp reminded me of my Southern influence and taught me how to embrace it," he says.

He moved to New Bern in January 2009 to open Persimmons. He has always loved the coast for its weather and hospitality.

When preparing food for himself, friends, and family, "I cook everything at home, mostly Chinese or grilling," he says. When he eats out, "I love pizza!"

The Restaurant

Persimmons Waterfront Restaurant

Persimmons is located on the Neuse River. Itinerant boats tie up alongside the docks adjacent to the restaurant. All seats provide water views. Outdoor deck seating overlooks the river. A separate private area is available in addition to the main dining room.

Chef Fong's motto is "Eat local! We cook everything as much as possible according to season. We deal with 12 to 18 local farmers weekly to pick their best products. We really do the farm thing! We are fresh local with an Asian perspective."

His produce acquisitions are based on "a lot of driving around. I never turn down a farmer, even if it's your grandma. So when people bring little Ziploc bags of stuff from their garden during dinner, we use it. Maintaining good communications and developing good relationships are the most important things you can do."

Pecan Shrimp
PHOTO BY JOHN BATCHELOR

The Recipes

Pecan Shrimp
Serves 3 or 4

CHEF'S NOTE "I created this from an old Asian dish my dad used to make. He would prepare it when he had friends and family at the restaurant. Its simplicity and the 'wow' factor make it one of my favorites."

Honey-Ginger Aioli
1 cup Hellman's mayonnaise
¼ cup maple syrup
¼ cup honey
2 tablespoons sugar
¼ cup ground ginger
salt and pepper to taste

Mix all ingredients well.

Shrimp

canola oil for pan-frying
2 cups all-purpose flour
½ cup cornstarch
pinch of salt
pinch of pepper
2 cups ice-cold soda water
1 pound large or jumbo North Carolina shrimp
½ cup chopped pecans, toasted

Add oil in a medium skillet until about ⅓ full. Heat oil to 375 degrees.

Mix flour, cornstarch, salt, and pepper in a medium bowl. Add soda water a little at a time and mix well until no lumps remain; mixture should have the texture of pancake batter.

When oil is hot, make sure shrimp are dry and add them to wet batter, coating thoroughly. Slowly place shrimp in oil. Do not overcrowd! Cook shrimp on each side for about 3 minutes until golden brown. Remove shrimp and place on a rack to allow excess oil to drip off.

PRESENTATION

Either toss shrimp in sauce and garnish with toasted pecans or serve sauce on the side with pecans sprinkled on top of sauce.

Pepsi-Brined Heritage Pork Tenderloin with Bacon-Braised Collards and Sweet Potato Purée

Serves 2 or 3

CHEF'S NOTE "This was one of the first dishes I originated when I moved to New Bern. Since New Bern is the birthplace of Pepsi-Cola, it only made sense to use it in a recipe. Our heritage pork is from Seven Springs, North Carolina. It is from a small, family-owned hog farm that has awesome beliefs about raising animals! It is the best pork you can find on the market!"

Bacon-Braised Collards

½ pound bacon, diced
1 large yellow onion, sliced
2 tablespoons chopped fresh ginger
2 tablespoons chopped fresh garlic

1 teaspoon red pepper flakes
2 cups rice wine vinegar
3 quarts chicken broth
salt and pepper to taste
2 pounds collard greens, ribs removed

In a stockpot large enough to hold 3 quarts of liquid plus the collards, add bacon and fry until crisp. Reserve bacon and leave fat in pot. Add onions and sauté in bacon fat until slightly caramel in color. Add ginger and garlic and sauté until you can smell the aroma. Add red pepper and toast quickly. Add vinegar. Reduce vinegar by ⅓. Add broth and sprinkle in salt and pepper. Add collards and bacon. Turn collards frequently to ensure they are immersed in hot liquid. Bring to a boil, reduce heat, and simmer until they reach desired texture. Drain and cool for at least 1 hour but no more than 3 hours to hold texture. Taste. Collards take a lot of seasoning. Depending on the strength of your chicken broth and the level of salt in your bacon, you may need to add salt and pepper.

Sweet Potato Purée

1½ pounds sweet potatoes, peeled and diced
¼ cup coconut milk
¼ cup maple syrup
1 cup heavy cream
½ stick butter
1 tablespoon ground coriander
1 tablespoon garam masala (Asian spice blend)
1 tablespoon fresh ginger juice
salt and white pepper to taste

Place sweet potatoes in a pot, cover with salted water, and boil until tender. Strain liquid and place potatoes in a food processor. Add remaining ingredients. (For ginger juice, grate ginger on a cheese grater, then squeeze pulp to yield juice.) Blend until smooth. Taste. Add salt as needed.

Pork Tenderloin

1½- to 2-pound pork tenderloin, silver skin removed
1 quart Pepsi-Cola
2 tablespoons canola oil

*Pepsi-Brined Heritage Pork Tenderloin with Bacon-Braised Collards
and Sweet Potato Purée*
PHOTO BY JOHN BATCHELOR

salt and pepper to taste
coarsely ground sea salt

Place tenderloin in Pepsi and allow at least 2 hours of brine time. Tenderloin can soak for up to 12 hours.

Preheat oven to 375 degrees. Use a large sauté pan that can be placed in the oven. Add canola oil and heat pan on medium-high. Remove tenderloin from brine and dry well. Season with salt and pepper. Carefully place tenderloin into pan. Sear on all sides, then place pan in oven. Roast tenderloin for 15 to 18 minutes to an internal temperature of 150 degrees (medium) or 160 degrees (medium-well). Allow 5 minutes of resting time before slicing. Reheat collards and sweet potatoes while pork is resting.

PRESENTATION

Using tongs, place collards in center of large plates. Blot any liquid with paper towels. Add a dollop of Sweet Potato Purée in middle of collards. Arrange slices of pork around half of the purée on top of greens. Garnish with sea salt if desired.

Jayson Foster
PHOTO BY TAYLOR MCCUNE, CCC, INC.

AQUA

114 Middle Lane

Beaufort, N.C. 28516

252-728-7777

aquaexperience.com/

The Chef

Jayson Foster

Jayson Foster grew up in Norwich, New York, near Syracuse. He cooked often with his grandmother and mother, especially in the Polish traditions of his family. The family moved to Beaufort when he was 16. His mother, who had always wanted to move to the South, picked Beaufort based on articles she read in *Coaster* magazine. He went to high school at East Carteret, then enrolled in the culinary program at Carteret Community College.

His class at CCC was the first to participate in an exchange program the culinary school had developed in collaboration with experienced chefs in France. As part of his training at CCC, he lived and worked in France, where he was taught by Chef Marc LaLaeut, a caterer, who served schools, businesses, and other events all over the area near Lille. LaLaeut specialized in French country cooking, accentuating the traditional. Jayson continued his studies under the supervision of Chef Marc Meurin at Le Chateau de Beaulieu in Bethune. The primary focus of his formal training is, therefore, classical French. "That tradition strongly influences what I am doing here at Aqua," he remarks.

While attending high school and CCC, and even after graduating, he cooked in several Crystal Coast restaurants, including DJ Shooters, the Channel Marker, and the Spouter Inn. His first executive chef position came at Williams' Fine Dining in Morehead City. Before rising to executive chef at Aqua, the highlight of his culinary career was participating on a team with Andy Hopper from Chefs 105 in Morehead City, which won the Fire on the Dock chefs' competition in 2012.

Regarding his "style" of cooking, he comments, "It starts with the ingredients. I try to imagine flavors in my mind, maybe experiment a little, but mostly it's in my head." He is particularly fond of fresh dill. "It's summery, light. I use it in roasted red potatoes with butter and a dill horseradish aioli. The aioli can be used on seafoods as well as meats. It's very versatile." His terrines and pates—unusual fare for the North Carolina coast—have attracted a following.

At home, he often returns to the Polish dishes that he enjoyed in his youth. One of his personal favorites is Gwumpkies-Polish stuffed cabbage rolls. He is thinking about trying them out as a winter special in the restaurant.

Jayson's son, Ethan, is a hunter. He loves duck. He brings them home and he and his uncle prepare jerky. Jayson's daughter, Jayden, loves spaghetti, but the only way she will eat it is the way Jayson's grandmother taught him to make it, a sweet version, using sweet sausage.

The Restaurant

Aqua

Aqua is located a block off the Beaufort waterfront on one of the town's picturesque back streets. It's a café providing a menu of tapas selections, as well as conventional entrées. Seasonal patio seating expands the opportunities for enjoyment. Inside, Calder and Miro prints decorate the aqua walls. Hand-blown vases and glassware and glass lighting shades in aqua, green, and blue cast hues of the ocean.

The owners, Fred and Joyce McCune and Joey McClure, also own Clawson's Restaurant (see pages 200-206). They wanted to try something no one else was doing in the area, so they drew up the model for Aqua on a paper napkin while sharing beer and talking. After Aqua opened, the eclectic small-plate concept took off.

The restaurant is relatively small, which allows the kitchen staff to spend time creating and refining dishes. The kitchen works with several area farms, including Laurel Farm in Beaufort, whose owner, Kim Safrit, drops off greens and other produce herself. Seafood comes from Bill Rice and Chris Conklin at Fishtowne Seafood. Aqua utilizes other North Carolina products such as Drake's fresh pasta, Ashe County cheese, and Joyce/Ashley Farms poultry as well.

The Recipes

Oven-Roasted Tomato Pie
Serves 8

Tomatoes
2½ pounds Roma tomatoes
2 teaspoons minced garlic
1 teaspoon chopped fresh parsley
1 teaspoon chopped fresh rosemary
1 teaspoon chopped fresh thyme
1 teaspoon salt
¼ teaspoon cracked five-peppercorn blend
2 tablespoons olive oil

Prepare tomatoes ahead. Preheat convection oven to 350 degrees. Core and halve tomatoes. Using fingers, scrape seeds and juice from insides. Remove as much moisture as possible. Don't be afraid to tear into them. Once you have cleaned tomatoes, mix all ingredients in a large bowl until tomatoes are completely coated. Using a cooling rack inside of a sheet pan, lay tomatoes cut side down on rack. Roast on center rack for 60 to 90 minutes. Press tomatoes down with a spatula 2 times during cooking time to get more juices out. You are looking for dry tomatoes with a light char on the skins. Allow to cool.

Pie
½ cup mayonnaise
½ cup sour cream

1 teaspoon minced garlic
1 teaspoon kosher salt
½ teaspoon cracked five-peppercorn blend
1½ tablespoons chopped fresh parsley, divided
1½ tablespoons chopped fresh rosemary, divided
1½ tablespoons chopped fresh thyme, divided
1 cup shredded mozzarella cheese
1 cup shredded Parmesan cheese
1 cup shredded smoked Gouda cheese
9-inch raw pie shell
½ cup basil chiffonade
¼ cup panko breadcrumbs
5-ounce package arugula
8 ounces balsamic glaze/reduction

Preheat convection oven to 425 degrees. In a large mixing bowl, combine mayonnaise, sour cream, garlic, salt, peppercorn blend, and 1 tablespoon of each of the herbs. Stir. Add cheeses and mix until well incorporated. Place cooled tomatoes evenly across bottom of pie shell. Top with basil chiffonade. Add cheese filling and top with breadcrumbs, pressing them just lightly into cheese. Bake on bottom center rack for 15 to 20 minutes. Allow 10 to 15 minutes to cool.

PRESENTATION
Sprinkle remaining herbs over top. Cut pie into 8 slices. Lay a bed of arugula in center of each plate. Drizzle 1 tablespoon balsamic glaze in center of arugula, with 1 line coming out of the center in either direction to rim of plate, forming a straight line across plate. Place a slice of pie on the center of the balsamic.

Shrimp and Prosciutto Pasta
Serves 4

3 ounces conchiglie (shell pasta), cooked al dente
8 ounces heavy cream
2 tablespoons grated Parmesan cheese, divided in half
4 tablespoons red onion, diced
4 tablespoons sweet green peas
2 tablespoons sun-dried tomatoes, julienned
4 tablespoons clam broth

Shrimp and Proscuitto Pasta
Photo by Taylor McCune, CCC, Inc.

2 tablespoons prosciutto, divided in half
8 large shrimp, tail on
3 tablespoon cooking oil (high-smoke-point, such as peanut oil)
pinch of salt

Heat a medium-sized saucepan on high for 2 minutes. Add oil, red onion, half the prosciutto, and the pinch of salt. Sauté until the onions start to caramelize and the prosciutto begins to crisp. Add the clam broth and reduce by ⅓. Incorporate shrimp, tomatoes, and peas into clam broth. Sauté one minute, then add cooked pasta. Add heavy cream and a half ounce of the Parmesan cheese. Cook 5 minutes on medium-high heat, stirring often.

PRESENTATION

Remove shrimp from pan and set aside. Place pasta in a shallow bowl. Arrange shrimp on top and sprinkle the remaining Parmesan cheese and prosciutto over top.

Spicy Saffron Cioppino with Wild Rice
Serves 8

Spicy Saffron Broth
¼ teaspoon saffron threads
1½ cups clam juice, divided
¾ cup diced yellow onion
½ red bell pepper, diced
½ cup dry white wine
1 tablespoon minced garlic
3 cups V8 juice
1 bay leaf
¼ cup fish sauce
3 cups canned diced tomatoes in juice
3 tablespoons shrimp base
3 tablespoons lobster base
1½ teaspoons crushed red pepper flakes
4 cups water

Prepare broth ahead. In a small bowl, steep saffron in ½ cup of the clam juice. In a large stockpot, sauté onions and peppers until caramelized. Add wine to deglaze pan and simmer until reduced by ½. Add all remaining ingredients to stockpot, including saffron and remaining clam juice. Bring to a boil over medium-high heat. Reduce heat and simmer for 1 hour, stirring occasionally.

Cioppino
wild rice
24 mussels
24 littleneck clams
1 pound shrimp, peeled and deveined
1 pound bay scallops
2 cups julienned shiitake mushrooms

3 tablespoons olive oil
1 loaf ciabatta bread, sliced and grilled

After broth is cooking, prepare wild rice according to package directions to yield 4 cups. Next, steam mussels and clams until they open. In a large sauté pan, sauté shrimp, scallops, and mushrooms in olive oil until cooked.

PRESENTATION

Add ½ cup cooked rice to center of large bowls. Place 3 mussels and 3 clams around rice on outer edge of each bowl. Spoon shrimp sauté over center of rice and ladle on 1½ cups Spicy Saffron Broth. Serve with ciabatta bread on the side.

BEAUFORT

Charles Park PHOTO BY JOHN BATCHELOR

BEAUFORT GROCERY COMPANY

117 Queen Street

Beaufort, N.C. 28516

252-728-3899

beaufortgrocery.com

The Chef

Charles Park

Charles Park savors memories of his aunt and grandmother, who were "always in the kitchen." His parents referred to his paternal grandmother's home as "the place where food came from."

"My parents were very knowledgeable about food," he recalls. "They had their own supper club in Charlotte, and they cooked there. They often tried to follow Julia Child and *The Galloping Gourmet* TV show. They traveled to Europe and Asia and brought back ideas. My grandparents, on the other hand, were home cooks. On my father's side, Granny cooked Southern-style. I remember fried chicken, spaghetti casserole, vegetables from the garden. My mother's parents were German. Her mother used to make kniffles [dumplings that are similar to spaetzle]. I remember seeing Grandma cut them off with a knife and drop them into boiling water. Family—that is the foundation for my cooking."

Charles is a graduate of the Culinary Institute of America in Hyde Park, New York. His first job after culinary school was with the Intercontinental Hotels group on Hilton Head Island in South Carolina, where he worked with European chefs. During winter, he was reassigned to the Intercontinental in Miami, where he picked up experience with South American chefs. He describes those years: "In school, you are allowed to make mistakes. Not in that setting. You work in a brigade system, per Escoffier. You are always trying to impress the upper-echelon chefs, directly in competition with other young chefs.

"There was a lot of hazing. I worked with a pastry chef who had what I call 'asbestos hands.' One time, he took a pan directly out of the oven with his bare hands, as he usually did, and just handed it to me. I screamed when I touched it. Then he screamed at me when I dropped it. It was just his way of showing me that I didn't know as much as I thought I did."

During his time with the Intercontinental chain, Charles developed a desire to move into management. So he went to work at Slug's 30th Edition in Charlotte. Slug Claiborne owned several restaurants in the North Carolina Piedmont and was a major force in the development of fine dining in the state. From there, Chef Park moved to a position as executive chef with the Beacon Hotel Corporation at Guest Quarters Suites in Charlotte.

He narrates his move to the coast: "Then the chance opened at The Cedars Inn in Beaufort. Once Wendy [his wife] and I moved here, this was where we wanted to stay. At that time, there were almost no chefs in the area who stayed more than a summer." So Charles was able to make a mark and establish a following from the outset. "The Wheatly family in Beaufort was really good to us when we moved here. Alice Wheatly patronized the restaurant. My father was an attorney, so was Claud Wheatly, and they became good friends. He's still around town, in his mid-90s. They helped us get off to a good start because they became our friends and told their friends about us, helped us get to know others who lived here, especially year-round."

Chef Park connected with the few other formally trained chefs in the area. They decided to establish an American Culinary Federation chapter. "We were fairly active, and one of them was a certified executive chef, so through the chapter I was able to gain the certification. The exam is very rigorous—even more so now than it used to be." With that degree, Chef Park joined the ranks of the most credentialed chefs in the area. He has also been a member of the prestigious Chaine des Rotisseurs (chainedesrotisseurs.com).

He considers himself the beneficiary of other chefs who have worked at Beaufort Grocery. "Some have been from Europe, others from South America. They brought new ideas. A lot of our dishes are named after friends, customers, or family members, but also after people who have worked here. If we had stayed the same, we would not have survived. That's how much cuisine has changed and improved in America."

He says that, at home, "Wendy and I like to cook family recipes and kind of play with them—anything fresh, sometimes leftover vegetables from the restaurant, or what looked good at Piggly Wiggly. I love fresh clams or scallops. Wendy makes spaghetti with sausage—maybe my favorite thing to eat. The way she adds one ingredient, lets it simmer, then adds another, it's like a painter painting on canvas."

The Restaurant

Beaufort Grocery Company

Charles and Wendy Park established Beaufort Grocery Company in 1991 on the site of Owens Grocery Store, just off the Beaufort waterfront. Wendy manages the front of the house and doubles as the pastry chef. The core elements of the grocery have been preserved in the restaurant's ambience, with old wood predominant. Takeout foods and desserts are available at the large deli counter. In 1994, Charles and Wendy added the adjacent property at 115 Queen Street, where private parties, wedding receptions, and other catered events are accommodated in the historic house and its landscaped garden.

Local connections with seafood suppliers and farmers are essential to the restaurant's operation. Chef Park says, "The seafood that is available here provides such a great opportunity for a chef. We have also developed partnerships with area farmers. They used to bring vegetables by the restaurant, but for some time now they have been asking what I want, and they plant according to what area chefs are seeking. I worked with one farmer, for example, who complained about the low price of squash. I told him to bring me the squash blossoms, and I would pay double for them. It had never occurred to him to cut the blossoms. He had been throwing them away. Stuffed squash blossoms have become a frequent special.

"Donnie Lewis in Otway grows lots of vegetables for me. His wife gave me the most delicious fig preserves recipe I have ever encountered. We use Beverly's preserves in some of our dishes. These are just people I feel fortunate and proud to know. I recently learned that Beaufort was a large exporter of figs 150 years ago. North Carolina was one of the largest fig producers in the country until California started growing them. In the last 15 years, we've learned to use figs in a lot of recipes. They're just so good. In winter, when there is no local fresh fruit, we often use preserved figs, especially combined with Vidalia onions."

The restaurant orders most of its seafood from Fishtowne Seafood (see page 142) and Blue Ocean Market. Chef Park finds that Bill Rice at Fishtowne seems to deal more with small fishermen, whereas David Tucker at Blue Ocean has contacts all up and down the Eastern Seaboard. Chef Park explains that "local" seafood has to cover an area from roughly Norfolk to the Low Country of South Carolina. Scallops, at least for part of the year, have to come from colder water, sometimes New Jersey. Grouper comes from Florida in winter. Certain fish that appear on the menu have to be available anytime. Yellowfin tuna and scallops are available fresh year-round from somewhere nearby. But Chef Park worries about local fishermen. "They are threatened. It's a really tough situation regarding overfishing, but the small-scale fishermen seem to get squeezed the most."

The Recipes

Aunt Marion's Apple and Onion Salad
Serves 2

Cranberry Vinaigrette
¾ cup cranberries, crushed
¼ cup sugar
1 tablespoon honey
2 teaspoons chopped garlic
½ cup balsamic vinegar
2 tablespoons cider vinegar
1 cup vegetable oil
salt and pepper to taste

Purée first 6 ingredients in a food processor. Slowly blend in oil. Season with salt and pepper.

Salad
½ head romaine lettuce, chopped
½ small red onion, sliced thin
1 Granny Smith apple, cored and sliced
6 ounces Gorgonzola cheese, crumbled

Line plates with ingredients in the order given.

Aunt Marion's Apple and Onion Salad
PHOTO BY JOHN BATCHELOR

PRESENTATION
Drizzle vinaigrette across top and serve.

Pork Tenderloin with Bourbon or Cognac Butter Sauce
Serves 4 to 6

6 tablespoons bourbon or cognac
2 tablespoons cider vinegar
2 tablespoons Worcestershire sauce
2 tablespoons soy sauce
2 teaspoons Dijon mustard
¼ cup onion, diced fine
2 cloves garlic, chopped fine
1 teaspoon hot sauce
1 stick cold unsalted butter, cut into cubes
salt and pepper to taste
2-pound pork tenderloin
mashed or sweet potatoes
greens

Pork Tenderloin with Bourbon or Cognac Butter Sauce
PHOTO BY JOHN BATCHELOR

Combine first 8 ingredients, bring to a boil, and reduce until thick. Remove from heat. Whisk in butter a little at a time until incorporated. Keep warm.

Preheat grill to high. Salt and pepper tenderloin. Place tenderloin on grill and reduce temperature to medium. Grill until internal temperature reaches 100 degrees. Turn over and make sure tenderloin looks done and is well marked from the grill. Grill second side until internal temperature reaches 160 degrees. Remove from grill and allow to rest on a warm surface for 2 to 3 minutes. Slice a little over ¼ inch thick.

PRESENTATION

Stack slices of tenderloin leaned on the diagonal on top of mashed or sweet potatoes. Drizzle with sauce. Place greens (collards, mustard-turnip mix, or kale) alongside.

BEAUFORT

BLUE MOON BISTRO

119 Queen Street

Beaufort, N.C. 28516

252-728-5800

bluemoonbistro.biz/

Kyle Swain
PHOTO BY
BRYAN DENEHY PHOTOGRAPHY

The Chef

Kyle Swain

Kyle Swain grew up riding skateboards and bicycles in front of the historic home on Queen Street that is now Blue Moon Bistro. Except for a four-year period working and going to school in the Chapel Hill–Durham area, he has never lived away from the North Carolina coast.

He started cooking after he woke up one morning and found that his mother had already left for work. "My brothers and I were hungry, and for whatever reason I decided I wanted some scrambled eggs. I had watched my mother cook scrambled eggs countless times and figured I'd give it a try. The first batch stuck to the pan, and after a minute of head scratching I hoped a little butter would do the trick. The second attempt was a success. I believe that positive result started the curiosity."

He landed his first paid gig at age 13 in Clawson's Restaurant (see pages 200-206). Kyle says that, over time, "I had the privilege of working with talented, hardworking, very patient mentors in some really great kitchens. I spent lots of long days and nights paying attention. I learned to take lots of notes, both actual written and mental, and learned the business from the bottom up."

He earned a bachelor's degree in anthropology from UNC-Wilmington and did a semester of graduate-level work at UNC–Chapel Hill. "The whole time I was in college, I always had a job in a restaurant. So I finally decided to admit to myself that cooking and food service was my real passion," he recalls.

"I guess my style began to develop while I was working with Gary Wein, a great chef in Durham. He and his business partner, Harold Tharrington, own and operate Savory Fare, an upscale catering company. I worked with these guys for a few years both in the kitchen each day prepping and in the field at catered events. Gary taught me about ingredient diversity, food and wine pairings, and the importance of using fresh local ingredients. There seemed to be a steady stream of food purveyors coming to his shop with the freshest foodstuffs. I guess Gary came from the Alice Waters era and was a product of the Chez Panisse influence. He was not formally trained, but he used his knowledge, skills, intellect, and passion to become the best at his profession. I guess it can be reduced down to having a strong desire to do your best to make your guests happy. Great food is only part of the equation. It's much more about the entire dining experience, which also includes direct contact with wait staff."

Kyle also spent some time cooking in country clubs. But he has made it a point not to move around the way so many chefs do. "I spent a fair amount of time at each place I have been associated with, and I always learned something different at each one—not only food and beverage service, but management skills and more about the business side of the industry. Food service is one of those industries where there will always have to be a critical mass of people doing the actual work, so the better you are at managing people, the more successful your operation will be."

In his first venture into ownership, Kyle was a founding partner at Windansea in Morehead City, where he ran the kitchen for about five years. He opened Blue Moon in 2002. He and two partners remodeled an old home in order to convert it into a restaurant.

When cooking at home, he loves fresh seafood most. "During the summer, the restaurant keeps me way too busy to cook at home. I try to eat out on my day off, usually sushi. During the off-season, I steam lots of local oysters and do some heartier winter fare such as stews, chowders, and slower-cooked dishes that keep the oven going. Holidays are special, because we get some family time to enjoy traditional dishes and take a little break from work."

The Restaurant

Blue Moon Bistro

Blue Moon Bistro occupies the historic Dill House, constructed circa 1827. Chef Swain wanted a small restaurant "so it would be easier to manage. My goal was to use the extra time that gave me to focus on sourcing great foodstuffs and creating something different with them. I wanted to create a restaurant where someone could eat with me every day and have something different each time. We dabble in regional cuisine, as well as international. We change the menu every month and offer several daily features, which are based on what fishermen and farmers are bringing in. Weather plays a role, too, and we pay careful attention and adjust our menus accordingly."

Because he grew up in Beaufort, Chef Swain has known many of his suppliers or their families most of his life. "In addition to actually going to the farms, docks, and fish houses, I try to keep lines of communication as open as possible. This allows us to keep a finger on the pulse of not only what's fresh and available today, but what we can start thinking about for the weeks ahead.

"The daily operation of a restaurant is a lot like staging a show, a theatrical event, circus, or even a concert," he says. "You have to make sure the front of the house and the back are in sync. There is lots of prep work that takes place long before the doors open. There are 'actors' and 'characters' who bring decades of experience, skill, and talent to the operation. Each one plays an essential role. It's up to the 'director' to keep everyone on task, working together. In our case, Blue Moon is chef/owner driven, and that works for us due to our small size."

The restaurant has been recognized as the "Best on the Coast" in *Metro Magazine* for several years and won a TripAdvisor "Award of Excellence" in 2012 and 2013. But Chef Swain concludes, "We depend mainly on word of mouth. Our customers bring in more business than any kind of self-promotion we ever tried."

Roasted Beet and Herbed Chevre "Napoleon"
PHOTO BY BRYAN DENEHY PHOTOGRAPHY

The Recipes

Roasted Beet and Herbed Chevre "Napoleon"

Serves 2

2 3-ounce red beets
olive oil
3 ounces fresh goat cheese
1 tablespoon fresh herbs (thyme, oregano, or basil)
1 Valencia orange
salt and pepper to taste
½ cup mixed greens (spinach, Bibb, mesclun, arugula)
2 tablespoons balsamic or other vinaigrette
2 tablespoons toasted nuts (pecans, walnuts, or hazelnuts)

Preheat oven to 325 degrees. Drizzle beets with olive oil and roast in a covered pan for approximately 3 hours until a fork is easily inserted in center. Cool, peel, slice, and dice the beet pulp. Reserve. (This can be done a day ahead.) Crumble goat cheese with a fork and fold in fresh herbs. Peel and slice orange and reserve segments.

To assemble, use a 3-inch ring mold on a plate. Place a layer of diced beets in the mold, pressing firmly to form a base. Season with salt and pepper and cover with goat cheese mixture. Repeat the beet/goat cheese layering until reaching top of ring. Dress mixed greens with vinaigrette and arrange on a plate. Place orange segments around edge. Hold the plate with the ring mold over the salad. Slide mold onto center of salad. Using the bottom of a small cup, gently apply pressure on the top while lifting the ring itself.

PRESENTATION

Drizzle with vinaigrette, dust with salt and pepper, garnish with toasted nuts, and serve.

Seared Sea Scallops in Penne Pasta
Photo by Bryan Denehy Photography

Seared Sea Scallops in Penne Pasta

Serves 1 or 2 as an appetizer; double quantities to serve as an entrée

olive oil
4 1-ounce sea scallops
salt and pepper to taste
1 tablespoon minced shallot
pinch of fresh thyme
1 portobello mushroom cap, chopped
2 tablespoons cognac
¼ cup heavy cream
¼ cup chicken stock
¼ cup penne pasta, cooked according to package directions
freshly grated Parmesan cheese

Heat a sauté pan on medium-high heat. Drizzle with olive oil and allow oil to get hot. Dust scallops with salt and pepper immediately before gently placing in hot oil. After 1 minute, reduce heat to medium and allow exterior of scallops to sear and caramelize. Turn scallops when they are dark golden brown and move to side of pan. Add shallots, thyme, and mushrooms to pan and sauté. Carefully deglaze pan with cognac and add cream and stock. Toss pasta in pan and heat until mushrooms are cooked and liquids are reduced and thickened.

PRESENTATION

Place everything on a plate with the scallops on top to protect their crispness. Garnish with Parmesan.

Steve Smid and Jennifer Mull   <small>PHOTO BY JOHN BATCHELOR</small>

THE CEDARS INN & RESTAURANT

305 Front Street

Beaufort, N.C. 28516

252-838-1463

cedarsinn.com

The Chef

Steve Smid

Although Steve Smid was born near Chicago, he grew up in North Carolina. His family moved to High Point in 1980 when his father, a photographer, took a position with the legendary Alderman Studios. At about age 17, Steve got a summer job in a little corner bar and grill. He worked nights and liked having mornings and afternoons free. Then he "just kind of stuck with it," he recalls. "I realized that cooking could be a lot of fun. When I began to consider that I could get paid for doing what I really liked, that became what I wanted to do as a career. I love good food, and I love to eat."

He confesses that he lied in order to get into a fine-dining chef's position. "Well, maybe not an outright lie, but certainly a stretch of the truth. By then, I could slice and dice and chop, but I had not made risotto and some of those other things the other guys on the line were doing. I read a lot of books. Over time, I worked with real professionals who were formally trained. They showed me lots of things books or even culinary school can't teach, things that only come from hands on."

He learned a good deal in three High Point restaurants that have since closed. "I learned about the business side from Charles Oaks at Act One—portion sizes, costs, that sort of thing. Matt Upchurch at M. Stevens taught me a lot of technique, French techniques especially. Ronnie Stevens at Pomodoro always emphasized the importance of fresh ingredients and letting them shine, not covering them up with heavy cream. Working for Ronnie helped me gain an understanding of what was required in a high-volume situation. Sometimes, we served 3,000 people a day during Furniture Market. The level of organization and planning was just incredible."

He moved to Hampton's at the J. H. Adams Inn in High Point when new ownership decided to change the restaurant operation. Six months later, management got rid of the chef who had been hired and asked Steve to take over. "I hated what happened, but it created a great opportunity for me. When I first went there, it was hard for us to pick up business, because so many people were loyal to the previous restaurant owner. Then to have another big change in so short a time created another handicap." Gradually, crowds were lured back in because Steve's food looked and tasted so good. His term at Hampton's lasted about five years.

His move to Beaufort came after K. J. Grissom, director of sales for the J. H. Adams Inn, introduced him to one of the owners of furniture maker Sarreid Ltd., Alex Sarratt, who had expressed admiration for Steve's cooking. Sarratt and his wife, Margaret Wilmerding, had been coming to Beaufort all their lives. They saw that The Cedars was closed and for sale. They had always loved the historic home, so they decided to buy it. They asked Steve to come down and inspect the condition of the restaurant and give them advice about what would be needed to make it operational again.

"Jenn [Steve's fiancée] and I came down to Beaufort one weekend. I had some vacation coming. We intended it to be a day trip, and we didn't even stay at The Cedars. We had never been to Beaufort. We sat around for hours talking with Alex and Margaret about what needed to be done. At some point, they ventured the idea of leasing the restaurant to us, but we declined. But we kept in touch with each other, and they eventually made us another offer. It was an opportunity for us to work together in a small, wonderful location. We got lucky and found a place to live a block away. That was in May 2012. We reopened the restaurant on Friday the 13th in July. Jenn was very apprehensive, even though she is not superstitious, but I thought the date signified good luck. Jenn became the restaurant and inn manager and special-events coordinator. The only thing I regret about the move is that it did not happen 10 years earlier."

Jennifer Mull met Steve when they both worked at Cleary's Hidden Shamrock Pub in High Point. She was in school, waiting tables as a part-time job. He was cooking. Now, in Beaufort, "we are off on Sundays," Steve says. "I don't want to spend all day in the kitchen, so I cook on the grill. Not just fish, but vegetables—squash, corn. When we're on our own, we crave what Mom made. We don't need a Bordelaise sauce at home!"

The Restaurant

The Cedars Inn & Restaurant

The Cedars is located in one of Beaufort's historic waterfront homes. Constructed in 1768 by William Borden, son of a Rhode Island shipwright, it played host to sailing-ship captains who stayed in the port town. Front porches upstairs and down look out on the water and the historic end of Front Street. The new owners made improvements in January 2014 while respecting the original details of the home. Elegant and stylish but casual furnishings came from the owners' company, Sarreid Ltd.

Although a fine-dining menu is served, there is no dress code beyond shirt and shoes. Chef Smid remarks, "Some of the locals who have been coming 20 years or so dress in coats and ties for a special occasion. But we want everybody to feel warm and welcome. We seat 40 maximum at any one time. There's nothing pretentious or snobby here. Everybody is family and friends.

"Good ingredients speak for themselves," he says. "What we do here is Southern coastal, because of the seasonal ingredients—the seafood, the squash, okra, heirloom tomatoes. Here, you know what's in season because you are talking to the fishermen, and they can only catch and sell what is within regulations. We get oysters super fresh from the Newport River, for example. It's just wonderful to be able to use ingredients that were harvested 30 minutes to an hour away and have just been caught or picked."

The main provider of seafood is Blue Ocean Market in Morehead City. "Dave Tucker is honest. He'll tell you when things were caught. He'll call ahead when he's out on his boat. Some restaurants won't buy the high-dollar stuff, but we will. Dave will send me a text at eight in the morning almost every day with what he has caught. It's in the restaurant by two in the afternoon, packed in ice chests. We shop the Beaufort Farmers' Market on weekends. Most area farms sell to wholesalers, and we buy from them. But we buy directly, too. One of our neighbors, who lives four houses down from The Cedars, has a farm in Virginia. She brings 50-pound boxes of sweet potatoes in the trunk of her Lincoln Town Car. She drives up, pops the trunk, and calls out, 'Here you are, honey!' "

Herb-Grilled Shrimp with Black-Eyed Pea Succotash
PHOTO BY JOHN BATCHELOR

The Recipes

Herb-Grilled Shrimp with Black-Eyed Pea Succotash
Serves 2

8 to 10 large shrimp, peeled and deveined
1 cup black-eyed peas (fresh, if available)
1 cup chopped cherry or grape tomatoes
⅓ cup heavy cream
½ cup fresh corn, cut off the cob
1 tablespoon chopped garlic
2 teaspoons Texas Pete hot sauce
1 teaspoon chopped fresh herbs (rosemary works well)
salt and pepper to taste
squeeze of lemon
chopped chives

Skewer shrimp and grill or sauté for 2 to 3 minutes per side until pink. Combine all remaining ingredients except chives in a sauté pan on medium-high heat for approximately 4 minutes until cream reduces and thickens.

PRESENTATION
Place shrimp on top of succotash and garnish with chives.

Red Snapper with Dijon Glaze and Heirloom Tomato, Corn, and Crab Relish
Serves 4

Heirloom Tomato, Corn, and Crab Relish
2 large heirloom tomatoes (German Johnsons or Purple Cherokees work well), chopped
2 ears cooked fresh corn, kernels removed from cobs
¼ pound jumbo lump crabmeat
¼ cup extra-virgin olive oil
2 tablespoons chopped fresh basil
1 tablespoon champagne vinegar
juice of 1 lemon
salt and pepper to taste

Combine all ingredients. Set aside.

Red Snapper with Dijon Glaze and Heirloom Tomato, Corn, and Crab Relish
PHOTO BY
JOHN BATCHELOR

Dijon Glaze

½ cup whole-grain Dijon mustard
2 tablespoons white wine
1 tablespoon sugar

Combine ingredients. Set aside.

Fish

2 pounds red snapper (grouper also works well)
salt and pepper to taste
1 tablespoon olive oil
fresh basil leaves

Preheat oven to 400 degrees. Portion snapper into 4 pieces and season with salt and pepper. Preheat a large nonstick sauté pan and add olive oil. Sear fish skin side up for 3 to 4 minutes. Turn over and apply Dijon Glaze. Finish in oven for 8 to 10 minutes until flaky.

PRESENTATION

Top snapper with relish and garnish with basil and a drizzle of olive oil.

Shrimp and Scallops with Collard Green–Parmesan Risotto and Garlic Prawn Sauce

Serves 4

Garlic Prawn Sauce

1 cup heavy cream
¼ cup shrimp stock
1 tablespoon chopped garlic
1 tablespoon paprika
1 teaspoon lemon juice

Prepare ahead. Whisk all ingredients in a saucepot over medium-high heat until reduced; mixture should coat the back of a spoon. Set aside and keep warm.

Risotto

1 tablespoon olive oil

1 large shallot, chopped

salt and pepper to taste

3 cups chicken stock

1 teaspoon chopped garlic

½ pound Arborio rice

1 tablespoon butter

¼ cup grated Parmesan cheese

2 cups cooked collard greens

*Shrimp and Scallops
with Collard Green-
Parmesan Risotto and
Garlic Prawn Sauce*

PHOTO BY
JOHN BATCHELOR

Add oil to a large sauté pan over medium heat. When oil is hot, add shallots and season with salt and pepper. Sauté for 3 minutes until shallots are slightly soft. Add stock and garlic. Bring to a boil, then reduce to a simmer. Cook for 6 minutes. Add rice and simmer for 18 minutes, stirring constantly until mixture is creamy and bubbly. Add butter, Parmesan, and greens to risotto after it has simmered 18 minutes. Season with salt and pepper. Simmer 2 more minutes and serve immediately.

Shrimp and Scallops

olive oil

12 large sea scallops

12 large or jumbo shrimp, deveined, tails on

While rice is simmering, heat a large nonstick sauté pan on medium-high heat and coat lightly with olive oil. Add scallops and shrimp. Cook for 3 minutes. Turn and cook an additional 3 minutes.

PRESENTATION

Place risotto in center of plates. Place shrimp and scallops over risotto. Spoon Garlic Prawn Sauce over shrimp.

FISHTOWNE SEAFOOD

100 Wellons Drive
Beaufort, N.C. 28516
252-728-6644
fishtowneseafood.com

The name *Fishtowne* dates back to colonial times, when people referred to a certain section of Beaufort as Fishtowne because of the constant smell of fish being caught, handled, and processed there. Fishing and fish processing have been important to Beaufort for a long time.

Bill Rice, owner and cofounder of Fishtowne Seafood, moved from Raleigh to the coast with his family when he was 12. He found he loved swimming, clamming, fishing, and the marine environment and just never wanted to leave. His family bought a commercial fishing boat. After college at Appalachian State, he applied with a friend for a fisheries resource grant and started buying and selling seafood. Fishtowne Seafood opened in 2004. It is both a retail seafood market and a wholesale facility. Fishtowne sells to residents and tourists, as well as area restaurants that specialize in local seafood.

Fishtowne's website points out that the first thing visitors notice when they enter is that "it smells good." The staff is meticulous about cleanliness and freshness. Charles Just, who cuts and processes fish, has over 30 years' experience in that role. Chris Conklin catches and sells fish to the market; he works as a cutter and is also involved in retail and restaurant sales when he is not on the water. Charles and Chris are both considered "master cutters."

Fishtowne buys seafood from local fishermen who work the waters of Carteret and Pamlico counties. Most of them are fourth- or fifth-generation watermen who learned the role from their families. They operate small-scale boats and equipment, catching finfish—flounder, trout, bluefish, mullet, mahi-mahi, tuna, grouper, and snapper—as well as shrimp, oysters, and clams. Blue crabs are caught in pots or traps.

The company participates in the North Carolina Department of Environment and Natural Resources' Oyster Shell Recycling Program. Shells are returned to the water and become habitat for tiny organisms that will develop other oyster beds over time.

Bill Rice reports that he likes "fresh-grilled fish, boiled shrimp, steamed clams, and fried oysters. We normally cook all of this at home."

Fishtowne is a member of Carteret Catch. Bill Rice is also actively involved in the Beaufort Historical Association.

Bryan Carithers
PHOTO BY JOHN BATCHELOR

CITY KITCHEN

Town Creek Marina

232 West Beaufort Road

Beaufort, N.C. 28516

252-648-8141

FRONT STREET GRILL AT STILLWATER

300 Front Street

Beaufort, N.C. 28516

252-728-4956

frontstreetgrillatstillwater.com

The Chef

Bryan Carithers

When he was growing up, Bryan Carithers told friends he wanted to own a restaurant someday. It was either that or stick with his gig as a drummer with the Insurgents. He waited tables at night and played with the band from D.C. to Georgia, most frequently in his hometown of Raleigh. Gradually, he moved into kitchens, washing dishes at first, then prepping and cooking. He worked in some of Raleigh's more prominent restaurants—Casa Carbone, Villa Capri, Cappers, Greenshields, and a few others. He started to learn about flavor in those jobs. He went to California when he was 18 and worked in a couple of restaurants there, but he didn't like the West and couldn't wait to get back to North Carolina.

Bryan returned to Raleigh and took a job as kitchen manager in a restaurant that must be unidentified. "It was not a good restaurant," he recalls. "The staff criticized me for cleaning too much." So he learned some things about how not to run a restaurant. His last job before leaving Raleigh was at the Horwitz Deli— "the only deli-type place that I had ever worked in."

In his mid-20s, he started looking for a location where he could start his own restaurant. Although he had never pursued formal culinary training, he had by then experienced "lots of trials, enough errors," and quite an education in the proverbial school of hard knocks. He stumbled upon an ice-cream shop on Front Street in Beaufort that had closed. "The owners offered it at what we considered a great price, so I talked my sister Tracey into moving back from Oregon to be my partner, and together we renovated it into what became Front Street Grill," he says.

Front Street Grill prospered, garnered good reviews, and earned a loyal following among residents and visitors alike. Things got even better after Bryan's marriage to Karen Burke, who had been food and beverage manager in hotels in the North and at the time of their marriage was director of sales and marketing for the Atlantic Beach Sheraton. She took over managing the front of the house and baking the restaurant's house-made desserts. They stayed in that location for 10 years. They had an option to buy the property, but when it was time to make a decision, Bryan and Tracey and their parents, Michael and Dianne, partnered to purchase a property on the waterfront, which they named Front Street Grill at Stillwater. Michael and Dianne had owned Carolina Glass and Interiors in Raleigh and moved to Beaufort in semi-retirement.

Bryan and Karen's son, Dylan, often works as host or helps bus tables. He is a member of the Future Business Leaders of America chapter at West Carteret High School. In order to qualify to attend the FBLA conference, students have to test in a field. He took the restaurant and hospitality management exam. From the conference, he texted his parents that he had placed second in the state out of 500 students, earning a trip to the Disney properties in California. "He had never taken a class in hospitality, and he did not study for the exam," Bryan says. "He just knew the procedures from hanging around the restaurant. He has decided now that he wants to go to Johnson & Wales."

The Restaurants

City Kitchen and Front Street Grill at Stillwater

When the Carithers family added "at Stillwater" to Front Street Grill, the revised restaurant name reflected a key element of the new restaurant's ambience—the lazy motion of the bay, where diners can watch boats enter and leave Beaufort, bound for the Intracoastal Waterway or the open ocean.

About six years after the move, Tracey and Michael took over management of Front Street Grill at Stillwater and Bryan and Karen opened City Kitchen in Morehead City. They moved City Kitchen to Town Creek Marina in Beaufort in 2014. Bryan continues as partner at Front Street and is executive chef for both properties.

City Kitchen is situated on the top floor of the Town Creek Marina building. A covered tiki bar is located on the docks adjacent to the restaurant and marina facility. The bar sells sandwiches and light fare, in addition to drinks. Upstairs in the main dining room, a copper-clad bar occupies center stage, with seating all around. The views of the bay and boats at anchor are wide-ranging. Most evenings when the sky is clear, people get up and go out on the deck to watch the sunset, then return to their tables to finish eating.

As far as a food style is concerned, Bryan says he tries "to seek a particular flavor profile. I've learned that simpler is better. So many young cooks have limited experience eating in good restaurants, and they tend to just pile stuff on. I cook what I like. I don't like lamb, so I don't cook it."

Karen observes, "Bryan's food is like the food and people of the United States. It's blended from different cultures and follows what different people enjoy. It is approachable food executed correctly. We test food with staff, and they give honest feedback." Many of his creations reflect the influence of family vacations in the Caribbean.

Bryan sticks to ingredients sourced nearby—sometimes very nearby. "We grow our own tomatoes. We like Cherokee Purples and Pink Ladies best of all. We buy day-boat fish. We pay more for it, but if you buy quality and you find ways to allow the ingredients to speak for themselves, you'll have better-tasting food."

Blue Ocean Market in Morehead City is a primary supplier, along with Fishtowne Seafood in Beaufort. "Everything they sell is caught by guys who live here," Bryan says. "These are not long-line boats, where fish hang and die over a long time. They are line-caught and reeled in. Our wait staff can tell customers where and when fish were caught and who caught them. Merrell Farm supplies lots of our vegetables."

Regular customers in both restaurants are greeted as friends, and new visitors feel the family ambience immediately.

The Recipes

Baked Oysters with Onion Bacon Jam and Creamed Collards
Serves 4

Creamed Collards
½ cup unsalted butter, cubed
5 cloves garlic, chopped
1 small onion, diced
½ cup cream
¼ teaspoon cracked pepper
1½ cups grated Parmesan cheese
2½ cups collards, chopped and cooked
1 cup panko breadcrumbs

Melt butter in a pan. Add garlic and onions and cook until translucent. Add cream, pepper, and cheese. Whisk until cheese melts. Fold in collards and simmer until warmed through. Remove from heat and stir in breadcrumbs.

Onion Bacon Jam
½ pound bacon, diced
1 small yellow onion, diced fine
2 tablespoons chopped garlic
1½ tablespoons dark brown sugar
1 tablespoon Sriracha sauce
¼ cup water
2 tablespoons apple cider vinegar
2 tablespoons maple syrup
1 tablespoon cracked pepper
salt to taste

Brown bacon in a heavy-bottomed saucepan. Remove bacon and reserve fat. Add onions to fat and sauté until caramelized. Add garlic and cook for 1 minute on low heat. Add remaining ingredients and cook over low heat until a thick, jam-like consistency develops.

Oysters

16 oysters, cleaned and shucked
rock salt
1 lemon, cut into 4 wedges

Preheat oven to 400 degrees. Open each oyster to the half shell. Top each with a dab of Creamed Collards. Bake about 6 minutes until warm. Remove from oven and add 1 teaspoon Onion Bacon Jam to each oyster.

PRESENTATION

Sprinkle rock salt on elongated plates to create a bed. Place 4 oysters in a row on each plate. Place a lemon wedge alongside.

Baked Oysters with Onion Bacon Jam and Creamed Collards
Photo by John Batchelor

Oven-Braised Chicken with Mushroom Curry and Fig Chutney
Photo by John Batchelor

Oven-Braised Chicken with Mushroom Curry and Fig Chutney
Serves 4

Fig Chutney
2 teaspoons canola oil
¼ cup onion, diced fine
1 cup plus 2 tablespoons fig preserves
juice of ½ lemon
3 tablespoons dark brown sugar
⅛ teaspoon ground cloves
¾ teaspoon ground allspice
¼ teaspoon ground nutmeg
¼ teaspoon cinnamon
1 tablespoon rice wine vinegar
1 tablespoon muscatel wine vinegar
¼ teaspoon pepper
pinch of salt

Add oil to a pan and heat to medium. Sauté onions until translucent. Lower heat and stir in fig preserves. Add remaining ingredients and cook over low heat for 15 minutes. Transfer to a nonreactive container and cool. Refrigerate until ready to serve.

Mushroom Curry Sauce

2 tablespoons canola oil
½ cup yellow onion, diced fine
3 tablespoons yellow curry powder
¼ cup plus 1 tablespoon water, divided
3 cups sliced mushroom caps
2½ cups heavy cream
1 teaspoon sherry vinegar
1 teaspoon cracked pepper
1 tablespoon sugar
1½ teaspoons salt
1 tablespoon butter

Add oil to a saucepan and heat to medium. Sauté onions until translucent. Add curry powder and simmer for 2 minutes, stirring constantly with a wooden spoon. Deglaze pan with 1 tablespoon of the water. Scrape bottom of pan and stir. Add mushrooms. Cook for 3 to 5 minutes. Add cream, vinegar, rest of water, pepper, sugar, and salt. Reduce heat to low and cook for 15 to 20 minutes until mixture reduces to a sauce consistency. Add butter just before serving and swirl into mixture.

Chicken

salt and pepper to taste
4 "airline" or French-cut chicken breasts, skin on, wing bones attached
oil
1 cup white wine
1 lemon, sliced into rounds
2 cups rice, prepared according to package directions

Preheat oven to 350 degrees. Salt and pepper skin side of chicken. Sprinkle a little oil in a pan and heat to high temperature. Add chicken skin side down and brown. Rotate to skin side up. Add wine and lemon slices and bake for 20 to 30 minutes. Keep warm in a covered dish.

PRESENTATION

Place chicken over beds of rice. Ladle with Mushroom Curry. Dab 1 tablespoon Fig Chutney alongside.

CLAWSON'S RESTAURANT

425 Front Street

Beaufort, N.C. 28516

252-728-2133

clawsonsrestaurant.com

Jon McGregor
PHOTO BY TAYLOR MCCUNE, CCC, INC.

The Chef

Jon McGregor

"I loved being a teenager in coastal Carolina. I enjoyed skating and surfing, cruising around in a convertible with the top down, just being a kid who always wanted to live at the beach."

Jon McGregor was born in Altavista, Virginia, but his family moved to the North Carolina coast when he was 15, due to his father's job-related relocation. When he grew up, he continued living in Beaufort. "Most of all, I enjoy the laid-back pace. I love spending time with my wife, Emily, and our three dogs, walking on the beach or the waterfront."

He began cooking around the time he moved to Beaufort, as a short-order cook in a summer job at a mom-and-pop ice-cream shop. "I knew nothing about cooking but enjoyed the job, learning to stay organized, to work clean and move fast," he says. He spent the next summer in a restaurant on the Morehead City waterfront, where he worked his way up from busboy to dishwasher to the pantry and ended the summer working across the street at a different restaurant. "I began learning how a professional kitchen operated. I would open the restaurant at 7 A.M., grab my clipboard, and start the coffee. It was my job to proof and bake bread, peel and devein shrimp, chop herbs, and set up *mise en place* for all stations before the line cooks and chef arrived around one or two. When my work was done, I would meet my friends at the beach or neighborhood pool for a couple of hours, then come back to the restaurant for dinner service at five. I made salads, desserts, and a couple of cold appetizers. I would always try to stay ahead of production so that I could try to learn what the cooks on the hot line were doing."

After graduating from high school, Jon moved to Boone for college at Appalachian State, where he intended to study business, music, or English. "But I kept coming back to restaurants. It seemed that anytime I couldn't land another job, I was always in a kitchen, working my way up from an entry job. It turned out that I just loved the atmosphere, the sense of controlled chaos. It was then that I decided to enroll at Johnson & Wales and take this cooking thing more seriously."

He graduated from the university's Charleston campus, then spent some time at the Renaissance Hotel in Charlotte, where working with experienced chefs helped him learn "how to produce very high-end food at very high volume, how to make sauces properly, and how to present classical dishes with a modern flair."

Reflecting on how he developed his own style, he remarks, "I think that growing up watching my grandmothers and great-grandmother canning and pickling, cleaning snap beans, and shucking corn in the summer had a great influence on the style of cooking I developed. I love making jams and jellies and adding some of the older Southern ideas that I remember from my childhood to the dishes that I'm making today. Also, a big influence on the way I cook comes from living in coastal Carolina and having the exposure to fresh, beautiful seafood. Knowing where that seafood comes from and the local methods of preparation, coupled with studying and living in Charleston, has helped to shape my culinary ideas."

When cooking at home, Jon likes grilling and smoking. "My wife and I are pizza fanatics. We love very simple dishes—pancakes and fresh jam, garlic bread and spaghetti. I have a good cast-iron skillet that we use to sear pork tenderloin and roast root vegetables in the fall."

The Restaurant

Clawson's Restaurant

Clawson's has nearly 300 seats. But instead of the prepackaged food that is characteristic of similarly sized chain restaurants, its kitchen focuses on preparing familiar dishes from scratch, using fresh ingredients. "We support local farms, and we like to serve fresh local seafood when available. We are a high-volume restaurant, but everything that comes from our kitchen is made in house," Chef McGregor explains.

The restaurant partners with a number of growers, including Merrell Farm and Laurel Farm (Beaufort), Simpson Farm (Bertie County), and Garner Farms (Newport). "Sometimes, the broccoli that customers are eating in the Broccoli Salad came from the field only an hour ago," Chef McGregor says. "We also feature local seafood, using Blue Ocean and Fishtowne markets. Overall, we serve very approachable food. We prepare classics that casual cooks can emulate at home."

The building constitutes a large part of the restaurant's identity. About half of the structure was built around 1905. The dining rooms are decorated with unusual antiques—RC Cola signs, grocery promotions, brass cash registers, and a big farmhouse stove, for example. The other half is only slightly newer, built in the 1930s. The pub is on the "new" side, framed by an enormous mahogany bar that dates back to the first half of the 20th century. Craft beers, most brewed in North Carolina, are an important element of the bar concept.

Jon was the chef at Clawson's sister restaurant, Aqua, when it opened. Then he moved to the North Carolina mountains. "My wife and I lived in the mountains for almost a year, but it seemed that we couldn't get back to the coast fast enough. I called the general manager at Clawson's and Aqua at the beginning of the summer and came back to Beaufort to work shortly thereafter. Don't get me wrong, my wife and I love the Asheville area, but just to visit!"

Clawson's has been featured in *Southern Living* for its Mud Pie, an ice-cream cake made with Rocky Road ice cream in an Oreo crust, with all the usual sundae toppings. The restaurant has been awarded a TripAdvisor Certificate of Excellence for several years.

The Recipes

Shrimp and Grits
Serves 4 to 6

Grits
1 tablespoon butter
1 quart milk
½ teaspoon salt
1 cup stone-ground grits
½ cup shredded cheddar cheese
pepper to taste

Use a large pot to prepare grits according to package directions, with the following modifications. Bring butter and milk to a slow boil. Add salt and stir until dissolved. Add grits and reduce heat. Stir frequently to keep grits from sticking. Once grits are cooked, stir in cheese and season to taste. Grits should be thick, creamy, and smooth.

Shrimp and Grits
PHOTO BY TAYLOR MCCUNE, CCC, INC.

Shrimp

8 slices bacon
½ cup diced red bell pepper
½ cup diced yellow onion
½ cup diced mushrooms
1 pound shrimp
2 teaspoons Tabasco sauce
2 teaspoons lemon juice
chopped parsley

While grits are cooking, fry bacon in a large skillet until crisp. Remove bacon, let cool, and break into small pieces. Sauté peppers, onions, and mushrooms in bacon grease for 2 to 3 minutes until onions are translucent. Add shrimp and sauté another 2 to 3 minutes, tossing frequently to ensure shrimp are cooked through. Add Tabasco and lemon juice just before serving.

PRESENTATION

Place grits in bottom of deep bowls. Add all other ingredients on top of grits and top with parsley. Serve in a platter if you want to let guests plate their own portions.

Fried Chicken and Tasso Gravy with Mashed Potatoes and Green Beans

Serves 4

Tasso Gravy

¼ cup butter
¼ cup flour
2 tablespoons diced celery
2 tablespoons diced red bell pepper
¼ cup diced yellow onion
½ cup diced tasso ham
1 teaspoon gumbo file
½ teaspoon cayenne pepper
1 cup chicken stock
½ cup heavy cream
salt and pepper to taste

Fried Chicken and Tasso Gravy with Mashed Sweet Potatoes and Green Beans
PHOTO BY TAYLOR McCUNE, CCC, INC.

Melt butter over low heat. Add flour 1 tablespoon at a time, stirring constantly. Cook butter and flour over low heat until it reaches a rich brown color. Set aside. This is a brown roux. Sauté vegetables and ham. When vegetables are about halfway done, add dry spices and chicken stock. Bring mixture to a slow boil, stir in brown roux, and allow sauce to thicken, stirring frequently. Add cream and salt and pepper. You can purée this mixture or leave it chunky. This gravy is also great with fried or seared fish, chicken-fried pork, chicken-fried steak, or just about any other protein.

Fried Chicken
4 chicken breasts
salt and pepper to taste
1 cup buttermilk
1 cup flour
1 teaspoon granulated garlic
1 teaspoon chili powder
oil for frying

Sprinkle chicken with salt and pepper. Soak overnight in buttermilk in a covered glass or ceramic bowl.

Mix together flour, garlic, and chili powder. Heat oil to medium-high.

Dredge chicken in flour mixture. When oil is hot, gently place chicken in pan and cook until done, turning once.

Green Beans
1 pound green beans, strings and ends removed, broken into 1-inch pieces
2 cloves garlic, peeled and diced
2 tablespoons butter
salt and pepper to taste

Sauté beans and garlic in butter. Sprinkle with salt and pepper. Feel free to add whatever is fresh and growing in your area, such as peas or tomatoes.

Mashed Potatoes
1½ pounds Yukon Gold potatoes
¼ cup butter
roasted garlic to taste (optional)
milk to taste
salt and white pepper to taste

Roughly chop potatoes into 1-inch cubes, place in boiling water, and cook until tender. Strain off water and transfer to a mixing bowl. Add butter and garlic and mix on low speed until fully incorporated. Add milk to achieve desired consistency. Season with salt and white pepper.

PRESENTATION
Place potatoes on plates and prop chicken on top of potatoes. Top chicken and potatoes with Tasso Gravy. Add sautéed beans on the side.

BEAUFORT WINE & FOOD WEEKEND

400 Front Street, Suite #8
Beaufort, N.C. 28516
252-515-0708
beaufortwineandfood.org

The Beaufort Wine & Food Weekend has been celebrated for over 10 years. During that time, it has established itself as one of the area's premier tourism draws. The main event is held the last full week in April, from Wednesday through Sunday. The festival has also expanded to host other wine and food events at different times of the year.

The 20-plus events during the five-day festival in April range from intimate wine dinners, with multi-course offerings set in some of the Crystal Coast's most sought-out restaurants, to the crowd favorite Vin de Mer, at which guests are offered tastings of up to 300 wines, as well as cuisine from dozens of area restaurants. Fashion-show luncheons, cooking demonstrations, beer tastings, and the Saturday-evening Beer, Bubbles and BBQ event round out the festival.

The festival has a strong emphasis on wine. North Carolina wineries are always well represented, but California, Oregon, Washington, and international producers have a strong presence as well. The winemakers themselves are often present for discussions. Because of the wide availability of alcoholic beverages, attendees at any event must be at least 21 years old.

During 2014, the organization sponsored additional events ranging from an "All Things Italian" al fresco dinner and bocce tournament to an oyster roast in November, as well as the popular Chef's Competition series in October, which featured a dozen local and regional chefs putting their best dishes forward.

One of the reasons the festival is so attractive is the historic ambience of Beaufort itself. *Travel & Leisure* magazine considers Beaufort one of the nation's most romantic towns, and *Budget Travel* named it America's "coolest small town." The Southeast Tourism Society has recognized the Beaufort Wine & Food Weekend as one of the top events in the region.

Beaufort Wine & Food is a nonprofit organization. Since its inception, it has raised over $400,000 for local nonprofits and charities including the Beaufort Historical Association, Carteret Catch, Carteret Community College's culinary program, and the North Carolina Maritime Museum.

Libby Eaton and Tim Coyne   PHOTO BY JOHN BATCHELOR

BISTRO BY THE SEA

4031 Arendell Street

Morehead City, N.C. 28557

252-247-2777

bistro-by-the-sea.com

The Chef

Tim Coyne

"I may own the place, but I still mop floors."

That is Tim Coyne's characterization of what it's like to be a restaurant own-er, in partnership with his wife, Libby Eaton.

Tim grew up in an Italian restaurant owned by relatives, where he worked every position from dishwasher to butcher to meat and fish prep to pasta mak-er to line cook to personnel manager. He earned a degree in culinary arts from Schoolcraft College in Livonia, Michigan, one of the largest culinary programs in the United States, located near his home.

Early in his career, Tim worked at the Golden Mushroom in Southfield, Michigan. The restaurant catered to a high-end clientele during the heyday of Detroit's prosperity. Chef Milos Cihelka, from Czechoslovakia, was one of the first master chefs in the United States and was widely regarded as one of the top

10 chefs in the country at the time. Under Chef Cihelka, Tim gained a lengthy exposure to European-style preparations, learning "a lot about French cuisine at its best. If you worked for him and lasted a year, you were good. The ones who lasted longer turned out to be great. Many are culinary-school instructors now, often certified master chefs," Tim says.

Later, Tim worked in chain restaurants, moving to Indiana, Kansas, and back to Lansing, Michigan, to a Houlihan's, "where I learned to crunch numbers. It's actually one of the better chains, with good corporate menu development."

He and Libby moved to the Morehead City area about 20 years ago. "We were working partners in a restaurant in Detroit, about 10,000 square feet and 600 seats. I had a cousin who worked on Topsail Island. After we had been through a few winters in Detroit, we visited him. Libby decided she wanted to move to the South. She was hired at Applebee's in Florence, South Carolina, and I got a position at the Ramada Inn in Florence. Then we became aware of a hotel opening at the Sheraton Atlantic Beach, owned by same company as the Ramada Inn where I was working. That's when we moved to North Carolina. About six months later, we saw that the original Bistro by the Sea property in Atlantic Beach was available, so we leased it with an option to buy. After the crowds outgrew the building, we decided to move, rather than buy and renovate."

When not at the restaurant, he and Libby sometimes go out to eat with friends. "But usually we eat at home," Tim says. "My favorite dish is roasted organic chicken with rosemary and Brussels sprouts, plus any leftovers from the restaurant. I only have time to actually sit down and eat once or twice a week."

The Restaurant

Bistro by the Sea

Bistro by the Sea is located adjacent to the Morehead City Hampton Inn on Bogue Sound. Chef Coyne runs the kitchen and cooks. Libby manages the front of the house. Every night the restaurant is open, Tim cooks and Libby greets guests. "Customers will find personality out front and good food coming out of the back," Chef Coyne observes. Guests pass through a piano bar on the way to their tables.

"As far as style goes, it's based on the region. We pay close attention to local fish and produce. We offer prime rib, too, because people like it. I don't do much French, because people want simpler food now. The high-demand items are grouper, prime rib, and liver. We get fresh liver. I've always had it on the menu wherever I had menu control. We make it with an orange liqueur glaze. The manager at the

Sheraton warned me, 'You'll never sell liver in eastern North Carolina.' I told him, 'They've never had mine.'

"Staying away from all the portion-controlled packages is good for us, because people can tell the difference. We still cut our liver and steaks to order. Grouper and scallops are all day-boat-caught in local waters. We make sure that what hits the table is colorful, fresh, and current in concept. There is no microwave in the building, no deep frying. You won't smell that fry-oil odor in this kitchen.

"A lot of local providers come to us. We are getting lionfish from Discovery Diving. Most fish comes from Blue Ocean Market in Morehead City and B & J Seafood in New Bern. We talk daily to the guys who actually catch the fish. There is a sturgeon farm in Marshallberg, and they are providing caviar as well as fish. There is a lot more connection between farms and restaurants going on now than in the past. Garner Farms brings us bushels of heirloom tomatoes, greens, peaches, and strawberries when they are in season. Organic beef and pork is available now. It did not exist in this area until a few years ago. It has a different flavor, less fat."

The Recipe

Carteret Catch Grouper and Sea Scallops with Chablis Dill Sauce
Serves 2

Chablis Dill Sauce
3 large shallots, chopped fine
1 tablespoon chopped garlic
2 bay leaves
2 tablespoons crushed peppercorns
2 springs thyme
2 leaves fresh basil
3 cups Chablis
2 cups cider vinegar
2 tablespoons clam base or reduced clam juice
3 cups heavy cream
½ cup fresh dill, chopped fine
2 tablespoons unsalted butter, softened to room temperature

Carteret Catch Grouper and Sea Scallops with Chablis Dill Sauce
PHOTO BY JOHN BATCHELOR

Prepare sauce ahead. In a medium saucepan over high heat, add all ingredients except cream, dill, and butter. Bring to a boil, then lower temperature to a simmer. Reduce until almost all liquid is evaporated, making sure mixture does not scorch. This is a simple process, but give it the needed time. The reduction may take 1 hour or more. Over 1 quart of liquid will reduce to about 5 tablespoons. Do not try to taste-test the reduction, as the vinegar will be overwhelming. When mixture is reduced, add cream and bring to a boil over medium heat. Reduce heat to low and simmer for 10 minutes. Remove from heat and strain liquid into another saucepan, using a wire-mesh strainer to achieve a smooth texture. Return sauce to low heat and simmer an additional 5 minutes. At this point, you can taste-test. Just before serving, add dill to sauce. Remove from heat and blend in butter with a wire whip.

Grouper and Sea Scallops
2 5-ounce grouper fillets
6 sea scallops
seasoned salt (kosher salt, pepper, and granulated garlic) to taste
paprika to taste
1 lemon, cut into wedges

Preheat oven to 450 degrees. Place grouper and scallops on a buttered cookie sheet. Sprinkle with seasoned salt and paprika. Bake for 5 to 8 minutes.

PRESENTATION
Place grouper and scallops on plates and cover with Chablis Dill Sauce. Serve with lemon wedges.

CIRCA 81

4650 Arendell Street

Morehead City, N.C. 28557

252-648-8300

circa-81.com

Clarke Merrell
PHOTO COURTESY OF CIRCA 81

The Chef

Clarke Merrell

Clarke Merrell recalls that he "kind of grew up in a restaurant kitchen. As a kid, you don't know any different. I thought everybody worked in a restaurant. I started washing dishes and began helping out in the kitchen around age 12. I got in the way a lot, probably. But I hung around the line, watched the cooking, and sometimes filled in on guys' days off."

He was born in Norfolk, Virginia, but grew up in Emerald Isle, North Carolina. His father, in partnership with his wife's stepfather, purchased D J Shooter's restaurant in Atlantic Beach in 1988. Clarke went to Carteret Community College in Morehead City after high school while working part-time in the restaurant. "I couldn't find my niche in the community-college program, though. I was taking general-education college classes with no real direction. I realized I had been cooking so long, I might as well learn how to do it right." So he went to Florida Culinary Institute in West Palm Beach.

"When I went off to culinary school, I thought I had a leg up on everybody," he says. "I did in one sense, at least regarding real restaurant experience. But the instructors were oriented toward formal French technique, and I had no idea about that. I knew how to work hard, and I knew how to take care of people, but I realized how limited my formal cooking knowledge was."

Clarke met his wife, Liza, through D J Shooter's. Her family owned a condo at Atlantic Beach, and she took summer jobs at the restaurant. "She and I kept in touch, and after she completed her junior year, we started dating. Her senior year at George Washington University in D.C., we maintained a long-distance relationship. She was finishing college, and I was just starting culinary school." They married in 2009.

Clarke opened Circa 81 in 2010 at age 28. "Everybody thought I was crazy to try to start my own place that young. I never had the opportunity to work with a lot of great chefs, because I was always in my own restaurant. But I had more experience in the real world than most chefs who were older." In order to continue his professional development, he does stages—short-term cooking stints in highly regarded restaurants. "I did one with Sean Brock at McCrady's in Charleston. I did another at Town House Restaurant in Chilhowie, Virginia, under John Shields. His wife was the pastry chef. He formerly worked at Charlie Trotter's and Alinea in Chicago."

Now, Clarke and Liza have two children and own six businesses—olive oil shops in Swansboro, Beaufort, and Morehead City, Twisted Spoon yogurt in Morehead City, a food truck called the Dank Burrito, and Circa 81.

At home, Liza does most of the cooking. "I'm not at home enough to cook at night," Clarke says. "If we go out, if I can get them, I love tacos and cheeseburgers. A soft taco with well-marinated meat gets me excited. I like anything bold and flavorful. I love French fries, when they are fresh-cut and cooked right."

The Restaurant

Circa 81

Circa 81 takes its name from the year Clarke and Liza were born: 1981. The restaurant has a lengthy tapas menu, plus a list of full-sized entrées. "We focus mainly on small plates with big flavors," Clarke says. "The large plates accommodate anyone who wants a full meal. But the creativity is in the tapas. It's a party in your mouth. I got interested in tapas as an outgrowth of what I remember about eating as a child. I'm one of four kids. My mom used to make spaghetti. I loved it. But halfway through, any novelty is over. You almost don't taste it anymore. What's cool about tapas is the adventure in every plate. It doesn't take us long to put out a plate. It's easy for people to eat a round, look over the menu, decide, order another. Sometimes, people will order six or seven different plates, although two or three is the norm.

"Running a tapas restaurant gives me a lot of flexibility to create things. We are a chef-driven restaurant, not a robotic chain. The team can use the guidelines and expectations that I have developed to execute at a high level. If somebody comes in and asks for something that is not on the menu, our attitude is, 'We're chefs. We know how to cook. Let's feed 'em.' I want my guys to feel free to make that judgment call even on a night when I may not be there. But it still will be within the parameters that define Circa 81. We want to stay wholesome, make sure we put out a quality product. I like Asian flavor profiles, also French and Italian. So what we develop incorporates a lot of fusion."

Chef Merrell has some advice for home cooks: "You start with the recipe—ingredients and method. In culinary school, that's what you see at first. But eventually the instructors start just giving you the ingredients. You're supposed to know what method should be used with each class of ingredient. Home cooks sometimes get uneasy when they can't get the exact ingredients in a recipe or feel intimidated if they can't execute each step as written. But they could probably create something on their own if they would just loosen up a little bit and not be afraid to screw it up once in a while. Just remember what you did the last time it worked, and try to do that with other ingredients."

Circa 81 uses "a ton of fresh products from nearby. Seafood especially. We work with Blue Ocean Market a lot. Garner Farms provides a lot of vegetables. We get farmers at the back door several days a week." The restaurant's website lists current local providers.

Chef Merrell enjoys being around other chefs and participates in competitions. He was a Best Dish North Carolina finalist in 2011. He has been featured in several magazine articles, including one in *Cooking Light*. He placed second out of 20 chefs in Fire on the Dock in 2013 and is active in both the Beaufort Wine & Food Weekend and the North Carolina Seafood Festival in Morehead City. The restaurant is a member of Carteret Catch.

The Recipes

Shrimp and Fried Grits Cakes

Serves 1 as an entrée or 2 as an appetizer

1 cup grits
oil for frying
1 tablespoon butter
1 small yellow onion, cut into rings
4 tablespoons sliced mushrooms
5 or 6 local green-tailed jumbo shrimp
4 tablespoons chorizo sausage, sliced
2 tablespoons prosciutto ham
2 tablespoons Marsala wine
salt and pepper to taste
2 tablespoons Cajun seasoning
¼ cup heavy cream

Cook grits ahead according to package directions until consistency is thick and creamy. Spread evenly about 1 inch thick in a casserole dish or sheet pan and allow to cool. Refrigerate. When firm, cut into 4-by-4-inch squares. To prepare grits cakes, place in hot oil and fry for approximately 4 minutes on each side until golden brown.

Shrimp and Fried Grits Cakes
PHOTO COURTESY OF CIRCA 81

Add butter to a pan over medium heat. Sauté onions and mushrooms. When onions are softened, add shrimp, chorizo, and ham and sauté for 2 minutes. Deglaze pan with Marsala. Add salt and pepper and Cajun seasoning. Add cream. Stir to incorporate all ingredients. Reduce sauce for about 2 minutes until thickened.

PRESENTATION

Top grits cakes with shrimp and sauce mixture and serve.

Duck Breast with Celery Root Purée and Apples

PHOTO COURTESY OF CIRCA 81

Duck Breast with Celery Root Purée with Beets and Apples
Serves 2 or 3

Duck
8-ounce duck breast (Ashley Farms recommended), cut in half
salt and pepper to taste
1 tablespoon duck fat or cooking oil

Start duck breast, skin side down, in a cold pan with salt and pepper on medium-high heat. Sear for 3 to 4 minutes, then cut heat to medium-low. Add fat or oil and baste duck with a spoon. Cook for 8 to 9 minutes until skin is crispy and duck is firm to the touch. Remove from heat and let rest.

Celery Root Purée with Beets and Apples

1 celery root
1 cup heavy cream
½ cup water, divided
kosher salt
1 beet
1 red apple
½ cup apple cider vinegar
2 tablespoons honey
2 stalks fresh tarragon, chopped
1 bulb fennel, sliced thin
1 kumquat, sliced thin

Peel celery root and dice into large pieces. Boil with cream and ¼ cup of the water until tender. Place in a blender and add enough of the cooking liquid to purée until smooth. Season with salt. Place beet in microwave oven on high. Check after 3 minutes. Continue until tender. (An alternative method is to char beet in hot coal embers until tender.) Peel when cool. Slice to desired size. Remove core from apple. Slice as thinly as possible with a knife or mandolin. Blend vinegar, remaining ¼ cup water, honey, and tarragon. Season with salt. Marinate apple in liquid for a couple of hours or overnight.

PRESENTATION

Smear Celery Root Purée on plates for a base. Thinly slice duck and place on plates skin side up. Arrange beets, fennel, apples, and kumquats around sliced duck.

CAPT. JIM'S SEAFOOD MARKET

4665 Arendell Street
Morehead City, N.C. 28557
252-726-3454
captjimsseafood.com

Marc and Pam Smith, originally from Tarboro, North Carolina, own Capt. Jim's Seafood Market. One of them usually works in the market each day. Chris Coble is the general manager.

Shortly after finishing college at East Carolina, Marc and Pam moved to Alabama, where Jim's career was in air-conditioner manufacturing for Rheem, Carrier, and Fedders. They stayed in Alabama for 25 years. They visited the Gulf Coast often and were always interested in the seafood markets there. They thought that one day they might like to do something like that in the Morehead City area.

In 2003, the Fedders plant moved to China. Marc and Pam decided to come back to North Carolina, where they still had family, and start their own business. They were looking at restaurants but came across Capt. Jim's, which was for sale.

"The first two or three years were certainly a learning curve," Marc recalls. "My previous work experience dictated that I recruit the best suppliers— fishermen, in this case—and target the best customers. We have gained considerable knowledge from association with the best available. Some of the commercial fishermen are indeed a rare breed."

Marc explains that all fish sold or served in North Carolina must be pur- chased from someone who holds a state-issued commercial fishing license. Capt. Jim's buys from 50 to 60 different people, some of whom provide shellfish from nets in the sound, others of whom fish on the beach or off- shore. "This includes everything from clams, oysters, flounder, trout, spots, and croakers to the offshore fish including grouper, snapper, trigger, sea bass, and others. Some fishermen are versatile with the seasons, and some are dedicated to one area."

Capt. Jim's has been under its current ownership for 10 years.

MOREHEAD CITY

Fabian Botta   PHOTO BY JOHN BATCHELOR

THE RUDDY DUCK TAVERN

509 Evans Street

Morehead City, N.C. 28557

252-726-7500

ruddyducktavern.com/

The Chef

Fabian Botta

When Fabian Botta was guest chef at the James Beard House in 2003, he cooked and served fish he had caught himself. At the time, he held a commercial fishing license, and he has always spent as much time as possible on the water.

He started working in restaurants in 1973, when he was still a boy, at Chateau Fleur de Lis in Atlanta, where he grew up. He was hired to bus tables in the bar, but he almost immediately went into the kitchen. In those years, he also worked at Joe Dale's Cajun House and Nikolai's Roof.

From Atlanta, he moved with his father to the North Carolina mountains. They opened and operated the Tack Room in Banner Elk, near Seven Devils, for

13 years. Fabian was a young chef, but his restaurant attracted quite a following and generated a lot of press. It was based on a novel concept for the times: forming partnerships with local farmers and serving food that was truly fresh. "We were doing then what so many chefs are trying to do now," he says.

His next ventures were Louisiana Purchase and the Village Café, both in Banner Elk. He remained in the mountains until about 1988. Louisiana Purchase expanded. He added one in Winston-Salem and another in Richmond. Fabian's, which opened in Winston-Salem in 1996, was his next venture. A path-breaking establishment for the Triad, it had no menu. The dinner price was fixed, and Fabian came out of the kitchen each evening to describe the day's fresh purchases.

He sold those operations and went into consulting, out of Richmond and Wilmington. Fabian moved to Morehead City in 2008 and joined up with William Kingery, whom he had met in Cape Hatteras years before. They opened The Ruddy Duck on the waterfront that same year.

Reflecting on his years in the business, Fabian says, "I like staying ahead, not following trends. I prefer to try to find my own way. Learning different cuisines has been interesting. I started out working with Swiss and German chefs who were strictly classical, and I incorporated those styles into the Tack Room. But I moved into Americana with Louisiana Purchase. Later, the prix fixe concept based on daily fresh ingredients was fun at Fabian's. Eventually, you realize that simplicity and quality ingredients are what real cooking is about."

He has traveled extensively—Argentina, Italy, Mexico, Venezuela, and the Caribbean, among other places—and incorporates those influences into his creations. "But I'm getting more into Americana foods again. Here, I just so enjoy Down East seafood, finding just the right kind of breading, not too heavy, something that complements the natural flavors of the fish."

He still spends as much time as possible on the water. Bill Kingery holds commercial wholesale and retail seafood licenses.

Fabian's wife, Silvana, is a great cook. "She worked with me in the kitchen at Fabian's. She is a really big part of what I do, and she helps manage The Ruddy Duck." They are both originally from Argentina. "Our parents lived 20 blocks away from each other in Buenos Aires," Fabian says. But the couple never knew each other in that country. They met in Winston-Salem.

The Restaurant

The Ruddy Duck Tavern

Chef Botta and Bill Kingery came up with the concept for The Ruddy Duck as an outgrowth of their combined experience in restaurants. Bill had been involved with steakhouses in the Pittsburgh area. They have about 40 years each in the business. They acquired the waterfront property and then "just talked about what to do," Fabian says. "I started with the idea of a big menu that would appeal to everybody. If we are going to do a hamburger, let's do a great hamburger. We followed the same idea for fried seafood. A full-scale menu, but with quality, and include 10 or so specials a day. The food is abundant, of high quality, and value priced. We finalized the menu four days before we opened. We never tested a recipe. We were more concerned about training the wait staff and getting the place organized.

"I incorporated some of my classical training. But we also have a smoker, and we smoke our own pork, beef, and some fish. We have added local stone-crab claws, which have to be cooked a very short time after you get them. So the menu is evolving constantly. We will probably incorporate more Caribbean flavors as we continue to grow."

Regarding his sources, Chef Botta says, "I know who caught any fish I serve. The regional, seasonal approach has always been part of my philosophy." In addition to local fishermen who sell directly to the restaurant, The Ruddy Duck buys from Blue Ocean Market in Morehead City and Pamlico Packing in Grantsboro. "We also try to incorporate fish that are part of this culture, but not often served in restaurants, such as jumping mullet and bluefish. We buy tomatoes from Merrell Farm near Beaufort. Farmers deliver produce directly to The Ruddy Duck.

"What I like here is, I can wear shorts, come out on the floor, and talk to customers, and I can be wide open about what I want to put on the menu. There is no formality here."

The Ruddy Duck won the North Carolina Seafood Festival Chef's Competition in 2013 for its Shrimp and Grits. But Chef Botta comments, "I don't much enjoy those kinds of things [competitions] anymore. What I really like is seeing crowds of people leaving happy."

Conch Chowder
PHOTO BY
JOHN BATCHELOR

The Recipes

Conch Chowder
Serves 6 to 8

2 quarts water
10 medium tomatoes, quartered
2 bay leaves
3 tablespoons fresh oregano
3 tablespoons fresh basil
3 cups raw conch or knob whelk
½ cup diced bacon, cooked, 4 tablespoons fat reserved
5 cloves garlic, minced
2 cups chopped onion
2 cups chopped celery
1 cup chopped carrots
4 potatoes, peeled and diced
1 tablespoon chipotle powder or hot smoked paprika
2 tablespoons allspice
salt and pepper to taste
fresh cilantro
lime wedges

In a large soup pot over high heat, bring water, tomatoes, bay leaves, oregano, basil, and conch to a boil. Reduce heat to medium and simmer until conch is tender. Take ½ of conch out of pot and reserve. Purée remaining conch and contents of pot until they form a soup consistency. In a large skillet over medium heat, add bacon pieces and fat. Stir in garlic, onions, celery, and carrots and sauté until browned. Transfer vegetables to soup pot. Add potatoes to pot and cook on low heat until tender. Slice reserved conch into small pieces and add to pot. Add chipotle powder, allspice, and salt and pepper.

PRESENTATION
Serve with fresh cilantro and lime wedges.

Cioppino
Serves 4 to 6

3 tablespoons olive oil
1 onion, chopped
1 large bulb fennel, sliced
5 cloves garlic, chopped
¾ teaspoon or more crushed red pepper flakes
3 tablespoons oregano
10 fresh ripe tomatoes, quartered
5 cups fish stock
2 cups dry white wine
1 bay leaf
12 red-skin potatoes, cut in half
3 dozen littleneck clams
3 dozen mussels
1½ pounds large shrimp, peeled and deveined
1½ pounds fresh firm fish (mahi-mahi, grouper, or triggerfish), cut into 6 large
    pieces
salt and pepper to taste
½ cup chopped fresh parsley
1 cup diced fresh tomato
crusty bread

Heat oil in a large pot over medium heat. Add onions and fennel. Sauté for about 8 minutes until onions are translucent. Add garlic, pepper flakes, oregano, and quartered tomatoes. Sauté for 3 to 4 minutes,

Cioppino
PHOTO BY JOHN BATCHELOR

stirring frequently with a wooden spoon. Add fish stock, wine, bay leaf, and potatoes. Cover and bring to a simmer. Reduce heat to medium-low. Cover and simmer until potatoes are tender. Add clams and mussels. Cover and continue to simmer for 5 minutes until clams and mussels open. Add shrimp and fish and simmer gently until cooked; discard any clams or mussels that do not open. Season with salt and pepper.

PRESENTATION

Ladle soup into bowls with equal amounts of seafood. Sprinkle parsley and diced tomatoes in bowls as garnish. Serve with crusty bread.

Pecan Fish
Serves 4

1 cup pecans, chopped fine
2 eggs
2 tablespoons milk
¼ cup yucca flour or cornstarch
4 8-ounce skinless flounder fillets
salt and white pepper to taste

2 tablespoons canola oil
2 tablespoons corn oil
lemon wedges
Cajun spice mix (Paul Proudhomme brand recommended)

Preheat oven to 350 degrees. Place pecans in a shallow bowl. Beat eggs and milk with a wire whisk or fork in another shallow bowl. Place yucca flour in a separate shallow plate or bowl. Sprinkle both sides of fillets with salt and white pepper. Place fillets in yucca flour and lightly press. Move fillets to egg mixture and coat well, then to chopped pecans, pressing pecans lightly into fillets. Heat oils in a large nonstick skillet over medium heat. Add fillets 1 or 2 at a time. Reduce heat to medium-low. Sauté for 3 to 4 minutes per side until pecans are toasted, turning once. Carefully lift fillets with a thin spatula into a separate oven-safe pan. Place in oven for 4 to 5 minutes. Fish should flake easily with a fork when done.

PRESENTATION
Serve fillets with lemon wedges and sprinkle with Cajun spice.

Pecan Fish
PHOTO BY JOHN BATCHELOR

NORTH CAROLINA SEAFOOD FESTIVAL

412 D Evans Street
Morehead City, N.C. 28557
252-726-6273
ncseafoodfestival.org

The North Carolina Seafood Festival has been held in Morehead City during the first weekend in October for almost 30 years. The festival promotes the positive social and economic impact of the seafood industry on citizens of North Carolina and provides information to the public about seafood and its importance to the state's economy. Revenue from the event supports a scholarship program for educational pursuits related to the seafood industry. Nonprofit, civic, church, and educational organizations raise funds through participation in the festival. Festival proceeds are shared with community organizations.

The Chef's Tent provides samplings from area chefs, who serve small portions typical of what they cook in their restaurants. A competition features chefs, mostly from Morehead City and Beaufort, who provide cooking demonstrations. Judges score each dish, after which a champion is announced at the end of the event.

More than 50 food booths scattered throughout town are sponsored by individual restaurants, civic groups, churches, and school groups. They serve everything from home-cooked fried seafood to smoked fish to shrimp or scallop burgers. Booths selling North Carolina seafood have yellow banners signifying "Fresh Local" and bearing the logo of the North Carolina Department of Agriculture's Seafood Division.

North Carolina State University's Center for Marine Sciences and Technology, North Carolina Sea Grant, the North Carolina Shellfish Growers, North Carolina Watermen United, NOAA, and the Division of Marine Fisheries provide opportunities for guests to see and touch various types of fish and learn what to look for when purchasing seafood. An open-air market sells

raw local shrimp. An area for free samples of North Carolina wines draws exhibitors from a dozen or more wineries.

Several downtown streets are blocked off for multiple music acts on various stages. Beach music is, of course, omnipresent. Country and rock are well represented, too.

Tours of the Morehead City port are provided. The waterman's heritage is celebrated in the Blessing of the Fleet, in which 30 or more fishing boats participate. A boat show featuring a wide range of sizes and types allows visitors to climb aboard and learn about small tenders, offshore power-boats designed for fishing, larger cruisers, and sometimes even sailboats and trawlers. Huge displays of fishing equipment are a standard offering.

The arts and crafts for sale at the festival—photography, paintings, blown glass, woodcarvings, wall hangings, pottery—usually follow beach and coastal themes. In previous years, dealers have taken advantage of the large crowds to show exotic automobiles including Ferraris, Lamborghinis, and Maseratis.

AMOS MOSQUITO'S RESTAURANT & BAR

703 East Fort Macon Blvd.

Atlantic Beach, N.C. 28512

252-247-6222

amosmosquitos.com

Luke Daniel Maguire and Hallock Howard
PHOTO PROVIDED BY
AMOS MOSQUITO'S RESTAURANT
& BAR

The Chefs

Hallock Howard and Luke Daniel Maguire

For Hallock Howard, following her father into the legal profession was always the plan.

An Atlantic Beach native, she graduated from the University of North Carolina at Chapel Hill, majoring in French and spending her junior year in Bordeaux. But when she began law-school applications, she found she just couldn't get through them. She recalls, "If I couldn't write one essay as part of the application process, how was I going to get through three years of law school? So I decided to change the plan. I like to travel, and I'd always enjoyed helping my mother, an excellent cook, in the kitchen, so I thought about culinary school. I could cook anywhere in the world, and school would be a quick way to find out if I was cut out for the job."

She enrolled at the Culinary Institute of America in Hyde Park, New York. "It had the best reputation, and my brother was in college down the road at Vassar. I loved every minute of it!"

After graduation, she spent some time cooking in Costa Rica and Greece but realized she would get the best experience where she faced no language barrier. She subsequently worked at Hawthorne Lane and Zinzino in San Francisco and Hula Grill and Merriman's in Hawaii. She also took two long tours through Southeast Asia, where she came to love the food and the minimalist approach to cooking. "This is why we have some Asian-flavored dishes at Amos Mosquito's," she says.

Hallock led the kitchen during the restaurant's early years. But when she and her husband, Sandy, had their second child, they brought in Luke Maguire as executive chef. Luke is originally from Key West. He grew up cooking with his mother. His first professional position came at the age of 15 at Camp Sea Gull in Arapahoe, North Carolina. He says, "Living by the water makes me feel alive. The salt in the air is palpable. The way the air smells gives me energy. I wake up every morning and think, 'It's another day in paradise.'"

Luke worked at Chefs 505 in Greenville while attending East Carolina University. Chef Scott McClelland, his mentor, allowed him to create a small handwritten menu nightly. Together, they developed a style they called "clean cuisine"—simply taking great ingredients and allowing them to speak for themselves, not overindulging in fats or sauces, and concentrating on fresh seafood and local vegetables. Luke also credits Bryan Carithers (of Front Street Grill at Stillwater and City Kitchen in Beaufort, see pages 193-99), Michael Santos (of Chefs 105 in Morehead City), and Hallock Howard for his professional growth.

Before Amos Mosquito's, he was executive chef of the Wilson Country Club, where the style was primarily Southern. But he had time to experiment with modernist cuisine, so he expanded his range during that time.

Hallock's favorite foods are scallops, triggerfish, and roasted chicken. "My husband, Sandy, runs the restaurant now, so at dinnertime I'm usually just cooking for the kids and myself. On occasion, we have fun making our own pizzas, but mostly I make a lot of soups and salads for myself and the usual kid stuff for them. We all enjoy a wide variety of fruits and vegetables."

Luke says he likes to eat everything, "but I don't always like everything I eat. I most certainly want to try everything at least once."

The Restaurant

Amos Mosquito's Restaurant & Bar

Amos Mosquito's opened in the spring of 1999 on the Morehead City waterfront, then moved to its current location in Atlantic Beach in 2003. The name came from an old knock-knock joke Hallock used to tell, incorrectly, as a child. Mosquito caricatures are painted on the walls throughout the restaurant.

Hallock and Sandy own the restaurant in partnership with Hallock's mother, Pam Cooper, and their friend, Dave Brumley. Sandy and Dave run the front of the house. Pam is the bookkeeper, and Hallock works closely with Executive Chef Luke Maguire in menu development.

The décor came from an incident that occurred during renovation of the original building. "One day, there must have been 30 pelicans lined up on the floating dock," Hallock recalls. "The winter sun was glinting off the water, and the wild island across the bay was the backdrop. I said to my mom, 'I wish we could make the inside of the restaurant look like that!' She replied, 'We can.' So we searched the woods for trees to mount on the walls and covered the branches with dried Spanish moss."

The restaurant's concept revolves around "flavorful made-from-scratch food with attentive service in a fun environment at an affordable price," Hallock explains. "We are a family-friendly restaurant that caters to adults, but the kids love it, too."

The owners insist on local seafood; they simply refuse to buy imports. Most fresh finfish comes from Blue Ocean Market in Morehead City. Garland Fulcher Seafood in Oriental provides flounder and scallops. The restaurant buys much of its North Carolina produce and dairy products through Fresh Point, a wholesaler that develops partnerships with area farms. Amos Mosquito's is a member of Carteret Catch.

The Recipes

Clams with Guajillo Chilies and Chorizo
Serves 1 or 2

*Clams with Guajillo Chilies
and Chorizo*

Chili Sauce

4 dried guajillo chilies
2 tablespoons tomato paste
2 cloves garlic
¼ onion, chopped rough
¾ teaspoon cumin
¼ teaspoon salt
¼ teaspoon cayenne pepper
¼ teaspoon coriander
¼ teaspoon white pepper
¼ cup cilantro, stems and all
4 cups vegetable broth

Cut stems off chilies and discard; don't throw out seeds. Cut chilies into 1-inch pieces and put into a small pot with tomato paste, garlic, onions, cumin, salt, cayenne, coriander, white pepper, and cilantro. Add broth. Cover and simmer for 1 hour, reducing a little. Purée mixture in a blender until smooth.

Clams

⅓ cup roasted chorizo sausage (any sausage may be substituted)
½ cup onion, sliced thin
oil for sautéing
1 teaspoon chopped garlic
12 middleneck clams
¾ cup clam juice
1 teaspoon butter
fresh cilantro

Preheat oven to 350 degrees. Bake chorizo for about 15 minutes until it reaches an internal temperature of 165 degrees. Slice into half-moons ¼ inch thick. In a large sauté pan over high heat, brown onions in a little oil. Add sausage and garlic. Add clams, clam juice, and 3 tablespoons Chili Sauce. Cover pan and steam about 10 minutes until clams open. Stir in butter.

PRESENTATION
Transfer to a bowl and garnish with cilantro.

Mixed Seafood Grill with Cilantro-Lime Vinaigrette and Caribbean-Style Black Beans
Serves 4

Caribbean-Style Black Beans
1½ teaspoons minced garlic
½ medium onion, diced small
½ medium red bell pepper, diced small
½ medium green bell pepper, diced small
2 15.5-ounce cans black beans, undrained
¼ cup chopped cilantro
1 teaspoon cumin
2 teaspoons salt
pinch of allspice
½ teaspoon white pepper

In a small pot, sauté garlic, onions, and peppers until soft. Add beans, cilantro, cumin, salt, allspice, and white pepper. Bring to a simmer and cook for 15 minutes. These will keep for a week in the refrigerator.

Mixed Seafood Grill
12 large shrimp, peeled and deveined
12 sea scallops
1 red bell pepper, cut into 1-inch squares
¼ cup lime juice
2 tablespoons cider vinegar
¼ cup chopped cilantro
1 tablespoon honey

*Mixed Seafood Grill
with Cilantro-Lime
Vinaigrette and
Caribbean-Style
Black Beans*

1 teaspoon chopped garlic
¼ teaspoon salt
½ teaspoon Dijon mustard
1 cup vegetable oil
4 5-ounce tuna steaks, cut small in diameter and thick
salt and pepper to taste
mixed salad greens
steamed jasmine rice

Soak four 10-inch bamboo skewers in water. Thread 3 shrimp, 3 scallops, and 7 bell pepper pieces onto each skewer: pepper, shrimp, pepper, scallop, pepper, shrimp, pepper, scallop, pepper, shrimp, pepper, scallop, pepper. Set aside.

Prepare vinaigrette ahead. Put lime juice, vinegar, cilantro, honey, garlic, salt, and mustard into a blender or a food processor and blend. With the motor running slowly, drizzle in oil. Set aside.

Season kabobs and tuna with salt and pepper. Grill kabobs for 2 to 3 minutes per side until shrimp turn pink and scallops are slightly firm and spongy but not hard. Grill tuna about 2 minutes per side until desired doneness is reached.

PRESENTATION
Place cooked seafood on beds of mixed greens and drizzle with vinaigrette. Serve with rice and Caribbean-Style Black Beans.

Scalloped Scallops
PHOTO PROVIDED BY
AMOS MOSQUITO'S
RESTAURANT & BAR

Scalloped Scallops

Serves 2 to 4

½ cup panko breadcrumbs
½ cup crushed saltine crackers
¼ cup melted butter
¾ teaspoon onion powder
¾ teaspoon salt
¼ teaspoon freshly ground pepper
1 pound fresh sea scallops
¾ cup grated Parmesan cheese, divided
1 cup half-and-half

Preheat oven to 350 degrees. Blend breadcrumbs and cracker crumbs in a food processor. With motor running, drizzle in butter. Set aside. Mix onion powder, salt, and pepper. Sprinkle on scallops. Add breadcrumb mixture and ½ cup of the Parmesan to scallops and toss together until all is evenly distributed. Spray a 9-inch pie pan with pan spray and transfer scallops and crumb mixture to pan. Sprinkle top with remaining ¼ cup Parmesan. Slowly drizzle half-and-half over top, allowing it to sink in. Bake for about 30 minutes to an internal temperature of 150 degrees. Scallops should be firm and spongy to the touch, not hard, and casserole should be bubbly around the edges.

PRESENTATION

Amos Mosquito's bakes this dish in individual casseroles. You may do the same by dividing the ingredients equally among individual dishes and baking at 350 degrees for 25 minutes. The restaurant recommends serving with mashed potatoes and spinach, sautéed with butter and garlic.

ISLAND GRILLE RESTAURANT & BAR

401 Money Island Drive

Atlantic Beach, N.C. 28512

252-240-0000

igrestaurant.net

Jason Scott
PHOTO BY JOHN BATCHELOR

The Chef

Jason Scott

Jason Scott's entry into professional cooking came by accident. He was about 15 years old. The owner of Mother Shapiro's, a large restaurant in Killington, Vermont, hired him to shovel snow off the roof. About the time he finished, he learned that the dishwasher had not shown up for work that night, so he asked if he could do that job, too. He has never left food service since then. He would go in every morning around daylight, shovel snow, then head back and wash dishes in the evening, finishing about nine o'clock after a day of more than 12 hours. From dishwasher, he moved up to the prep station.

After about a year of that schedule, Jason started looking for something nearer to a normal range of hours. He moved to Sabby's, an Italian restaurant in nearby Rutland, closer to home, where he was a line cook for about five years. The owner, a good business manager, taught him about the business side of restaurants. While living in Rutland, Jason became best friends with Amiee Dykeman, who had grown up in the Summit Lodge, the oldest ski lodge on Killington Mountain. Her dad, a Hyde Park CIA alumnus (class of 1976), was the chef there. Amiee and Jason started dating after a two-year friendship and married in 2010.

They relocated to North Carolina when Jason landed a job at Kelsey's in Emerald Isle. He started out working on the line but quickly took over as head chef. He stayed about three years until the restaurant closed. Patrick Hogan, the chef-proprietor of Carlton's in Salter Path, hired him, and that was where he learned about fine dining. He migrated up the road to Atlantic Beach about five years ago, when he heard that Chef Mike Mahoney was looking for a sous chef at Island Grille. Jason became executive chef within a year. Amiee is now the manager.

"I don't really think I have a specific style," Jason says. "I don't think a chef should be that limited. I just take a little here, a little there, and combine it into whatever is good."

He especially enjoys meals his mother-in-law cooks. When he and Amiee cook for themselves, they "tend to eat what we grew up with—New England food such as shepherd's pie. I have a file of recipe cards from my mother that I still use when I'm cooking for friends and family."

The Restaurant

Island Grille Restaurant & Bar

David Bradley owns Island Grille. It has been in operation for 15 years. Located across the street from the beach, it appears small and unassuming from the outside. But that impression belies the wildly popular following the restaurant has earned because of its food. The kitchen focuses on fresh local seafood. At least one, and usually two, Carteret Catch fish dishes appear on the "Specials" chalkboard.

One of the servers is a granddaughter of the family that owns Garner Farms in Newport. She brings vegetables directly from the farm. The wait staff is remarkably stable for a coastal location. "Most of the service staff has been here 10 years, except for a few seasonal additions, and two helped start the restaurant when it first opened," Chef Scott says. "The staff has parties together, Christmas and other holidays. It's a close group. Many customers are old friends. When you sit at a table, the people at the next table will probably talk to you. It's just a real open kind of place."

The wine list has won multiple *Wine Spectator* awards, earning praise for both quality and value. Amiee is working on sommelier certification. She will be one of only a handful of certified sommeliers in the state, a breed that is especially rare in eastern North Carolina.

Island Grille's beachfront catering facility, under construction across the street, is scheduled to open by 2015.

The Recipes

Pan-Seared Sea Scallops with Bacon Jalapeño Jam
Serves 2 as an appetizer or 1 as an entrée

Bacon Jalapeño Jam
1 fresh jalapeño pepper, diced
¼ cup rice wine vinegar
1 pound bacon, cut into 1-inch squares
4 small shallots, diced
1 teaspoon chopped garlic
¼ cup dark brown sugar

Soak jalapeño in vinegar for 1 hour. Drain and set aside, reserving ½ of the vinegar. Render bacon in a 12-inch saucepan until crisp. Strain, saving drippings. Set bacon aside. Pour drippings back into pan. On medium-high heat, sauté shallots until golden. Add garlic and continue to cook for 1 minute. Add bacon mixture to shallots mixture. Add reserved vinegar and reduce heat to a simmer. Add brown sugar and stir constantly for 4 to 5 minutes until fully incorporated and sticky. Remove pan from heat and set aside.

Scallops
salt and pepper to taste
4 sea scallops
canola oil or bacon drippings

Pan-Seared Sea Scallops with Bacon-Jalapeño Jam
PHOTO BY JOHN BATCHELOR

Salt and pepper scallops. Using canola oil or bacon drippings in a new pan, sear scallops for 2 minutes per side.

PRESENTATION

Plate each scallop with a dollop of Bacon Jalapeño Jam.

Stuffed and Grilled Filet Mignon
Serves 4

4 center-cut filet mignon steaks
½ cup crumbled feta cheese
¼ cup chopped sun-dried tomatoes
4 or 5 slices bacon, cooked and crumbled
4 large fresh basil leaves, chopped
salt and pepper to taste

Cut a small opening in each fillet to create a pocket for stuffing. Try to make an opening the size of a Ping-Pong ball in the middle of fillets. Set aside. In a small dish, combine feta, tomatoes, bacon, and basil. Divide into 4 equal portions. Roll portions into small balls and stuff into fillets. Let rest in refrigerator for 45 minutes.

Stuffed and Grilled Filet Mignon

Preheat a grill to high. Remove fillets from refrigerator 15 minutes before grilling and let the surfaces come close to room temperature. Salt and pepper fillets on both sides. Sear fillets for 3 minutes on top and bottom, plus 1 additional minute on edges, until internal temperature reaches 135 degrees. This should produce an evenly cooked medium-rare filet. Let rest 1 minute before serving.

PRESENTATION
The restaurant recommends stacking fillets on edge over mashed potatoes and serving with your favorite vegetable side dish.

Bourbon Chocolate Torte with Raspberry Sauce
Yields 2 tortes

Tortes
1 pound butter
18 eggs
4 cups sugar
1 pound Hershey's milk chocolate
¼ cup bourbon

Melt butter in a small saucepan over low heat. Crack eggs into a large bowl and add sugar. Combine thoroughly. Add chocolate and bourbon to melted butter and stir until smooth. Add a small amount of chocolate mixture to egg mixture, stirring constantly. (If you use too

Bourbon Chocolate Torte with Raspberry Sauce
PHOTO BY JOHN BATCHELOR

much chocolate mixture, eggs will scramble. Do not rush this step.) Repeat until all is blended thoroughly.

Preheat oven to 350 degrees. Line two 8-inch round cake pans with aluminum foil and spray foil with nonstick spray. Pour mixture into pans and bake for 25 to 35 minutes. Start checking after 25 minutes by inserting a toothpick into cakes. When it comes out dry, cakes are done. Remove tortes and let cool to room temperature.

Raspberry Sauce
2 cups sparkling wine
1 pint fresh raspberries
¼ cup sugar
juice of ½ lemon

In a saucepan on medium heat, add wine, raspberries, and sugar, stirring constantly. Cook until raspberries are softened and mixture is combined. Add lemon juice and simmer for 3 minutes. Remove from heat.

PRESENTATION
Once sauce has cooled, cut tortes into 16 slices (8 per torte). Plate individual slices and top with Raspberry Sauce.

CAP'N WILLIS SEAFOOD MARKET

7803 Emerald Drive

Emerald Isle, N.C. 28594

252-354-2500

WILLIS SEAFOOD

130 Headen Lane

Salter Path, N.C. 28575

252-247-2752

Trey Willis
PHOTO BY JOHN BATCHELOR

The Willis family was among the early settlers of Bogue Banks, the island that now contains the towns of Emerald Isle, Salter Path, Pine Knoll Shores, Indian Beach, and Atlantic Beach. The Willises came in the mid-1800s, drawn by the opportunity to catch fish and live the life of watermen. In the early years, boats delivered the mail. A ferry conveyed vehicles from the mainland. Development of the area took off in earnest after bridges were built across the sound.

The Salter Path and Emerald Isle markets are separate businesses, although the owners are members of the same family. Both locations sell a full range of seafood in season, caught fresh in nearby waters. The only non-local seafood products are popular varieties that just do not live off the Southern coast, such as salmon and snow crab legs.

Four generations of the Willis family have been in the seafood business. Trey Willis, who works at the Emerald Isle location, is the great-grandson of Headen Willis. Wade Willis, Trey's grandfather, worked on the water, catching and packing fish, scallops, and shrimp. Wade and his wife, Vesta, own the Salter Path location, on the sound side just off the main road.

Trey's father, Donald (1959–2013), fished from Pamlico Sound to the Beaufort bar, following shrimp as they migrated. Donald's boat, 40 feet long, was the *Wade Donald*. Trey describes it: "It had almost no living quarters. Dad 'clocked it,' which means staying awake and looking for shrimp until you find them, so he didn't need much living space. The *Wade Donald* was one of the smallest boats in the area, but Dad either beat the big boats or came close most of the time, just because of how he stuck with it around the clock. You have to quit Friday night on the inside [in the sound], but you can stay out all the time on the ocean. He came in most Friday nights, and people wouldn't believe how much shrimp he had caught. My dad and his one deck hand, Edward Chadwick, did the same level of work as the big boats with four deck hands." Edward's son, Alex Chadwick, now works at the Emerald Isle shop with Trey.

Donald started out operating several roadside shrimp stands, mostly in the Emerald Isle vicinity. But he saw that roadside businesses were on the decline. So the family found land on Emerald Drive that they could buy. Trey's mother, Telena, got her contractor's license, and the family constructed the building with a red roof that now houses Cap'n Willis Seafood Market.

Trey catches shrimp for the Emerald Isle shop himself. He explains that three varieties of shrimp are caught along the North Carolina coast. Spotted shrimp run from approximately May through June. Brownies show up big in July, then move south late in summer. Green tails are most prominent in the fall. The shrimp migrate with the full moon, along with weather changes.

Trey's family eats a lot of shrimp. He likes them boiled with a little Old Bay or fried. "Don't add too much to them," he advises. "Don't cover up the taste. Just sprinkle them with the least amount of flour possible. Use just enough vegetable oil to cover them. Don't deep-fry. Put the pan on medium-high. They cook fairly fast. When they're browned, take them out. Or boil water, take it off the burner, then put in the shrimp. Just leave them in the hot water, don't boil it again."

Trey's favorite fish is hardhead mullet, or jumping mullet. "In summer, they have a lot of fat in their bellies. When you cook them, it melts and goes into the meat, just like bacon. Salt them and fry them like frying shrimp. In fall, they start producing roe, and the taste changes. They are like bluefish. They have to be really fresh. You have to get ones caught in salt water, not rivers, or they'll taste like mud. Late in fall, they are full of roe. You either love roe or you hate it. Lightly salt the roe, fry it lightly in peanut or olive oil at medium-high heat, cook slow, about five minutes. Put it on a brown paper sack to drain. The fat holds heat. There is huge demand for mullet and mullet roe in Asia. They buy it and dry it."

SWANSBORO

Edward Aikin
<small>PHOTO BY JOHN BATCHELOR</small>

ICEHOUSE WATERFRONT RESTAURANT AND THE BORO CAFÉ

103 Moore Street

Swansboro, N.C. 28584

910-325-0501

SwansboroIcehouse.com

BoroCafeNC.com

The Chef

Edward Aikin

Edward Aikin started cooking on a Sunday morning. "My dad woke me up early, we took a trip to the grocery store, and when we got home he taught me how to make biscuits and sausage gravy. I will never forget his lessons on how to make a roux. Later, my mom would teach me how to make some of the best chicken and dumplings I have ever had. I never thought I would be a chef when I was little. I had dreams of being an astronomer, then a chemist, then a rock star, but I wound up in the kitchen!"

When he was 16, living in his hometown of Jacksonville, Florida, he "ventured out into the world. I started washing dishes at a place called the West Inn Cantina, a small family-owned Mexican restaurant in Jacksonville. I learned a lot about the basics of traditional Mexican cuisine. Then I hit the road, off to New Orleans, where I wound up washing dishes at Angelica Café on Magazine Street. From the Big Easy, I went to Houston, then on to California, in the Monterey Bay area. Finally, I moved back to Jacksonville."

By then, Edward was 19. "I had some experience on the line, so I wound up at Harpoon Louie's, a little bar and grill. That's where I really started grilling and sautéing. I started getting good fast, and my dream of being a rock star dwindled. I started reading about cuisine and became eager to learn more, realizing that reading and doing were two different things.

"I knew I had to make a change, so I applied to Biscottis of Avondale/ Jacksonville, a casual/fine-dining establishment, and that was the period when I really had a chance to expand my knowledge of food. One of the chefs there introduced me to *The Food Lover's Companion*. I must have read that book 20 times! That reading, coupled with three very good chefs from different ethnic backgrounds, really taught me a lot. There was Cary, well versed in Italian cuisine; Carlos from Venezuela, who I thank for teaching me that all Latin cuisine isn't Mexican; and Chris, from the Philippines and Canada, who demonstrated how the French influence is strong and alive in the fundamentals of almost all cuisine. I was doing very well at Biscottis, and one day the chef asked how I would feel about writing the specials on Sundays. Of course, I said yes, and that's when I really began creating in the art of food. So there I was, 23 years old, sautéing and writing specials. It felt good, but the more I read and created, the more insatiable I became.

"I knew I had to learn more, so off I went to St. Augustine, where I met Chef John Janette at La Parisienne Restaurant. I became his sous chef. John would take the weekends off and drive to Miami to learn chocolate and sugar, paying $500 per class at the time, and when he came back I would get to learn for free.

"I started creating my definition of what I thought being a real chef was. I feel that chefs should be able to make every part of the meal themselves, from the bread to the dessert course. I craved to be well rounded but until then had really only focused on the hot side. When John left, I was promoted—my first time as 'the chef.' Wow! Guess what. I wasn't ready. I knew how to cook, but I didn't know how to manage people.

"So I found the best fine-dining restaurant in town, Opus 39. Chef Michael McMillan graduated from the Culinary Institute of America in Hyde Park, New York, at the top of his class. That was the first time an interview consisted of actually cooking, not just answering questions. I learned classic French baking and *garde-manger* from the sous chef, who was from Provence.

"Living arrangements eventually forced me to move back to Jacksonville, where I secured a position as chef of the Village Café & Bakery. They wanted to expand into a dinner format, so I tried being the chef again. I didn't do as badly as in St. Augustine, but I knew there was still a lot more to learn."

Edward worked briefly at a few other places but became dissatisfied with life in Florida. He moved to Jacksonville, North Carolina, in 2008, to join his sister, a marine who was stationed nearby.

"I was looking for a change of scenery, the availability of fresh seafood, and I was fed up with the Florida coast—condos, chain restaurants, and just too many people," he says. "One day after I moved to North Carolina, I drove from Jacksonville to Swansboro, and from there I never looked back. The beautiful White Oak River, the unspoiled coastline, the friendly people, the abundant fresh local seafood, and the family-owned businesses—they all reminded me of the way Jacksonville, Florida, was when I was growing up."

After spending some time in Swansboro, he met the Icehouse Waterfront Restaurant's Randy Swanson, whom he considers "the best restaurant owner I have ever had the privilege of working for. I have been able to see my and his dreams become a reality. Last winter, he opened The Boro Café in the same building. It was just a little bakery and coffee shop, but he has since transformed it into a full tapas-style restaurant in the evenings." So now Edward is executive chef of both the Icehouse Waterfront Restaurant and The Boro Café.

The Restaurants

Icehouse Waterfront Restaurant and The Boro Café

The Icehouse Waterfront Restaurant is situated on the White Oak River in downtown Swansboro. One end of the dining room hangs out over the water. Guests look out on three sides to views of the Intracoastal Waterway and waterfront piers. A wild island, an occasional spot for waterborne adventurers, lies just across the bay. The look is casual, as befits this historic port town. Additional seating is available on the outdoor patio.

A list of daily specials, primarily freshly caught seafood, supplements the large printed menu. The prices reflect a concentration on value as well as quality; thanks in part to wine prices that are especially attractive, the final check will not come as an unpleasant surprise. Sixteen microbrews are available on tap.

The Swanson family opened the Icehouse in 2005. The Boro Café, which began service in 2014, occupies the front of the building, facing the street in Swansboro's historic section. The Boro offers tapas servings in a small, casual setting; the emphasis is also on wine and desserts.

Buffalo Shrimp
PHOTO BY JOHN BATCHELOR

The Recipes

Buffalo Shrimp

Serves 2 to 4 as an appetizer

1 tablespoon melted butter
¼ cup Texas Pete hot sauce
12 large shrimp, peeled and deveined
1 cup buttermilk
3 cups Atkins seafood breading
oil for deep frying
¼ cup blue cheese dressing
¼ cup ranch dressing
6 stalks celery
shredded kale
2 slices lemon

Combine butter and Texas Pete. Butter mellows some of the heat and makes a milder sauce. If you like it hot, use less butter or omit it altogether. Soak shrimp in buttermilk, then drop in seafood breading. Deep-fry in 350-degree oil until golden brown.

PRESENTATION

Place dressings side by side next to celery. Array shrimp on other end of plate. Place kale alongside shrimp and lemon slices next to kale.

Grouper Royale
PHOTO BY JOHN BATCHELOR

Grouper Royale
Serves 6

Beurre Blanc Sauce
1 sprig fresh thyme
1 bay leaf
2 whole peppercorns
1¼ cups white wine
1 pint heavy cream
1 pound butter
salt and white pepper to taste
cornstarch if needed

Add thyme, bay leaf, and peppercorns to wine. Simmer until reduced by ½. Add cream. Continue to simmer until reduced by ½. Remove peppercorns. Slowly swirl in butter and season with salt and white pepper. Tighten with cornstarch if necessary.

Grouper
6 cups panko breadcrumbs
12 strips bacon, fried crisp and chopped
1 tablespoon dried chives
3 large potatoes, cooked and shredded
6 4- to 6-ounce pieces grouper
1½ cups flour
1½ cups liquid egg or 9 whole eggs, whisked
6 tablespoons cooking oil

Mix breadcrumbs, bacon, and chives. Stir into shredded potatoes. Dredge each side of fish in flour, then eggs. Remove and lay in breadcrumb-potato mixture. Turn over to coat both sides. Heat as many tablespoons of oil as you are cooking pieces of fish in each sequence; do not crowd pan. Sauté fish in hot pan until lightly browned, starting with service side down; cooking time should be 3 to 4 minutes per inch of thickness. Turn and cook skin side down.

PRESENTATION

The restaurant recommends placing fish over potatoes, rice, or orzo. Ladle with Beurre Blanc Sauce.

CAPE FEAR SEAFOOD COMPANY

5226 South College Road #5

Wilmington, N.C. 28412

910-799-7077

capefearseafoodcompany.com

Richard Aaron Martin
PHOTO COURTESY OF CAPE FEAR
SEAFOOD COMPANY

The Chef

Richard Aaron Martin

Richard Martin grew up on a canal in Carolina Beach, where he remembers pulling crab cages with his grandfather. "I have always felt at one with nature," he explains, "and food is a way for me to express this love for all things natural that I learned from these first experiences as a young boy."

He got his first cooking job at the Hanover Seaside Club in Wrightsville Beach at the age of 16. "My interest in food service started from the potential of a free meal after working construction jobs. Not having much money in my youth always brought me to a dish pit or a kitchen to earn extra cash and scavenge a free meal."

After six years of washing dishes, frying, and grilling in various restaurants, he landed at another Wrightsville Beach restaurant, Middle of the Island. Then, "after two years of 70-hour weeks from busing to the dish pit to peeling mountains of potatoes, I found myself needing to move on to something more."

He applied for a position at Riverboat Landing in downtown Wilmington. "This was where my true love for food creation began. Riverboat Landing introduced me to fine cuisine. The kitchen was filled with ingredients I had never even heard of, from escargot to black truffles. That place really lit the fire for a passion that has grown ever since. I tasted my first lobster citrus sauté dish and immediately began to read everything about cooking that I could find. Barry Sweatt, one of the experienced chefs there, had been a culinary instructor, and he really took me under his wing." After two years, Richard took over the Riverboat Landing kitchen.

Eight years later, he moved to Ruth's Chris when the chain opened a steakhouse in Wilmington. "I didn't have the opportunity to expand my creativity in this corporate environment, but I learned another level of management and how to ensure consistency," he says.

From Ruth's Chris, he moved to the Country Club of Landfall. He describes his experience there: "It was a beautiful place to work, and since the club had both a fine-dining restaurant and a tavern, I was able to put out fires in whatever department needed my experience. We did a lot of volume. But with so many chefs in one building, it was sometimes hard to get all the hours I needed."

So Richard began to work outside the club. "Cape Fear Seafood Company was growing its business at a rapid rate. There was an off-premises catering facility, and the owner, Evans Trawick, asked if I would be interested in feeding 120 people. I said yes, although I knew nothing about what I was going to do other than grill.

"For our first event together, we drove to Burgaw to cater a wedding reception. There was a pig cooker hooked to the back of the truck. When we arrived, I realized that Evans was a native, and the event would include people who had watched him grow up and branch out. That raised my level of concern a bit. Then, not long after we arrived, clouds came rolling in, and this was no ordinary storm. The sky went to black, and lightning began to decorate the sky. Our original location was compromised. So Evans and I started the truck while the grill was still cooking, and we began to pull this cooker through downtown Burgaw, looking for a dry spot. We finally pulled under an overhang at a local barn, where a red tractor turned into a backdrop for what was to be my kitchen that afternoon.

"The delay raised the pressure of the situation even more, and I was left to grill everything on my own, in time for the party. When Evans returned to pick me up, I had all but the last round of chicken on the grill. I turned the grill down to low, we hooked up the trailer, and then we filled that town with a great aroma as we made our way to the party site with chickens still cooking on the grill."

At Cape Fear Seafood Company, Chef Martin has developed a style that he says "comes from the energy of the food. When I look at the ingredients, they tell me what to do. I love to incorporate vegetables and fruits into my seafood creations."

When he cooks at home, it's usually for his children. "We visit the local produce market and learn about the things we are going to have for dinner. Sautéed Brussels sprouts with couscous and crushed honey almonds with grilled red onion. Cucumber and tomato salad and citrus vinaigrette. These always produce empty plates at the Martin family table. A mountain of steamed edamame is no stranger to our starter list."

The Restaurant

Cape Fear Seafood Company

Evans Trawick's first restaurant job was outside: he delivered pizzas. After a couple of years, he began cooking pizzas, and eventually he became the manager. That job supported him through college. He graduated from UNC-Wilmington, then spent a year in law school. Although he made good grades, he decided the law was not to be his chosen profession. He returned to Wilmington, and he and his wife, Nikki, opened a sandwich shop where Cape Fear Seafood Company is now located. But it was a franchise, and the franchising company folded.

So, in 2008, just before the greatest downturn in the American economy since the 1920s, Evans and Nikki opened Cape Fear Seafood Company. "I wanted Wilmington to have a go-to destination for seafood, which I believe we have created," he says.

The restaurant grew steadily, bucking the trend by developing a strong local following and earning a reputation that appealed to visitors as well. By 2012, Evans was thinking about moving from chef to an arrangement that would allow him to continue monitoring and conceptualizing the food while spending his time actively managing and growing the business.

The restaurant's website states the owners' goal: "CFSC strives to provide every customer with a wonderful dining experience at a reasonable price. Simply great food in a comfortable relaxed atmosphere has become our creed." The interior is decorated with local artwork. Situated in a small, unassuming shopping center, the restaurant is located off the proverbial beaten path.

It maintains relationships with local seafood wholesalers and buys produce from local farms. "I just ask for whatever is in season and go from there," says

Richard Martin, whom Evans hired as executive chef in January 2013.

Cape Fear Seafood Company has been recognized repeatedly by area publications and food bloggers as one of the best and most reliable restaurants on the Southern coast. It has also developed a major catering operation, serving as many as 2,000 people a day.

The Recipes

Ginger-Seared Tuna with Lemon-Garlic Sautéed Purple Kale over Fruit Couscous and Quinoa
Serves 6

Fruit Couscous and Quinoa
3 cups couscous and quinoa (multicolored blend, or 1½ cups of each)
9 cups chicken stock
2 cups pineapple, diced ¼ inch
½ cup diced tri-color peppers
1 tablespoon chopped cilantro
½ cup diced red onion
2 tablespoons olive oil

Prepare couscous and quinoa according to package directions. Drain and cool to room temperature. Place couscous and quinoa in a medium mixing bowl and fold in remaining ingredients lightly.

Tuna
¼ cup canola oil
6 6-ounce tuna steaks
salt and pepper to taste
¼ cup chopped ginger

In a large skillet, heat oil until hot but not smoking. Dab tuna with oil and salt and pepper. Press chopped ginger into surface. Place in a hot pan and sear for 1 to 2 minutes, then repeat on other side. This will produce medium-rare tuna steaks. Finish in a 400-degree oven to desired doneness.

Kale

1½ tablespoons chopped
  garlic
¼ cup canola oil
1 large head purple kale,
  shredded
2 tablespoons lemon juice
salt and pepper to taste
lime juice

In a skillet, add garlic and oil. Bring oil up to medium-high heat. Add kale and lemon juice and lightly sauté. Finish with salt and pepper and a squirt of lime juice.

Ginger-Seared Tuna with Lemon-Garlic Sautéed Purple Kale over Fruit Couscous and Quinoa
PHOTO BY JASON ARMOND PHOTOGRAPHY

PRESENTATION

Slice tuna about ¼ inch thick. Mound couscous mixture slightly to right of center of plates. Mound kale next to couscous. Place edge of each tuna slices on mound so they create a slightly vertical stack.

Baked White Fish with Herb Shrimp Tapenade

Serves 4

Marinade

¼ cup fresh lemon juice
½ cup white wine
¼ cup minced onion
½ cup olive oil
4 6- to 7-ounce fillets white, firm fish (grouper, mahi-mahi, or triggerfish, for
  example)

In a mixing bowl, whisk together lemon juice, wine, onion, and olive oil. Lay fillets out flat in a baking dish and pour all but ¼ cup of

Baked White Fish with Herb Shrimp Tapenade
PHOTO BY JASON ARMOND PHOTOGRAPHY

marinade over top. Place in refrigerator for about 4 hours, turning fillets twice.

Herb Shrimp Tapenade

½ pound peeled and deveined shrimp, cooked (use small shrimp or dice large shrimp into small pieces)
2 tablespoons minced fresh parsley
1 tablespoon capers, drained and chopped fine
¼ cup chopped fresh basil
1 cup panko breadcrumbs
¼ cup mayonnaise
⅓ cup grated Parmesan cheese
salt and pepper to taste
lemon wedges

Combine first 7 ingredients in a mixing bowl. Preheat oven to 400 degrees. Remove fillets from marinade and pat dry with a towel. Add salt and pepper. Place fillets in a baking dish and bake for about 10 minutes. Remove from oven. Spread tapenade onto fish generously and return to oven. Bake for another 3 minutes, then turn on broiler and brown tapenade for 2 minutes for added color and crispness.

PRESENTATION
Garnish plates with lemon wedges, add fillets, and serve.

CAPRICE BISTRO

10 Market Street

Wilmington, N.C. 28401

910-815-0810

capricebistro.com

Thierry Moity

The Chef

Thierry Moity

Thierry Moity cooked in what were at the time some of New York's most illustrious restaurants, including Le Chantilly, La Caravelle, and La Gauloise.

His grandmother provided his earliest food-related experiences, when he baked cookies with her in Nantua, a small town in eastern France. His wife, Patricia, is from northern France, near Belgium. He began cooking professionally as an apprentice in a small, rural bistro in 1967. He attended culinary school on his days off, eventually completing a chef's diploma. He cooked in several restaurants in France and other locations in Europe before moving to the United States in 1977.

One night at La Gauloise in New York, he was training a new cook-saucier to make *sauce au poivre* for pepper steak. "I showed him exactly what to do. I had no idea that the customer it was going to was Bryan Miller, the restaurant reviewer from the *New York Times*. The review came out a couple of weeks later, and it was great. One of his comments was, 'Speaking of pepper steak, of which I am an ardent fan, the version prepared by Thierry Moity, the French-born chef, is among the best I have found in town.' "

Like so many chefs, Thierry yearned for his own restaurant. That ambition came to fruition when he and Patricia opened Café de Bruxelles, named after the Belgian city of Brussels. Although the restaurant was successful and received good reviews in the New York press, after 18 years in the city, Thierry and Patricia began to yearn for a slower pace.

They moved to Charlotte in 1995, where they owned the well-regarded Patou. They liked North Carolina but still wanted to live someplace smaller. A good friend in Wilmington helped them get acquainted with the city. They relocated to the coast and opened Caprice Bistro in 2001.

At home, they like to grill. If they go out to eat, they enjoy sushi. Thierry has a special love for ice cream and local goat cheese with a French baguette.

The Restaurant

Caprice Bistro

Caprice Bistro is located near the waterfront in downtown Wilmington. It is a classic French bistro with a Belgian twist, reflecting the influence of Patricia Moity. Downstairs in the main dining room, guests are seated in cafeteria-style chairs at wooden tables. Daily specials are posted on a chalkboard. The upstairs houses a sofa bar, an idea Thierry and Patricia brought from New York.

"I love to work with fresh local fish," Chef Moity says. "Waterzooi, a fish stew that is always on the menu due to its strong local following, is a good example. Local fishermen bring the day's catch to the restaurant early in the morning. Grouper and shrimp are especially reliable in this area, but we feature other seafood that is caught fresh. For produce, I use Feast Down East. They only deal with local products—one truck, one delivery, all from local farmers.

"I believe in simplicity, respecting the integrity of the main dish, not using too many spices that cover up the original taste. For example, carrot soup should taste like carrot, not curry or cumin. I always try to find the best, the freshest ingredients, but they do not have to be the most expensive. We always try to provide good value for our customers."

Caprice Bistro has received good reviews from the *Wilmington Star-News* and the *Greensboro News & Record*, as well as *Encore, Coastal Carolina*, and *Focus on the Coast* magazines. It has been featured on *North Carolina Weekend* on UNC-TV.

The Recipes

Tomato Tartelette
Serves 6

CHEF'S NOTE "This is a very easy recipe. You just proceed the same way as you would to make a pastry tart. Instead of using sweet cherries or apricots, use tomatoes. Instead of using pastry cream, use goat cheese."

1 9-inch pastry shell or 6 smaller shells
48 vine-ripened cherry tomatoes
12 Kalamata olives
1 cup balsamic vinegar
1 cup olive oil, divided
salt and pepper to taste
½ cup chopped basil
1 teaspoon chopped garlic
1½ cups goat cheese
½ cup grated Parmesan cheese

Bake tart shells (according to package directions if premade or according to recipe if you make your own) until they just slightly begin to brown. Remove from oven and place in refrigerator overnight.

Tomato Tartelette

Preheat oven to 425 degrees. Cut tomatoes and olives in half. Marinate for about 1 hour in balsamic vinegar and ½ cup of the olive oil. Remove tomatoes and olives. Save balsamic mixture. Add salt and pepper, basil, and garlic to tomato mixture. Cream goat cheese in a mixer. Remove tart shells from refrigerator and spread goat cheese in shells. Arrange tomato mixture over goat cheese. Sprinkle tarts with olive oil and Parmesan. Bake about 20 minutes. While tarts are baking, simmer balsamic mixture until reduced to the consistency of syrup.

PRESENTATION
Serve hot, drizzled with reduced marinade.

Beef Bourguignon
Serves 8

CHEF'S NOTE "This is an abbreviated version of what we do in the restaurant. It is designed to minimize the use of too many pots and pans, so there is less cleaning when cooking at home."

1 cup canola oil
4 pounds trimmed beef chuck, cut into 2-inch cubes
½ pound bacon, cut into 1-inch pieces
3 onions, minced
3 cello carrots, minced
3 cloves garlic, crushed
⅓ cup all-purpose flour
1 bottle red wine (Merlot recommended)
5 cups veal or beef stock
pinch of thyme
2 bay leaves
1 tablespoon tomato paste
2 tablespoons brown sugar
salt and pepper to taste
½ pound white mushrooms, quartered
½ cup Dijon mustard
chopped parsley
crostini

Preheat oven to 425 degrees. Heat oil in a Dutch oven. Sear beef a few pieces at a time until browned. Remove and set aside. In the same

Beef Bourguignon
PHOTO COURTESY OF THIERRY MOITY AND CAPRICE BISTRO

pot, sauté bacon until crisp. Drain off some of the fat, then add on-ions, carrots, and garlic. Return beef to pot and mix with vegetables. Sprinkle with flour and stir. Place in oven for 10 minutes. Remove pot from oven, remove ingredients from Dutch oven, and deglaze bottom of Dutch oven with red wine. Simmer over medium heat until reduced by ½. Add stock, thyme, bay leaves, tomato paste, brown sugar, and salt and pepper. Bring stew to a boil, then return to oven and cook, covered, for about 1 hour. Add mushrooms and cook for another 20 minutes. When beef is cooked, skim off any surface fat, check seasoning, and stir in mustard.

PRESENTATION

Serve in shallow plates with a side of boiled potatoes or pasta. Finish with parsley and crostini.

Oeufs à la Neige (Floating Islands)
Serves 6

CHEF'S NOTE "This is an old-fashioned dessert. The *oeufs*—eggs—are baked meringues. We used to serve it with crème anglaise, but the lighter and easier way is to serve it with any seasonal fruit coulis of your choice. It is also gluten-free."

Strawberry Coulis

½ cup water
½ cup sugar
10 strawberries, hulled

Bring water to a boil. Stir in sugar until fully dissolved. This makes simple syrup. Place strawberries in a blender. Slowly add simple syrup while blending until puréed into a fine liquid. Set aside.

Islands

8 egg whites
pinch of salt
1 cup organic sugar
1 drop lemon extract
powdered sugar
cocoa powder
fresh mint leaves
fresh strawberries

Oeufs à la Neige
PHOTO COURTESY OF THIERRY MOITY AND CAPRICE BISTRO

Preheat oven to 300 degrees. Butter 6 ramekins and dust with sugar. Put egg whites and salt in a mixing bowl and whip until stiff. Fold in sugar and lemon extract. Using a pastry bag, fill ramekins to the rim with egg-white mixture. Bake for about 55 minutes until firm and lightly brown on top. Let meringues cool for a few hours in the refrigerator.

PRESENTATION

Spoon equal amounts of Strawberry Coulis in 6 small dessert plates. Unmold a meringue onto each plate. Top with powdered sugar and chocolate powder. Garnish with mint leaves and strawberries.

Keith Rhodes   PHOTO COURTESY OF CATCH

CATCH

6623 Market Street

Wilmington, N.C. 28405

910-799-3847

catchwilmington.com

The Chef

Keith Rhodes

Keith Rhodes is one of North Carolina's celebrity chefs.

A big guy (six foot five) with a big beard, he is easily and often recognized. He won the Best Dish North Carolina competition, sponsored by the North Carolina Department of Agriculture, in both the casual and fine-dining categories in 2007. He was nominated for a James Beard Award in 2011, reaching the semifinals for Best Chef in the Southeast, and has also appeared on the television show *Top Chef*. He considers the James Beard nomination his highest honor as a chef so far.

Originally from Philadelphia, he moved with his sister to Wilmington at age 13 to live with family in the Porters Neck neighborhood after the death of his mother. He credits Royce Rhodes, his paternal grandfather, for his interest in food and cooking. After a career in passenger restaurant service on railroads, Royce retired and became a bartender at Figure Eight Island Yacht Club and a private butler, booking and managing personnel for parties in Wilmington. He helped Keith get a job as a dishwasher at the yacht club. There, Keith observed some classically trained chefs and started to think about becoming a chef.

He had to drop out of school in order to work. Keith eventually got into some trouble but overcame his difficulties and continued to pursue restaurant work. He learned by observing and doing. He was hired as a prep cook at Deluxe in Wilmington and worked his way up to executive chef. Patrons and critics alike praised his work.

Chef Rhodes helps others avoid the troubles he has seen in his own life. He participates in outreach projects for young people and is a mentor to aspiring chefs. He and his wife, Angela, have two daughters in college.

The Restaurant

Catch

Angela and Keith Rhodes opened Catch in 2006. At first, the restaurant served only lunch. Keith operated Catch by day and continued as executive chef at Deluxe at night. Later, he left Deluxe in order to operate his own restaurant full-time.

He describes the concept at Catch: "We wanted to serve the best local ingredients but with a modern twist, striving to support local farmers, local fisheries, and sustainable fishing practices." Organic produce is emphasized. The restaurant, decorated in colors of the sea, is small and casual.

Catch, as the name implies, is best known for its seafood, prepared mostly in the Southern style but often with French and Vietnamese influences and flavors. Meats and fowl appear on the menu as well. Chef Rhodes has joined an initiative to control lionfish, an invasive species, by buying and serving fillets of the diver-caught fish.

Catch is popular with Wilmington's film community. Robert Downey Jr. took one of his gatherings there during the filming of *Iron Man 3*.

Chef Rhodes has added a food truck to his enterprises.

NOTE This profile contains information from articles on the *Raleigh News & Observer* website (newsobserver.com/2012/06/06/2114902/chef-keith-rhodes-star-of-wilmington.html) and the Bravo website (bravotv.com/people/keith-rhodes/bio).

Carolina Crab Cakes with Texas Pete Aioli
PHOTO COURTESY OF CATCH

The Recipe

Carolina Crab Cakes with Texas Pete Aioli
Serves 4 as an appetizer or 2 as entrée

Texas Pete Aioli
1 cup mayonnaise
⅓ cup Texas Pete hot sauce
1 teaspoon minced garlic
1 teaspoon white pepper
1½ teaspoons honey

Prepare aioli ahead. Mix all ingredients together and blend thoroughly.

Crab Cakes

1½ teaspoons minced fresh ginger
1 egg yolk
2 tablespoons mayonnaise
1 teaspoon sea salt
1 teaspoon white pepper
6 saltine crackers, crushed
1 pound North Carolina jumbo lump crabmeat, picked
⅓ cup soybean oil

Mix ginger, egg yolk, and mayonnaise. Add salt and white pepper. Stir in crushed crackers and mix thoroughly. Allow to soak for 10 minutes. Add crabmeat a little at a time, taking care not to break up lumps. Form into 4 cakes, using about ⅓ cup of mixture per cake. Press about ¾ inch thick. Heat oil in a skillet over medium heat. Carefully place cakes in hot oil and cook for 4 minutes per side until exterior turns brown. Drain on paper towels.

PRESENTATION

Serve cakes with Texas Pete Aioli alongside. For extra impact, buy mini bottles of Texas Pete and place on plates so guests can increase heat if they want to.

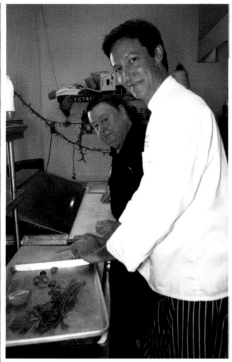

JERRY'S FOOD, WINE, SPIRITS

7220 Wrightsville Avenue

Wilmington, N.C. 28403

910-256-8847

jerrysfoodandwine.com

Left: *Jerry Rouse,* right: *Steven Powell*
PHOTO BY JOHN BATCHELOR

The Chef

Steven Powell

Steven Powell grew up with a grandmother who cooked all the time. She was raised on a farm in Wallace, North Carolina. "As a child, I loved helping her cook but never put much thought into it," Steven recalls. "On the other hand, I also grew up with a mother who had trouble boiling water. So out of necessity, I started cooking for myself, and it just progressed."

He is a Wilmington native. When he was 15, he got a job busing tables on weekends at Leon's, a family diner. That turned into washing dishes and some light prep work. He started washing dishes for Jerry Rouse, owner and founder of Jerry's Food, Wine, Spirits, when he was 17. "One night, the fry cook didn't show up, so Jerry asked me to help out. That's when my professional culinary career started. I went on learning to cook for the next three years until I decided to further my education. I went to Johnson & Wales in Charleston and graduated with honors in the top of my class. While attending school, I worked at a local fine-dining restaurant, Jasmine, for two years. After school, I made a tough choice and took a job inland, at the Biltmore Estate in Asheville. I quickly moved to the sous chef position at The Bistro on the estate and stayed in that position for three years. But I was missing the coast, and I was tired of freezing in the winter, so I moved back home in 2004 and started working for Jerry the second time, as his sous chef." Steven took over as executive chef in 2010.

"There is only one way to really become a chef, and that's working at it," he observes. "Culinary school didn't teach me how to be a chef or how to cook well or even how to develop a style. School just gave me the tools. The rest comes from practicing, reading, exploring, reading some more, trial and error—oh, and did I mention reading? It's about watching and learning from other people in real kitchens. Working at the Biltmore Estate was one of the best learning experiences I could have had. The experience really introduced me to the farm-to-table style of cooking. We used to take field trips to the local slaughterhouse and participate in the butchering of estate cows, make trips to local trout farms. And we even made a trip to a local bison farm. It really opened my mind up and changed the way I think about food.

"Being born and raised on the North Carolina coast meant I grew up going to the beach, surfing, boating, and enjoying great seafood. There's nothing like right-off-the-boat fresh. The love of the ocean and surfing is a big reason why I like where I am. Other family members live in the area as well, so being close to them is a bonus."

The Restaurant

Jerry's Food, Wine, Spirits

Jerry's Food, Wine, Spirits is located just before the Wrightsville Beach drawbridge. Jerry Rouse started the restaurant over 18 years ago. He is a Wilmington native with more than 40 years' experience in the restaurant business. The restaurant's website describes Jerry's food as "progressive continental cuisine with a heavy southern coastal influence, paired with a great wine selection, and of course the spirits of your liking." Jerry's is unassuming from the outside, but the interior is elegant, although the ambience is casual.

Reflecting on how he grew into the style of cooking at Jerry's, Chef Powell remarks, "The first time I saw Thomas Keller's *French Laundry Cookbook*, I was blown away by his style, his presentations. I knew this is what I liked and what I wanted to do. When creating a dish, I try to keep it simple. Don't mask the main ingredient. Try to only add a couple of things to accentuate that item, then take it from there.

"We are one of the few restaurants in town to get fresh soft-shell crabs all summer from our special local crab fisherman. We not only serve great seafood of all varieties, but also châteaubriand, filet mignon, spring lamb, and vegetarian options as well. With an excellent wine selection and a wait staff with more experience than you can count."

Chef Powell collaborates with several local seafood purveyors, plus local produce companies. "Deliveries arrive daily, providing great produce from eastern North Carolina farms. Now, even the big food purveyors have started reaching out to smaller farms for local products."

Jerry's has received positive reviews in *Focus on the Coast* magazine and the *Greensboro News and Record*, as well as a TripAdvisor Certificate of Excellence and recognition by the Bravo Awards Best of Readers Poll in 2011 and 2012. Chef Powell has participated in a young chefs' competition held by the Chaine des Rotisseurs.

Jerry's also provides catering that can accommodate any dietary or religious requirements.

The Recipes

Fried Green Tomato Tower with Fresh Mozzarella, Crispy Smoked Bacon, Green Tomato Chutney, Rosemary Honey, and Salted Pecans
Serves 4

CHEF'S NOTE "One hot summer afternoon, staring at my garden full of tomatoes, I thought about the classic Caprese salad with fresh mozzarella but thought, 'Let's put a little twist on it.' Then fried green tomatoes popped into my head. From there, it was how to use green tomatoes a little differently. Enter the sweet and sour Green Tomato Chutney and some saltiness from the bacon and nuts, and add the refreshing rosemary. Done, sold, call it a day!"

Fried Green Tomato Tower with Fresh Mozzarella, Crispy Smoked Bacon, Green Tomato Chutney, Rosemary Honey, and Salted Pecans

PHOTO BY JOHN BATCHELOR

Green Tomato Chutney

3 medium green tomatoes, diced ½ inch
1 cup sugar
pinch of kosher salt
pinch of red pepper flakes
2 tablespoons apple cider vinegar
2 tablespoons apple cider

Combine all ingredients in a small nonstick sauté pan. Simmer over medium heat for 25 to 30 minutes, stirring occasionally, until thickened and glossy in appearance. Remove from heat, pour into a small bowl, and allow to cool completely. Set aside. This can be made the day before; refrigerate if preparing ahead.

Rosemary Honey and Salted Pecans

½ cup honey
1 tablespoon fresh rosemary, chopped fine
½ cup pecans, chopped coarse
1 teaspoon kosher salt
1 tablespoon unsalted butter, melted

In a small mixing bowl, combine honey and rosemary. Reserve. This can also be made the day before.

Mix pecans, salt, and butter in another small bowl. Place on a cookie sheet and bake at 400 degrees for 4 to 6 minutes until browned and toasted.

Fried Green Tomatoes

3 cups vegetable oil for frying
1 cup all-purpose flour
½ cup cornmeal
2¼ teaspoons kosher salt
½ teaspoon pepper
½ teaspoon granulated garlic
4 medium green tomatoes, sliced ½ inch thick (12 slices total)
2 cups buttermilk
8 1-ounce slices fresh mozzarella
4 slices smoked bacon, cooked crisp and broken in half
4 sprigs rosemary

In a cast-iron skillet or a home frying device, heat oil to 350 degrees. Combine flour, cornmeal, salt, pepper, and garlic in a medium mixing bowl. Add sliced tomatoes 1 at a time and coat with flour mix. In another bowl, add buttermilk. Add floured tomatoes to buttermilk and coat evenly. Drain tomatoes and add back into flour mix again, coating evenly. Working in batches, carefully place tomatoes in hot oil and fry for 2 minutes on each side until golden brown. Using a slotted spoon, remove tomatoes onto a plate lined with paper towels. Season with a touch of salt.

PRESENTATION

Place 2 tablespoons Green Tomato Chutney in center of 4 large, round plates. Stack a fried tomato slice on top of chutney. Stack a slice of mozzarella, then bacon. Repeat with tomato, mozzarella, bacon, and end with tomato, creating a "tower" or stack. Drizzle 1 tablespoon Rosemary Honey over tower. Add ¼ of toasted nuts to tower. Place a sprig of rosemary into top of tower and serve.

Applewood Bacon–Wrapped Grouper with Chilled Poached Shrimp-Tomato Relish

Serves 4

CHEF'S NOTE "I love to make this at home and add some grilled garden vegetables, such as asparagus or squash."

Applewood Bacon–Wrapped Grouper with Chilled Poached Shrimp-Tomato Relish
Photo by John Batchelor

Chilled Poached Shrimp-Tomato Relish

1 cup water
1 cup dry white wine
⅓ cup lemon juice
1 tablespoon crab seasoning (Old Bay recommended)
1 bay leaf
6 ounces medium to large shrimp, peeled and deveined, tails on
2 large ripe tomatoes (about 1 pound)
¼ cup red onion, diced fine
¼ cup green bell pepper, diced small
2 teaspoons minced garlic
1 tablespoon fresh Italian parsley, chopped rough
1 teaspoon fresh thyme, chopped fine
3 tablespoons red wine vinegar
1½ tablespoons extra-virgin olive oil
salt and freshly ground pepper to taste

In a small saucepan on high heat, add water, wine, lemon juice, crab seasoning, and bay leaf. Bring to a simmer, then keep on low heat. Fill a medium-sized mixing bowl with ice and water. Add shrimp all at once to poaching liquid, stirring occasionally for 5 to 6 minutes. Remove from heat and drain in a colander. Place shrimp in ice bath and cool for 15 to 20 minutes. Remove and drain. Pinch tails off shrimp and rough-chop the meat. In a medium-sized mixing bowl, add shrimp, tomatoes, onions, bell peppers, garlic, parsley, thyme, vinegar, olive oil, and salt and pepper. Mix well and refrigerate for at least 1 hour, preferably 4 hours. This can be made a day in advance.

Grouper

8 thick slices applewood bacon
4 8-ounce grouper fillets, about ½ inch thick (any white fish will do)
salt and pepper to taste
2 tablespoons olive oil
4 lemon wedges
4 sprigs parsley

On a large work surface, lay down 2 slices of bacon side by side, overlapping just slightly. Season a fillet lightly with salt and pepper. Place fillet at end of bacon and wrap bacon around fillet, making sure seam side is down when finished. If necessary, trim excess bacon off end to "clean it up." Repeat with remaining fillets. Fillets can be wrapped in advance of day of service.

Preheat oven to 400 degrees. In a large nonstick sauté pan on high heat, add olive oil. When oil is hot, it will "run around" pan very fast when pan is tilted back and forth. At this point, add wrapped fillets, working in batches of 2 at a time, seam side up. Place edge of fillets in hot oil first, then gently lower fillets in the direction away from you, so hot oil does not splash back. Sear for 3 to 5 minutes until golden brown. Carefully flip fillets over to seam side down and cook for 3 to 5 minutes more. Remove to a sheet pan. Repeat with remaining fillets. Bake for 15 to 18 minutes until internal temperature reaches 145 degrees. Fish should be opaque and flaky.

PRESENTATION

Place fillets on large, round white bowls or plates. Place 2 or 3 tablespoons relish on top of fillets, cascading it off the side, making sure to get some liquid on the dishes, too. Garnish with lemon wedges and parsley.

KORNERSTONE BISTRO

8262 Market Street

Wilmington, N.C. 28411

910-686-2296

kornerstonebistro.com

Robert Pickens
PHOTO BY JIM RAYCROFT

The Chef

Robert Pickens

Robert Pickens was the chef on board the mega yacht *Nadine* when it sank in the Mediterranean. The yacht belonged to Jordan Belfort, the subject of the film *The Wolf of Wall Street*.

Robert has spent most of his adult life at sea, after being born and raised in Mississippi. "I suppose my grandmother Geneva laid the groundwork for my cooking. She owned a well-known steakhouse, Geneva's Lizard Thicket in New Albany, Mississippi. She dry-aged her beef and cooked all her steaks over an open-flame pit. The fish she served was raised in her own ponds. At home, the family grew their own vegetables, canned, made desserts from scratch, and lived simply."

His professional career began when he was 19, after he moved to California and was exposed to a broader range of foods. "My culinary education was self-styled, in addition to formal. By the time I left California, I knew I wanted to become a chef, so I worked on towboats as a deck hand, pushing barges up and down the Mississippi River, in order to pay my way through culinary school. I attended the Memphis Culinary Academy and furthered my education by working in the best restaurants I could find wherever I lived."

He eventually went to sea as a chef on private yachts. "Being a chef on yachts is an education in itself. You get paid to travel and provision in markets and remote locations all over the world, while cooking with an unlimited budget for some of the wealthiest people on the planet. There are also many opportunities to dine and cook on a short-term basis in some of the best restaurants around the world. It's a priceless education for experiencing different food cultures." During his yacht-chef years, Robert cooked for numerous celebrities, high-profile professional athletes, and billionaire business titans.

On Belfort's *Nadine*, "we were in a horrific storm for 19 hours, with 40-foot seas and 60-knot winds, before being rescued by the Italian navy," he says. "The galley flooded, and I was almost electrocuted by stray current. There are other stories about experiences on that boat and others, but I've signed so many non-disclosure agreements, I'll have to keep those to myself."

He came to love "the simplicity of the food of the Mediterranean. I cook with the seasons, generally narrowing my focus to three or four flavors on a plate that complement each other with a conscious refinement. Ideally, I try to highlight the flavor of an ingredient without masking it. I'm still Southern at heart, with a wide range of cultures to pull from when cooking for clients. I try to match my own style to the people I'm cooking for and create things I think they will like."

He moved to North Carolina in 2005. "I was working on yachts and traveling quite a bit back and forth to the Bahamas from South Florida. My first child had been born, and I did not want to miss out on her growing up, so when an opportunity arose at Eagle Point Golf Club in Wilmington, I took it. It seemed like a natural fit. The fact that Wilmington is a Southern coastal town with plenty of farming nearby was very appealing. My kids will get to grow up surfing and also have a sense of rural country life." Robert continues to oversee the food and beverage operations at Eagle Point.

At home, he tries to "cook healthy in a macrobiotic style, using a lot of whole grains and vegetables. However, I do like to splurge occasionally on the foods I grew up with, such as fried catfish, hush puppies, rib-eyes, and cat-head biscuits with country ham and red-eye gravy!"

The Restaurant

Kornerstone Bistro

Kornerstone Bistro is a Mediterranean restaurant with an emphasis on fresh local ingredients. "We prepare them with the same simplicity as the food of the Riviera," Robert says. "It's a healthy cuisine that uses a lot of whole grains, seafood, tomatoes, capers, and lemons, with nods to French, Spanish, Italian, and Greek flavors." Pizza is baked in a wood-fired oven.

"I based the Kornerstone concept on the food of the Mediterranean. As in the Riviera, we strive to be the local neighborhood restaurant cornerstone, or gathering place, where people come together and enjoy well-prepared, healthy food and libations. One of our employees dubbed us, 'a local place for worldly taste.' "

The kitchen staff frequents the Poplar Grove Farmers' Market, located a couple of miles up the road on U.S. 17, and Cape Fear Seafood, a couple of miles in the other direction. Feast Down East provides a liaison between farmers and chefs in the area.

Kornerstone Bistro has been honored twice in North Carolina's Best Dish contest. The restaurant participates in local fundraisers and puts on an annual event to raise money for wounded soldiers. Chef Pickens is the author of *Caribbean Cuisine: A Culinary Voyage*.

The Recipes

North Carolina Bouillabaisse
Serves 6

CHEF'S NOTE "Bouillabaisse is a classic fish soup from the Mediterranean region of Provence. You can find some version of it throughout the Mediterranean. Traditionally, bouillabaisse was made with Mediterranean fish and seafood, such as scorpion fish and conger eel, as well as shellfish, such as mussels and crab. Modern bouillabaisse can be made with a variety of white fish and shellfish. In the traditional method of serving bouillabaisse, the broth is presented in a bowl, along with toast rounds garnished with rouille, similar to aioli, with the fish and seafood presented on a separate platter. Modern bouillabaisse is served with all

North Carolina Bouillabaisse
Photo by Cory Marie Noonan

the ingredients together in a single bowl. The pronunciation is BOOL-yuh-bayz or bool-yuh-BAYZ."

Fish Stock

2 tablespoons olive oil
1 cup chopped onions
2 carrots, chopped rough
½ cup chopped celery
salt and pepper to taste
3 cloves garlic, minced
1 bay leaf
8 whole peppercorns
2 cups 74/40 tomatoes (canned, peeled, vine-ripened tomatoes, sometimes called tomato fillets)
2 to 3 pounds fish bones
water to cover

Heat olive oil in a large saucepan. Add onions, carrots, and celery. Season with salt and pepper. Sauté for 3 minutes. Add garlic and cook for 1 minute. Add bay leaf, peppercorns, and tomatoes. Add fish bones and water. Bring to a boil, then reduce to a simmer. Cook for 30 to 45 minutes. Remove from heat and strain. This will keep in the refrigerator for 3 days. It freezes well.

Soup Base

2 tablespoons chopped garlic
1 cup white wine
pinch of saffron
2 cups julienned leeks
zest and juice of 1 orange
2 cups julienned fennel, seeds removed
4 cups diced potatoes
salt and pepper to taste

Place Fish Stock on heat and bring to a simmer. Add first 7 ingredients. Season with salt and pepper. Cook for 8 minutes.

Rouille

2 cups roasted red peppers, chopped
2 slices bread
3 cloves garlic, roasted
1 teaspoon Dijon mustard
1 teaspoon lemon juice
½ cup olive oil
salt and pepper to taste

Combine first 5 ingredients in a food processor. Purée until smooth. With machine running, slowly add olive oil. Season the emulsion with salt and pepper.

Bouillabaisse

30 littleneck clams
30 mussels
12 2- to 3-ounce pieces sea bass, flounder, and/or salmon
2 cups calamari
36 shrimp, peeled and deveined, tails removed
¼ cup tomatoes, peeled, seeded, and chopped
2 tablespoons parsley, chopped fine
salt and pepper to taste
12 crostini, grilled

Heat 1½ quarts of Soup Base (including pieces of potato, fennel, and leek) in a pan. Add clams and mussels and heat for 3 to 4 minutes until they begin to pop open. Add fish, calamari, and shrimp. Cook for about 2 minutes until fish is almost cooked through. Add tomatoes and parsley and season with salt and pepper.

PRESENTATION

Distribute evenly in large, deep bowls. Place bowls on large white plates with side ramekins of Rouille and 2 crostini per person.

Mediterranean Flounder

PHOTO BY CORY MARIE NOONAN

Mediterranean Flounder

Serves 4

CHEF'S NOTE "The Mediterranean diet focuses largely on fresh seafood, lemons, tomatoes, olives, and other sun-drenched delights from the coastlines of Italy, Greece, Morocco, France, and Spain. Living on the North Carolina coast, we are fortunate to have phenomenal fresh seafood, as well as farmers to provide us with fresh homegrown vegetables reminiscent of that region. In this dish, flounder is the perfect light North Carolina white fish. The fish is sautéed to a golden brown and highlighted with flavors of lemon, tomatoes, olives, and feta. Although tabbouleh is traditionally Lebanese in origin and made with bulgur or cracked wheat, our variation is quinoa-based and tossed with arugula to provide a healthy, light coastal alternative."

Lemon Vinaigrette

¼ cup lemon juice
1 tablespoon honey
1 teaspoon chopped garlic
½ cup extra-virgin olive oil
1 tablespoon chopped parsley
salt and white pepper to taste

In a bowl, add lemon juice, honey, and garlic. Whisk together. Continue whisking while slowly pouring in olive oil. Add parsley and season with salt and white pepper.

Flounder

4 6- to 8-ounce flounder fillets
flour seasoned with salt and pepper
¼ cup olive oil
½ cup white wine
1 tablespoon lemon juice
1½ cups diced tomatoes
4 tablespoons feta cheese
¼ cup sliced Kalamata olives
salt and white pepper to taste
1 teaspoon chilled butter

Dredge fillets in seasoned flour and shake off excess. Heat a sauté pan until hot. Add olive oil and fillets. Cook for about 3 minutes on each side until golden brown. Add white wine to pan and reduce for about 2 minutes. Add lemon juice and remainder of ingredients except butter. Add butter and gently swirl pan to incorporate. Adjust seasonings. Hold sauce and fillets.

Taboulleh

6 cups quinoa
4 cups chopped fresh parsley
½ cup chopped fresh mint
1 cup chickpeas
1 cup diced tomato
1 cup diced cucumber
salt and pepper to taste
4 cups arugula

Cook quinoa according to package directions. Toss quinoa, next 5 ingredients, and 4 tablespoons of Lemon Vinaigrette together in a mixing bowl. Season with salt and pepper.

PRESENTATION

Mound Taboulleh and arugula on plates. Lay fillets over top. Divide reserved sauce over tops of fillets.

MOTTS CHANNEL SEAFOOD

120 Short Street
Wrightsville Beach, N.C. 28480
910-256-3474
mottschannelseafood.com

Motts Channel Seafood has been in operation for over 20 years. Founder Gene Long set out to find the freshest seafood he could and to provide friendly, well-informed service to customers.

He started fishing when he was around eight and continued as a part-time commercial fisherman as an adult. He spent some time in New York in the smoked seafood business but came back home to the Wrightsville Beach area after a few years. Gene sold boats for a while at Carolina Inlet Marina and Pages Creek Marine but found himself lured back to seafood. He had fished with Captain Linwood Roberts since he was young, and when he got the opportunity to open a market on property owned by Captain Roberts, he jumped at it.

Tom Franz, the manager, explains that Motts Channel Seafood is a "primary handler," meaning that fish in the market come directly from the boats that caught them. The market is located on the water, and boats tie up at the Motts dock. Visitors can watch them unload and observe cleaning and butchering. The concrete floors contain dozens of drains, so the entire facility can be washed down and disinfected.

Motts is frequently mentioned by area chefs as a favored supplier. The market also offers a few non-local seafood items—Chilean sea bass and salmon, for example—in order to accommodate customer demand. Side displays offer local vegetables and produce, as well as seafood preparation condiments.

The company's website provides preparation tips, in addition to a recipe for Motts Channel Grouper, the market's own creation.

Pierre Penegre
Photo courtesy of Le Catalan French Café & Wine Bar

LE CATALAN FRENCH CAFÉ & WINE BAR

224 South Water Street
Wilmington, N.C. 28401
910-815-0200
lecatalan.com

The Chef

Pierre Penegre

"I do not pretend to be a chef in the true French meaning; I consider myself a cook," says Pierre Penegre. He was born in Perpignan, near the border of Spain in the historic region of Catalonia. Most of his family still lives there. The weather of the North Carolina coast reminds him of home.

"My wife, Marie, is American. I met her in Paris at the end of 1988. We got married in 1990, and we lived in Paris until 1999 before moving to Wilmington," he explains. They originally planned to move somewhere in the Triangle area, but after visiting friends in Wilmington, they fell in love with the surroundings.

Pierre started to cook for himself at age 16, making *croque-monsieur* (grilled ham and cheese sandwich) after school. "With regard to my first experience of cooking with *croque-monsieur,* I can tell you that is when I discovered that the way you cook and the equipment you use produces different results. I do not know for what purpose, but my parents had bought a two-sided electric grill. I am speaking of 1969, well before the craze of paninis. I used that grill to cook the *croque-monsieur* by pressing the grill on the bread and rotating the *croque* several times. I succeeded in making the bread very thin and crisp all the way through, because it was absorbing the fat of the butter and Gruyère cheese. I loved it!"

From that point, he developed a love for food and wine and began cooking for family and friends. Over the next 40 years, he constantly read culinary books and learned from experience. He also attended Le Cordon Bleu in Paris, earning certification in oenology, the study of wine. He calls his work today his third professional life. He started in the corporate world as a chemical engineer. Then he worked as a consultant for large corporations. Finally, when he moved to the United States, he decided to transform his love of cooking into a business.

"Obviously, the strongest influence on my cooking is from the Mediterranean region, with their traditional extensive use of olive oil, garlic, spices, and produce growing in the area. My cooking is simple. The key to success is the quality of the ingredients and the respect for the product.

"Just before opening the restaurant in January 2001, I sat down with a representative of a food distributor and explained what I intended to do. He looked at me and told me with a sad voice, 'Cheese and pâté are not going to work in Wilmington.' Fortunately, I proved him wrong."

His personal tastes are wide ranging. "For everyday, I will use whatever I find in my fridge and try to make a dish out of it. When I have the time, I invite friends and experiment with a recipe that I have worked on." Lately, he has become fascinated with the cuisines of Morocco and Mexico.

The Restaurant

Le Catalan French Café & Wine Bar

Le Catalan opened in January 2001. It is based on the combination of two concepts: a French café and a wine bar. "These two types of places have a precise meaning in France," Pierre says. "A French café is a place that usually provides outside seating on the street with specific furniture [bamboo woven chairs and round tables with cast-iron feet]. The menu is limited to a few items. It does not close between lunch and dinner, and people feel comfortable to order just coffee. A wine bar has a more intimate atmosphere and is a little more sophisticated. For example, we have a 12-bottle machine to preserve opened bottles under nitrogen, with three different levels of temperature. I believe Le Catalan represents the combination of these two concepts."

The restaurant offers patio seating on the river. In the interior, an elegant custom wood bar joins tables and benches designed and constructed by a local carpenter from France. In addition, corks from the restaurant add to the ambience. "If you've had a glass of wine at Le Catalan, you have added to the décor," explains Marie. The restaurant hosts "Le Cork Contest" once a year, during which customers guess how many corks are affixed around the restaurant.

Marie is responsible for the front of the house, the website, social media, and special events. The restaurant celebrates the Fourth of July and "Bleu, Blanc, Rouge Bastille Day" with French dinner specials; the annual Fête de Beaujolais Nouveau with regional wines and cuisine; and "Midnight in Paris," a New Year's celebration on Paris time.

A retail wine shop is part of the restaurant. Menu prices range from moderate to inexpensive. Charcuterie, pâtés, cheese plates, quiches, soups, creative salads, seasonal entrées such as stews and gratins, and desserts including Chocolate Mousse with Espresso are standard offerings.

Pierre likes to buy produce himself. "In my region in the south of France, farms are everywhere. Therefore, it is easier to use local produce at a competitive price. I buy locally, we use an artisan sausage, and I grow my own basil. Because my mother-in-law has retired—she lives in Antigua—I use that connection for whole nutmeg and a special hot sauce."

The Host Room in the wine shop is ideal for private dining. It can accommodate groups of eight to 12 people for meetings, birthdays, showers, personal wine tastings, or other events.

Le Catalan's unique concept has been featured on *North Carolina Weekend* on UNC-TV and in *Southern Living* and the *Wilmington Star-News*. The restaurant has been highly praised by customers in social media. In 2014, the "romantic café" scene in the television series *Sleepy Hollow* was shot in Le Catalan.

The Recipes

Les Tartines du Catalan
Serves 4

CHEF'S NOTE "Tartine is a piece of French bread on which you add a spread."

Les Tartines du Catalan

Black Olive Tapenade
1 cup Kalamata olives
1 teaspoon or more capers
2 anchovies
3 cloves garlic
¼ cup olive oil

Rinse olives, capers, and anchovies in a colander. Add garlic and olive oil. Place in a food processor and pulse until you obtain a smooth paste.

Tartines
8 slices French bread (preferably sourdough)
1 tomato, sliced very thin
8 thin slices Parmigiano Reggiano cheese

Toast bread. On each warm slice, spread a layer of Black Olive Tapenade, slices of tomato, and a slice of Parmesan. To avoid soggy bread, do not prepare in advance.

PRESENTATION
Serve 2 Tartines per person, accompanied with a green salad tossed in balsamic vinaigrette.

Shrimp and Orzo Gratin
PHOTO COURTESY OF LE CATALAN FRENCH CAFÉ & WINE BAR

Shrimp and Orzo Gratin
Serves 6

CHEF'S NOTE "Gratin is a dish which is covered with grated cheese and baked in the oven."

1 medium onion, diced (red onion adds color)
1 carrot, diced
1 stalk celery, diced
3 tablespoons olive oil
4 cloves garlic, pressed
½ cup dry white wine
1 large tomato, diced
pinch of saffron, crushed
salt and pepper to taste
pinch of cayenne pepper (optional)
1½ pounds medium shrimp, peeled
¾ cup heavy cream
¼ cup water
1 cup orzo
½ to ¾ cup grated Swiss cheese

In a pot, cook onions, carrots, and celery in olive oil until they start to caramelize. Add garlic. Stir for 1 minute, then add wine, tomatoes, saffron, salt and pepper, and cayenne (if desired). Add shrimp and cook until they get pink and wine has nearly evaporated. Add cream and water and remove from heat. Cook orzo in salted water until al dente, according to package directions. Add orzo to shrimp and vegetables and mix well. Poor into a gratin dish and cover with Swiss. Finish cooking in a 425-degree oven for 15 minutes.

PRESENTATION

Place a scoop of mixture in center of colorful plates. This goes especially well with sautéed spinach or *haricots verts*.

Crème Catalane
Serves 4

CHEF'S NOTE "This is a traditional dessert of Catalonia."

1 cup milk
1 cup heavy cream
½ teaspoon orange zest
½ teaspoon lemon zest
¾ teaspoon vanilla
⅛ teaspoon cinnamon
⅛ teaspoon anis
4 egg yolks
1 tablespoon flour
1 tablespoon cornstarch
2½ tablespoons sugar, plus extra
  for caramelization

Crème Catalane
Photo courtesy of Le Catalan French Café & Wine Bar

In a pot, combine milk, cream, orange zest, lemon zest, vanilla, cinnamon, and anis. Simmer for 8 minutes. Cool in an ice bath. In a bowl, whisk together yolks, flour, cornstarch, and sugar, then add to cooled milk mixture. Bring slowly to a boil, stirring constantly until you obtain a smooth custard. Cool custard immediately in an ice bath. Pour custard into 4 ramekins. Refrigerate until serving.

PRESENTATION

Just before serving, sprinkle surface of each custard with sugar and caramelize with a torch or under grill of oven. Place ramekins in refrigerator for 2 minutes until caramel forms a solid layer.

MANNA

123 Princess Street

Wilmington, N.C. 28401

910-763-5252

mannaavenue.com

Jameson Chavez
PHOTO COURTESY OF MANNA

The Chef

Jameson Chavez

"What distinguishes this kitchen from others is the care that is taken with the ingredients, with each other. All our people want to share knowledge in a way that is not pretentious. We try to provide something that is familiar, but in a way that is uniquely us," observes Jameson Chavez.

He is from Las Cruces, New Mexico, where his first restaurant job was flipping burgers. He worked in food service while attending Dona Ana Community College, part of New Mexico State University. EMT students were required to take courses in a minor field, so he signed up for two classes in the culinary program. About halfway through the paramedic program, he decided he liked cooking better than dealing with medical emergencies. His parents were good cooks at home, and he went out to eat with them about once a week. "They made enchiladas that were great," he recalls. From then on, he constantly read cookbooks and food-related articles.

Jameson got a job in catering at New Mexico State. There, Chef Chris Beardsley provided "what was really a crash course in professional cooking. I could already cook, but he refined what I did. This was in a huge production kitchen, so I learned pacing and quantities, how to run a big kitchen. We did occasional plated dinners for the university president and his functions, for example. We produced refined dishes for those events."

Later, Jameson took a position at Restaurant Martin, one of Santa Fe's premier establishments, under Chef Martin Rios. "He would jump on the line most weekends, and observing his precision and skills were lessons in themselves." Then he got a call from an old friend, asking if he might be interested in coming to Wilmington. "It sounded like a good opportunity, and I would get to see other parts of the country." So he made the move in 2010. Jameson was promoted to executive chef at manna in 2012.

When cooking at home, he tries to keep it simple. "Homey things are what I really like to eat best—roasted pork with collards or kale and sweet potatoes. I didn't know how much I loved sweet potatoes until I moved to the South. My girlfriend likes barbecue, so I do that for her, and we make barbecue in the restaurant, too."

The Restaurant

manna

William Mellon is owner-manager at manna. Not long after he got out of the army, he was living in Raleigh and saw a Help Wanted sign on the window of a restaurant. He went in, applied, and got the job the same day. "I am certain I was hired because I was the first to apply, not for anything related to training or experience," he recalls. That was 20 years ago. He moved to Wilmington in 1995 to help open Harvest Moon. He has had "the pleasure of working under top chefs since the early days of scrubbing pots and mopping a sweaty kitchen. Aside from actually being the chef, I've done everything in restaurant operations. I've also worked with the area's best chefs: James Bain [Harvest Moon, Dockside], Pete Baxley [Harvest Moon, City Club], Tom Mills [Gardenias, Little Pond], Aaron Peterson [Deluxe], Keith Rhodes [Deluxe, Catch], Kevin O'Connell [Seldom Blues], Shawn Wellersdick [Undercurrent, Port Land Grille], and Josh Woo

[YoSake]. They've all shaped my love for this industry."

The restaurant's website states the chef and owner's aspiration: "American cooking is rooted in survival; it is rugged, it is wild, and somehow it is elegant. At manna we use local, regional, and other American ingredients almost exclusively. We are trying to paint a picture of American food that uses colors that are only born and hued here, and the result is often pure and stunning. Come see America through our eyes."

Chef Chavez uses classical techniques with local ingredients to create sophisticated American cuisine. The menu changes frequently, reflecting seasonal ingredients. If the restaurant is not too busy, requests for things that are not on the menu are accommodated. A four-course tasting menu is available on weekdays.

Reflecting on how he creates dishes, Chef Chavez says, "Sometimes, I kind of wonder where my food ideas come from. Sometimes, I start with a single ingredient or a sauce or a flavor combination that I get my mind set on, then build a dish around that. Sometimes, there is a dish that I see or remember from somewhere else—a classic stew, for example—and I want to do something like it."

Area providers include Motts Channel Seafood in Wilmington, Cottle Organics in Rose Hill, Smac Down Fishing in Wanchese, Shelton Herb Farm in Leland, Feast Down East in Burgaw, and Heritage Farms in Seven Springs.

The Recipes

OBX Tuna, Tomato, Tomatillo, Grilled Okra, and Mojo de Ajo
Serves 4

Mojo de Ajo
10 cloves garlic
1½ cups extra-virgin olive oil
pinch of salt
1 lime
2 tablespoons water
1 cup parsley leaves
1 cup cilantro leaves

Preheat oven to 300 degrees. Put garlic in an ovenproof dish, cover in olive oil, add salt, and place in oven until golden brown and fragrant.

OBX Tuna, Tomato, Tomatillo, Grilled Okra, and Mojo de Ajo

Zest and squeeze lime into olive oil. Put halved lime into oil and bake for 10 more minutes. Remove from oven and let cool to room temperature. Remove lime. In a blender, add oil and garlic. Add water, parsley, and cilantro. Blend until smooth. Remove and chill. Mixture keeps for 4 to 5 days chilled but will lose some color.

Tuna and Vegetables
1 pound or more okra
4 5-ounce portions tuna
salt and pepper to taste
4 large tomatoes (heirloom varieties recommended)
8 small tomatillos
olive oil

Preheat a grill. Slice okra into quarters the long way and set aside. Season tuna with salt and pepper. Cut tomatoes and tomatillos into chunks. Season tomatoes, tomatillos, and okra with salt and pepper and sprinkle with olive oil. Sear or grill tuna to desired doneness. While tuna is cooking, grill okra.

PRESENTATION
Spread Mojo de Ajo on base of plates. Arrange tomatoes and tomatillos over top. Slice tuna. Place tuna and okra over tomatoes and tomatillos.

Pork Belly Roulade with Ragout of Butter Beans, Corn, Padron Peppers, Smoked Paprika, and Sherry Vinaigrette

Serves 6

3 pounds pork belly, skin removed
salt and pepper to taste
3 tablespoons brown sugar, divided
2 tablespoons smoked paprika, divided
1 onion, diced large
1 carrot, diced large
2 tablespoons cooking oil
2 quarts chicken stock
3 dried ancho chilies
4 tablespoons sherry vinegar, divided
2 shallots, diced, divided
2 cups corn kernels
4 cups butter beans, cooked
20 padron peppers
1 head fresh cilantro, chopped

Preheat oven to 200 degrees. Place pork belly on a cutting board skin side up. Using a sharp knife, butterfly belly down the center from the side without cutting all the way through. (You are trying to open the belly like a book.) Season with salt and pepper, 1 tablespoon of the brown sugar, and 1 tablespoon of the paprika. Roll belly starting with meat side, trying to end with skin side on the outside. Truss full length of roll with kitchen twine. Tying individual knots will work, too, if that is easier. In a hot pan, sear belly on all sides until browned. Set aside. Sweat onions and carrots in oil in a pan for about 5 minutes until translucent. Place belly in a deep, ovenproof dish. Add stock, carrots, onions, chilies, remaining 2 tablespoons brown sugar, and 2 tablespoons of the vinegar. Cover and place in oven. Cook for 5 or 6 hours or overnight until tender. When done, keep belly in its dish and chill until cold. This will help with slicing.

Slice belly into portions. Strain and reserve cooking liquid. In a medium warm pan, add ½ of the shallots and some oil to sweat. Add corn, beans, and 1 cup of belly. Braise and simmer until almost all liquid is gone. Taste and season with salt if needed. Sear belly in medium-hot

Pork Belly Roulade with Ragout of Butter Beans, Corn, Padron Peppers, Smoked Paprika, and Sherry Vinaigrette

pan, taking care not to burn. When belly is hot and crispy, remove to a warm plate covered with paper towels. Keep 4 or 5 tablespoons of pork fat for the vinaigrette. In a separate hot pan, add padron peppers (with no oil) and char. Add oil and salt and pepper at the end.

For vinaigrette, add rest of shallots, rest of paprika, and rest of vinegar to the pan used for the pork belly. Warm up and reserve for plating.

PRESENTATION

Put beans in small piles on plates. Top with pork belly, then padron peppers. Finish with cilantro and reserved vinaigrette.

Left: *James Doss,* above: *Scott Grimm*
PHOTOS PROVIDED BY PEMBROKE'S

PEMBROKE'S

1125 A Military Cutoff Drive

Wilmington, N.C. 28405

910-239-9153

pembrokescuisine.com

The Chefs

James Doss and Scott Grimm

"We don't make the menu, then search for product. We buy what farmers have and design the menu around that," explains Scott Grimm, *chef de cuisine* at Pembroke's.

James Doss founded Rx in Wilmington in 2012. Pembroke's came about, he says, because "we could not put everything we wanted into Rx. We discussed adding a new location with our partners when we learned that this property was going to be available. The time and the opportunity were just there, and we figured we ought to take it. The kitchen had already been built, and it was really good, so we could avoid kitchen-remodeling expenses. It had a wood-fired grill and rotisserie, and I fell in love with that thing as soon as I saw it. We also observed that Wilmington tends to be a neighborhood-oriented city, and people tend to go to places that are near home. I approached Scott Grimm. He was interested in coming in with us, so that sealed the deal. We probably lost a few Rx customers to Pembroke's, but our overall business has more than doubled."

Scott started cooking at Dockside in Wilmington when he was 18. "I loved the fast pace. I just fell in love with cooking and presentation. About a year later, I went to Vinnie's Steak House in Wilmington, where Chef Jeff Burr was a big influence. I moved to Charleston to attend Johnson & Wales, then worked at Peninsula Grill under Chef Robert Carter. That was one of the best experiences I've ever had—a lot of talented cooks, and they all wanted to be execs. I got to cook for and meet lots of celebrities. I moved back to Wilmington to work with James Bain at the original Harvest Moon, who really brought the farm-to-table and local foods idea to Wilmington. I moved to Nashville, where I cooked at the Capitol Grille in the Hermitage Hotel. Then I was able to work with Sean Brock for two years. He's now the godfather of Southern cuisine. I came back to North Carolina in my first executive chef job at Nelson's in Raleigh. I was pleased to see a few articles written about me while I was there. But I always wanted to be in Wilmington. So when James called me, I was really excited. I run the kitchen here. He is over both Rx and Pembroke's, and we share a passion for cooking the right way and paying homage to the products we have available locally."

James is especially interested in smoking meats. "I built a smoker at home, and I really like to play with it," he says. "Mostly, I am smoking pork these days. What I cook at home is a lot like what we do in the restaurant. I don't plan much for home. I just buy what is appealing and wing it. I have a garden, and I go fishing whenever I can, so that determines what I cook. I'm not able to cook at home as much as I would like these days. I cook the way people cooked 80 to 100 years ago, when they had to depend on what was growing nearby."

The Restaurant

Pembroke's

The phrase "keeping up with the Joneses" is thought to have come from Pembroke Jones, a financier and railroad owner whose hunting estate has been developed as Landfall. He and his wife owned several other properties in the Wilmington area, including what is now Airlie Gardens. He was part of the Vanderbilts' circle of friends. The restaurant is named after him, in recognition of the neighborhood where it is located, part of his original holdings.

Pembroke's provides a "seasonally inspired, locally-sourced Southern Cuisine dining experience," according to the website. "All of our seafood, protein, and produce are purchased from local fishermen, vendors, and farmers, so your meal will not only be freshly grown and hand chosen, but you can enjoy supporting our local suppliers too!" The menu changes daily.

"The idea is fine-dining technique and quality of ingredients and presentation, but in a relaxed environment where you can just enjoy yourself," Chef Doss says. "We take our food and our menu, as well as the wine list and our cocktails, very seriously. But we don't take ourselves too seriously. We have evolved into what we hope is a leader in the community with the local food movement. Our menus are not just seasonal, they are micro seasonal, because everything comes from local producers. The dishes are listed according to where the ingredients came from. Some of the suppliers are so small, they don't sell to anyone except us. Harvest Moon was the first place in Wilmington that tried to stick to local foods. Sean Brock made that such a focus at Husk, when I was working for him in Charleston. So when I moved back to Wilmington, I spent a lot of time visiting farms, and now we are so well known, they come to us." The restaurant's website has an up-to-date list of suppliers.

In particular, Pembroke's buys from Bill and Tina Moore at Nature's Way (natureswayfarmandseafood.com). "Bill is a clammer, oysterman, and fisherman. Tina is an excellent cheesemaker, and she has a goat farm," Chef Doss says. The other primary seafood source is Motts Channel Seafood in Wrightsville Beach. "They have been around forever, and that is where the bulk of our seafood comes from. I have some friends who are fishermen, and they sell to Motts. Gene Long owns it. Tom Franz is the guy I work with. We have learned a lot about seafood from him. It's hard to even keep up with what is in season, but he always knows."

A special-functions room is separate from the main dining area at Pembroke's. Wedding rehearsal dinners, art exhibitions, wine dinners, and other private parties are served there.

Pembroke's has received an Agrarian Stewardship Award from Feast Down East, as selected by farmers who are members of the co-op. It has been nominated for Best New Restaurant in *Encore* magazine; Chef Doss was nominated for Best Chef the last two years.

Crab Cakes

The Recipes

Crab Cakes
Serves 4

1 local farm egg
½ cup Duke's mayonnaise
2 dashes Lea & Perrins Worcestershire sauce
2 dashes Texas Pete hot sauce
2 dashes lemon juice
1 tablespoon Dijon mustard
zest of 1 lemon
½ teaspoon salt
¼ teaspoon pepper
1 tablespoon chopped herbs (parsley, chives, tarragon, chervil)
1 pound North Carolina unpasteurized lump blue crabmeat
cracker crumbs
¼ cup butter

Combine first 10 ingredients in a bowl. Fold crab into mixture, being careful not to break up lumps. Form 4 or 5 cakes, 3 to 4 ounces each, and roll in cracker crumbs. Pan-sear in butter over medium heat until both sides are browned and crisp.

PRESENTATION
Serve with remoulade or tartar sauce.

Butterbeans
Serves 4

4 strips hardwood smoked bacon
1 onion, diced small
2 cloves garlic, minced
1½ cups beer
2 cups butterbeans
2 tablespoons apple cider vinegar
1 bay leaf
6 sprigs thyme
hot sauce to taste
sea salt and freshly ground pepper to taste
4 cups chicken stock

Render bacon until crisp. Add onions and cook until soft. Add garlic. Deglaze pan with beer. Add remaining ingredients and bring to a simmer. Cook until butterbeans are tender, adjusting seasonings and adding stock as needed.

Grilled Heritage Pork Chops and Collards
Serves 1 or 2

CHEF'S NOTE "Collards are best after the first frost."

Pork Chops
1 gallon water
1½ cups kosher salt
½ pound heritage pork chops (Heritage Farms recommended)
olive oil
pepper to taste
several sprigs fresh thyme

Bring water to a boil. Dissolve salt in hot water. Allow to cool. Brine pork chops for 1 hour. Pat dry. Lightly marinate in olive oil, pepper, and thyme for up to 24 hours. Season with salt and pepper.

Cook pork chops on a wood or charcoal grill to an internal temperature of 135 degrees. Let rest for 5 minutes. Slice against the grain and finish with a high-quality sea salt.

Grilled Heritage Pork Chops and Collards
Photo provided by Pembroke's

Collards
4 quarts chicken or pork stock
1½ cups beer
1 cup apple cider vinegar
1 cup light brown sugar
1 tablespoon red pepper flakes
hot sauce to taste
2 heads collards, tough stems removed, cut into wide strips
2 onions, julienned
1 smoked ham hock
sea salt and freshly ground pepper to taste

Bring stock and beer to a boil. Add vinegar, brown sugar, chili flakes, and hot sauce and stir until sugar is dissolved. Add collards, onions, and ham hock. Lower heat and simmer until tender. Remove ham hock, pick lean meat out, and return to pot. Season with salt and pepper.

PRESENTATION
Mound collards (over a starch, if desired) in center of plate. Stack pork chops on top, angled so they fall off either side.

PORT LAND GRILLE

Lumina Station

1908 Eastwood Road, Suite 111

Wilmington, N.C. 28403

910-256-6056

portlandgrille.com

Shawn Wellersdick and Anne Steketee
PHOTO COURTESY OF PORT LAND GRILLE

The Chefs

Shawn Wellersdick and Anne Steketee

Shawn Wellersdick was born in Colorado but moved with his family to Connecticut when he was young. He grew up near the Berkshire Mountains. At age 13, he began working at the famed Tollgate Hill Inn and Restaurant in Litchfield as a dishwasher and prep cook. After a few years, Executive Chef Michael Louchen encouraged him to enroll in culinary school. He graduated at the top of his class from Johnson & Wales in Providence, Rhode Island.

Shawn interned at the Halcyon Restaurant in the Rihga Royal Hotel in New York. He moved to North Carolina in 1993 and was executive chef for the Noble's restaurant group at Lo Spiedo di Noble in Greensboro in 1994. While he was there, Noble's earned acclaim from *National Restaurant News* and the Food Network.

Anne Steketee was born in Miami. She came to North Carolina for college, graduating from Guilford College in Greensboro with a baccalaureate degree in psychology. She worked in restaurants in the Greensboro area for 20 years, including 13 years at Southern Lights Bistro as general manager and wine buyer.

Anne and Shawn married in 1996. After the birth of their son, Logan, the following year, Anne became pastry chef at Lo Spiedo di Noble. They relocated to Wilmington to open their own restaurant, Under Currant, in 1998.

The Restaurant

Port Land Grille

Shawn and Anne opened Port Land Grille in November 2000. During a trip to Portland, Oregon, they were impressed with how chefs created menus that capitalized on quality ingredients from the ocean and nearby farms and rivers. They seriously considered moving to Oregon but were drawn back by their love of the North Carolina coast. The name *Port Land* is a play on words, based on Wilmington's role as the state's primary port, plus their commitment to using nature's bounty from the sea and the land, as they had witnessed in Oregon. Chef Wellersdick buys foods only when in season, from local sources, so he not only gets the best, he supports farmers and the men and women who work the sea nearby.

Port Land Grille seats 85 to 100 in its main dining area, which has large windows overlooking a beautifully landscaped patio area decorated with a fountain and live oak trees. Separate, smaller dining rooms can accommodate private parties. The ambience is casual, yet elegant. Light green walls accented in black and white host framed historical photos of Wilmington and Wrightsville Beach.

The restaurant has received multiple accolades, including reviews that place it among the elite. Esteemed restaurateur and food writer Moreton Neal, writing in Raleigh's *Metro* magazine, termed Port Land Grille "one of the most exciting restaurants in the State." *Wrightsville Beach* magazine named it "Best Overall" restaurant for four consecutive years and also acknowledged it for "Best Service," "Best Creative Menu," and "Best Seafood." *Santé*, *Wine Enthusiast*, and *Wine Spectator* magazines have honored the wine list on multiple occasions.

Chef Wellersdick is a member of the American Culinary Association and the Chaine des Rotisseurs. He also serves on the North Carolina Seafood Commission and the chefs' advisory boards of the North Carolina Sweet Potato Commission and the North Carolina Pork Council. As part of his role with the seafood commission, he represented the state in 2006 and 2007 in the Great American Seafood Challenge in New Orleans. The 2006 event was filmed by the Food Network. Anne was his sous chef, which generated press attention.

He has won a silver medal from the American Culinary Federation and was a finalist in the Chaine des Rotisseurs National Hot Food Competition at the Culinary Institute of America. The restaurant won a DiRoNA award in 2005.

The Recipes

Watermelon Gazpacho with Carolina Peanuts, Feta Cheese, and Mint
Serves 8 to 10

1 ripe large watermelon, seeded and cubed
1 ripe cantaloupe, seeded and cubed
½ cup lemon-infused olive oil
½ cup orange blossom honey
2 dashes Texas Pete hot sauce
¾ to 1 cup fresh orange juice
¼ cup cider vinegar or rice wine vinegar
2 tablespoons minced dried tarragon leaves
½ cup minced fresh basil
1½ tablespoons minced ginger
2 cucumbers, peeled, seeded, and diced
1 yellow bell pepper, seeded and diced
1 green bell pepper, seeded and diced
1 bunch scallion greens, minced
salt and pepper to taste
crumbled feta cheese
Carolina roasted peanuts
mint sprigs
julienned red pepper
julienned watermelon
julienned cantaloupe

Purée watermelon, cantaloupe, olive oil, honey, Texas Pete, orange juice, vinegar, tarragon, basil, and ginger in food processor, then place in a large mixing bowl. (Can be done in several batches as necessary.)

Watermelon Gazpacho with Carolina Peanuts, Feta Cheese, and Mint

PHOTO COURTESY OF PORT LAND GRILLE

Stir in cucumbers, peppers, and scallion greens. Season with salt and pepper. Chill at least 6 hours or overnight.

PRESENTATION

Ladle gazpacho into chilled bowls. Garnish with feta, peanuts, mint sprigs, and 1 strip each of red pepper, watermelon, and cantaloupe.

Country Duck Terrine with Pistachios and Cherries

Serves 12 to 16

1¾ pounds raw duck meat, trimmed and cubed, divided
½ pound fatback, chopped
1 tablespoon sea salt
2 tablespoons chopped sage
1 tablespoon white pepper
1 tablespoon lemon thyme
1 tablespoon Madeira wine
½ cup ham, diced small
¾ cup pistachios, roasted and peeled
2½ ounces dried cherries
8 slices uncooked smoked bacon

Combine 1 pound of the duck meat, fatback, and seasonings. Grind first through the medium plate (¼ inch) and then the fine plate

Country Duck Terrine with Pistachios and Cherries
PHOTO COURTESY OF PORT LAND GRILLE

(⅛ inch) of a meat grinder or food processor. Stir in Madeira. Cover and refrigerate. Sear remaining duck meat and diced ham over medium heat. Let cool over an ice bath. Fold cooked and cooled duck pieces, ham, pistachios, and cherries into ground meat mixture until evenly distributed. Line a terrine mold first with plastic wrap, then with bacon slices, leaving an overhang for both, and pack with meat mixture. Fold bacon and then plastic wrap over terrine, then cover with the mold lid. Poach in a 170-degree water bath in a 300-degree oven to an internal temperature of 165 degrees; this will take about 50 to 60 minutes. Let terrine rest for 1 hour. Remove lid and cover with a 2-pound weight at least overnight and up to 3 days under refrigeration. The terrine will then be ready to slice and serve. It can be wrapped in plastic wrap and held in refrigerator for up to 7 days.

PRESENTATION

Serve cool or at room temperature garnished with crostini, whole-grain mustard, pickles or cornichons, and spiced fruit jellies or conserves.

Risotto with Butter-Poached Lobster, Leeks, Pistachio Nuts, and Mascarpone

Serves 4 as an appetizer or 2 as an entrée

1 whole leek with greens, julienned
¼ cup julienned fresh basil leaves

Risotto with Butter-Poached Lobster, Leeks, Pistachio Nuts, and Mascarpone
PHOTO COURTESY OF PORT LAND GRILLE

¼ cup julienned fresh Italian parsley
2 cloves garlic, peeled and minced
2 tablespoons olive oil
2 cups Arborio rice
6 cups chicken or vegetable stock
2 tablespoons unsalted butter
6 ounces lobster meat, cooked
3 ounces shelled, roasted pistachio nuts
¼ pound mascarpone cheese
¼ cup grated asiago cheese
salt and pepper to taste
fresh basil leaves and flowers

Sauté leeks, basil, parsley, and garlic in olive oil over low heat in a large, heavy-bottomed pan for about 10 minutes until leeks are well softened. Add dry rice. Stir to coat rice kernels with oil. Cook another 2 to 4 minutes over low heat, stirring occasionally. In a separate heavy-bottomed saucepan, heat stock to boiling, then turn off heat. Ladle a few ounces of hot stock into rice mixture to temper. Continue to add hot stock a ladle at a time, stirring after each addition until rice absorbs liquid. Repeat until all stock is used. Rice mixture should become smooth and creamy but remain al dente. In another small pan, melt butter. Add lobster and stir over low heat until just warmed. Fold lobster into finished risotto. Add pistachios, mascarpone, and asiago. Season with salt and pepper.

PRESENTATION
Scoop risotto in middle of small, colorful dishes. Garnish with basil.

WILMINGTON

Left: *James Doss,* above: *Will Doss*
PHOTOS PROVIDED BY RX RESTAURANT & BAR

Rx RESTAURANT & BAR

421 Castle Street
Wilmington, N.C. 28401
910-399-3080
rxwilmington.com

The Chefs

James Doss and Will Doss

James Doss explains, "The name *Rx* comes from the history of the building, still owned by the family that built it 100 years ago. It was originally Hall's Drugstore. We kept the sign on the front but remodeled the interior to facilitate a bar and restaurant."

James grew up in Goldsboro. His father is from Wilmington, as is his mother's family. "We spent a lot of time going to Morehead City, Wrightsville Beach, and the Wilmington area when I was growing up," he recalls. He moved to town in 1996 to go to UNC-Wilmington. "I kind of bounced around among majors—business and economics, mostly."

His grandmother was a country-club manager for about 30 years. The properties where she worked included Walnut Creek in Goldsboro, Highland in Fayetteville, and the Dunes Club in Atlantic Beach. The summer before college, James began working in Atlantic Beach under her supervision—busing tables, washing dishes, waiting tables, plus "just a little cooking." In college, he "worked at dishwashing in a chain restaurant, then moved into the kitchen at Vinnie's Steak House. I went to Dockside for about three years, starting as fry cook, later working up to a supervisor role. I also spent some time at Elijah's, on the docks. I left there to work at Harvest Moon for James Bain.

"That was the job that made me think about becoming a chef. I was still in school, but his influence caused me to focus on professional kitchens. That restaurant was sold while I was working there. I moved over to Sweet and Savory, working for Dave Herring, then Port Land Grille for Shawn Wellersdick, then kitchen manager at K38. I also worked for Ash Aziz at Max's Prime Steakhouse about two years. I spent some time as line cook, then sous chef, and finally executive chef at the Bridge Tender in Wrightsville Beach before moving to Charleston to work for Sean Brock at Husk. I had written a paper about him while I was in school, and I had admired him for a long time. Scott Grimm and I had worked together at Harvest Moon. Scott had moved to Nashville, where he was working for Sean, and he introduced us. I stayed at Husk about two years.

"The concept for Husk fit what I had imagined I would like to have if I owned my own restaurant, and the concept seemed to fit Wilmington as well. Josh Novicki, a childhood friend from Goldsboro, found the ideal spot for a restaurant in Wilmington. He contacted me, I came up, we signed a lease, and that became Rx. We opened July 2012."

Will Doss, James's younger brother, is *chef de cuisine* at Rx. He also spent his early restaurant career working for their grandmother at the Dunes Club, starting about age 15. He attended UNC-Wilmington, then cooked in several Wilmington restaurants, including Elijah's, Kiva Grill, and Port City Chop House. He also worked for highly regarded chef-owner Jim Noble in Greensboro, Winston-Salem, and High Point. He had been in the Charleston area for eight or nine years, at High Thyme Cuisine on Sullivan's Island, when he got the call from his brother about Rx.

The Restaurant

Rx Restaurant & Bar

Chef James describes the cuisine at Rx as "definitely Southern. Most of our ideas come from our ingredients. We base our menu on the ingredients we get at the time. We have to be really creative in winter, when kale and collards and sweet potatoes are about all the local vegetables we can get. In summer, we have an abundance of local produce—heirloom tomatoes, corn, butter beans, melons, just so much to work with, something new popping up every week."

Among the farmers and farms that source fruits and vegetables for Rx are Herbie Cottle in Rose Hill; Black River Organic Farm in Ivanhoe (blackriverorganicfarm.com), where the chefs consider Stefan Hartmann to be the "Zen master of organic vegetables"; Humble Roots Farm in Wilmington (humblerootsfarm.com); Red Beard Farms in Burgaw, especially for blueberries, figs, okra, and vegetables grown specifically for Rx. "We can get things nobody else has," remarks Chef Will.

Two pig farmers are especially important to Rx. A. J. Carroll at Dirty Pig Pork Company (thedirtypigporkco.com) in Riegelwood "does all pasture-raised, hormone-free heritage breeds—Berkshire Duroc, for example," Chef Will says. "Those pigs are beautiful. The meat has fantastic marbling. They raise their own soybeans, peanuts, and corn to feed the pigs." The Doss brothers grew up with Esther and Marlowe Ivey of Heritage Farms (heritagecheshire.com). The Iveys' father had a business selling Chester White hogs to Japan because Americans weren't interested in such high-quality pork. The daughters started Heritage Farms to try to market high-quality pork in the United States. Their timing was right, and they've been highly successful.

"We also get fresh herbs from Shelton Herb Farm in Leland," Chef Will says. "And we've just started working with Troy Haithcock. He is a culinary-school graduate who worked as sous chef at Gramercy Tavern in New York. His parents have a big pecan farm. He has started a vegetable farm and is trying to produce mushrooms.

"The farmers love that we put their names on our menu and website."

Rx has been nominated for Best New Restaurant in *Encore* magazine. Chef James was nominated for Best Chef the last two years.

The Recipes

Butterbean Hummus with Poppy-Benne Seed Crackers
Serves 4

Butterbean Hummus
1 pound butterbeans, blanched
3 tablespoons benne seeds, toasted
zest and juice of 1 lemon
3 cloves garlic
1 tablespoon Texas Pete hot sauce
½ to ¾ cup high-quality olive oil
sea salt and cracked pepper to taste

Combine butterbeans, benne seeds, lemon zest and juice, garlic, and Texas Pete in a food processor. Purée while slowly drizzling in oil until smooth and spreadable. Season with salt and pepper.

Butterbean Hummus with Poppy-Benne Seed Crackers
PHOTO PROVIDED BY RX RESTAURANT & BAR

Poppy-Benne Seed Crackers

2 cups all-purpose flour
1 tablespoon sea salt
1 teaspoon pepper
1 tablespoon sugar
1 tablespoon baking powder
6 tablespoons cold butter, diced
2 tablespoons high-quality olive oil
⅔ cup water
1½ tablespoons benne seeds
1½ tablespoons poppy seeds

Preheat oven to 400 degrees. Combine dry ingredients and butter in a food processor. Pulse. Drizzle in olive oil until mixture resembles wet sand. Add water until it forms a ball. Roll out as thin as possible. Sprinkle seeds on dough and lightly roll again to embed seeds. Cut and bake for about 7 minutes until golden brown.

PRESENTATION

Scoop hummus into center of plate. Surround with crackers stacked with edges over each other. Add condiments such as tomatoes, cucumber pickles, or pickled onions as desired.

Pan-Seared Grouper with Local Organic Ratatouille

Serves 4 to 6

Grouper

4 to 6 6-ounce grouper fillets
sea salt
butter
lemon juice

Season fillets with salt and pan-sear or grill to medium temperature. Baste with butter and lemon juice.

Local Organic Ratatouille

1 tablespoon olive oil
½ cup chopped onion

Pan-Seared Grouper with Local Organic Ratatouille

½ cup diced bell pepper
1 tablespoon diced garlic
2 cups diced tomatoes
2 cups chopped squash
2 cups chopped eggplant
1 cup loosely packed chiffonaded basil
1 tablespoon butter
lemon juice to taste
salt and pepper to taste
Texas Pete hot sauce to taste

Add olive oil, onions, and peppers to a pan and sweat over medium heat until onions are translucent. Add garlic and sauté for 2 to 3 minutes. Add tomatoes and increase heat to high. Reduce by ½. Add squash and eggplant and heat for 2 to 3 minutes. Finish with basil, butter, lemon juice, salt and pepper, and Texas Pete.

PRESENTATION
Spread Ratatouille in center of plates. Stack fillets on top.

WILMINGTON

Kymberlei DiNapoli

TASTE THE OLIVE CAFÉ & WINE BAR

1125-E Military Cutoff Road

Wilmington, N.C. 28405

910-679-4772

olivecafenc.com

tastetheolive.com

The Chef

Kymberlei DiNapoli

"It's easy to love living life in the Carolina sunshine wearing flip-flops. It is a relaxing, beautiful atmosphere with such nice people. I am so grateful that I can let the sound of the ocean take my stress away, even if it's only for a moment. Living here also provides such a variety of access to local farmers, fishmongers, and produce, which brings me a little closer to my childhood memories."

Kymberlei DiNapoli is from the mountains of West Virginia. She moved to the District of Columbia area when she was 20. She began coming to the North Carolina coast for vacations and became a resident in 2010.

She started cooking when she was five years old, standing on a chair beside her great-aunt. "I was taught good old-fashioned country cooking," she says. "It was a way of life. We grew our own vegetables and fruits. I lived in apple country.

We even had a local butcher, along with a general store. Growing up poor, even though I had no idea we were poor, I just thought breakfast for dinner was a treat. I didn't know it meant the money had run out. The valuable lesson learned from those early years was to create ways to use all of my food; don't waste anything. Trendy restaurants think they are the ones that coined the phrase 'nose to tail.' I heard that phrase all of the time growing up!

"I became fascinated with every type of cuisine once I moved to D.C. You can only imagine how wide-eyed a West Virginia girl would get, moving into that multicultural-cuisine melting pot. My interest in professional food service developed with the input of friends and family. I don't really refer to myself as a chef. I have no formal training. I'm a self-taught, at-home cook, with just enough craziness to open my own restaurant.

"I experiment all the time. I have some great friends who are amazing cooks. They have always encouraged me to try new things, and they have shared their knowledge. That is how the food passion began. I have one friend from New Delhi, India, who is a fabulous cook. He utilized me as his 'sous' often. That was the beginning of my love for Indian cuisine. I have so much fun incorporating those flavors into unsuspecting places. I can honestly say I learned to cook 'real' Indian food. You should see the clerks' questioning looks when I visit an Indian market and purchase items such as curry leaves, red lentils, mung beans, and mustard seeds. One time, a woman asked, 'You know how to cook real Indian? Most Americans come and buy spice packages ready to use.' Then she smiled, asking another question: 'How did you learn?' I told her, 'Thanks to my dear friend Savio,' and just hearing the name satisfied her. I don't think many non-Indians are named Savio!"

Kymberlei says her early focus was turning her country-cooking family recipes into healthier alternatives. "This is the reason my world is a pool of extra-virgin olive oil." Taste the Olive is an "ultra-premium" olive oil and balsamic vinegar emporium. "Those ingredients have become the backbone of every recipe I create. Taste the Olive is the passion that drives me, specifically to get information about the flavorful health benefits that certified extra-virgin olive oil and balsamic vinegars have, and why they should be incorporated into daily living. I have always preferred using whole, quality foods instead of processed foods. With quality, you don't need numerous ingredients to make your dish flavorful."

At home, she likes to cook things that are fresh, easy, and quick. "I try to follow a more European way of shopping for dinner. I don't buy too much at one time—back to not wasting food. It's easier to go to the grocery store and get just a few things, depending on what you are in the mood for."

The Restaurant

Taste the Olive Café & Wine Bar is "an epicurean emporium devoted to taste," Kymberlei says. "We use quality ingredients prepared in a comforting way. I want to serve food that guests understand.

"I love wine. Our wine bar is about helping people travel the world one grape at a time. I love to learn about wine and experience it, everything from *terroir* to flavor profiles.

"I have also been obsessed with owning a cheese shop and introducing people to the world of cheese. Our cheese boards are show-stoppers, and that is why there is a cheese counter in my restaurant. Not only can guests enjoy cheeses in the restaurant, they can buy some to take home as well.

"Our motto is 'an upscale atmosphere without an uptight attitude.' I want people to enjoy being in a beautiful place, eating delicious food, and feeling comfortable just as they are.

"I love traveling. I designed my restaurant after some of my favorite places. It is French-inspired, starting with Paris. (My husband proposed to me at the Eiffel Tower.) We have several large tables. It's like having a big family dinner, going back to the comfort aspect.

"We believe that it is very important to use local vendors. We do what we can to use as many as possible. We are fortunate enough to have many local resources here on the coast to get our produce, fish, and meats."

Taste the Olive was named "Best New Restaurant of 2013" by Shore Picks.

The Recipes

Bacon Pops
Serves 4 to 6 as an appetizer

1 cup brown sugar
2 teaspoons cayenne pepper
2 teaspoons onion powder
1 teaspoon cinnamon
1 pound North Carolina bacon

Bacon Pops
PHOTO COURTESY OF TASTE THE OLIVE CAFÉ & WINE BAR

Taste the Olive's Maple-Infused Aged Balsamic Vinegar (maple syrup can be substituted but won't be as rich in flavor)

Soak wooden skewers in water for 30 minutes. Preheat oven to 350 degrees. Mix together brown sugar, cayenne, onion powder, and cinnamon. Press each side of bacon strips into mixture. Thread bacon on to skewers. Place on a baking sheet lined with parchment paper. Drizzle with balsamic and bake until appropriately crisp.

PRESENTATION
Add more balsamic before serving.

Seared Scallops with Balsamic Bacon Onion Jam
Serves 4

½ pound North Carolina bacon, diced
2 large sweet onions, sliced
½ cup Taste the Olive's Aged 18 Traditional Balsamic Vinegar
1 teaspoon freshly cracked pepper
2 tablespoons Taste the Olive's Garlic-Infused Extra-Virgin Olive Oil
1 pound large scallops
salt and pepper to taste

Seared Scallops with Balsamic Bacon Onion Jam
Photo courtesy of Taste the Olive Café & Wine Bar

In a medium pan, cook bacon until it begins to crisp. Remove and place on a plate lined with paper towels to drain. Drain all but 2 tablespoons of bacon drippings and add onions to pan. Reduce heat to low and cook onions until they start to caramelize; this could take up to 30 minutes. Add balsamic and pepper. Return bacon to pan and continue to cook about 5 minutes until balsamic reduces somewhat. Let cool while cooking scallops. Jam will thicken.

Heat a nonstick skillet over medium-high heat for 1 to 2 minutes. Add olive oil and heat until hot. Pat scallops dry and put them in pan in a single uncrowded layer. Season with salt and pepper and sear for 2 to 4 minutes until browned and crisp. Using tongs, turn scallops and sear another 2 to 4 minutes until second side is well browned and scallops are almost firm to the touch.

PRESENTATION

Transfer scallops to plates, top with Balsamic Bacon Onion Jam, and serve.

YOSAKE DOWNTOWN SUSHI LOUNGE

33 South Front Street

Wilmington, N.C. 28401

910-763-3172

yosake.com

Andrew C. Post

PHOTO COURTESY OF YOSAKE DOWNTOWN SUSHI LOUNGE

The Chef

Andrew C. Post

"Let's face it, the beach wins hands down in comparison to the icy-cold tundra that is Upstate New York."

Andrew Post came to Wilmington from Syracuse, where he lived for 23 years. He played guitar in an instrumental band named Coup de Grace, which booked gigs in Wilmington. He intended to remain for only a few months while performing, but "the whole vibe was so great, I decided to stay." That was seven years ago.

He started out working part-time as a dishwasher at "an amazing place in Syracuse called Alto Cinco," he says. "All the chefs that I worked with took me under their wings, and I was kind of their project. I was young and eager to work and learn. The chefs came from different culinary backgrounds and different parts of the world, so I got to dabble in a lot of different cuisines, Mexican and Caribbean most often. I eventually worked my way to the lead kitchen position and was in charge of day-to-day service and functionality of the restaurant. But I was only 22 at the time, and I was quickly burning myself out doing 80-hour workweeks and hardly touching my instruments. Playing music is my other passion in life. So I decided to pack it up and come to Wilmington to pursue music.

"I just busted my ass for years; that's how I learned to cook. I've worked under a lot of amazing chefs and done a lot of study on my own time. Between keeping my nose buried in cookbooks and obeying different chefs' demands, I think I've learned a lot, but when it comes to my own style, I like to have fun. I'm a food snob. I know what I like. Generally, I like to accentuate fresh local veggies, but I'm also a fan of robust flavors, so I try to find a happy medium between letting veggies speak for themselves and turning them into something totally different. I was a vegetarian for years, so I know how to develop flavor in the absence of proteins. I'm not knocking meat, but there's a whole lot that can be done without its presence."

Andrew has been at YoSake since he came to Wilmington. He rose from the line to sous chef, then was promoted to executive chef in 2014.

When he's not cooking professionally, he is a big fan of Mexican and Caribbean cuisines—as well as Spanish, Moroccan, and Asian. "As long as it's done right, I'm a fan," he says.

The Restaurant

YoSake Downtown Sushi Lounge

YoSake is exhilarating. Behind the sushi bar, bright red over black tile sets the tone, while aqua wood slats wall the space behind the regular bar. Big eyes in the large anime characters by local artist Sullivan Dunn observe the scene from the side brick walls. The original wood floors have been retained from the historic Roudabush Building. Pulsating techno music helps establish the ambience and fits the mood of the crowd.

YoSake is an Asian fusion restaurant featuring local produce and seafood. "We base all our food around what ingredients are available locally," Chef Post says. "We have a large sushi menu, and all our sushi sourcing and preparation strictly follows North Carolina health codes. This adds up to an array of different options that cater to anyone's interests. We try to have fun ourselves and create a fun atmosphere for our patrons, where both our staff and customers have a great experience and everyone walks away happy. We make all our food and all our cocktails from scratch, and we do our best to combine fun pairings with our menu items and featured items and our menu cocktails and featured cocktails.

"We have an array of local farmers that we communicate with on a weekly basis, but we also use a wonderful company called Feast Down East, which helps local farmers distribute their goods to local restaurants."

YoSake was voted Best New Restaurant by readers of *Encore* magazine. *Wilmington* magazine recognized it for "Best Happy Hour" in 2014.

The Recipes

Sambuca Grouper
Serves 4

4 6-ounce grouper fillets
salt and pepper to taste
1¼ cups fresh-squeezed orange juice, divided
1 cup quartered Yukon Gold potatoes
2 tablespoons extra-virgin olive oil
2 tablespoons diced garlic
2 tablespoons minced fresh ginger
¾ cup white onion, diced small
1 cup chopped celery
1 cup diced carrots
½ cup sambuca
¾ cup heirloom cherry tomatoes, halved
4 tablespoons fresh tarragon, plus a little extra for garnish
1 cup vegetable stock
4 tablespoons unsalted butter
zest of 1 orange

Sprinkle fillets with salt and pepper. Marinate in ¼ cup of the orange juice for 2 to 3 hours.

Roast potatoes for 15 minutes at 400 degrees. Swirl a sauté pan with olive oil, heat to medium, and sear service side of fillets. Flip fillets. Add garlic, ginger, and onions. Sauté about 1 more minute. Add celery, carrots, and roasted potatoes. Continue sautéing about 1 more minute. Deglaze pan with sambuca. Add tomatoes and tarragon. Continue sautéing

Sambuca Grouper

about 2 minutes. Add remaining orange juice and vegetable stock. Reduce by ½. Add butter and swirl until melted and blended in.

PRESENTATION

Place veggies in bowls. Place fillets on top. Garnish with orange zest and tarragon.

Hot and Cold Pork Noodles
Serves 4

CHEF'S NOTE "This is a great dish for a hot day on the Carolina coast, with cold noodles, citrus, and crunchy vegetables. The sugar in the sauce gives the pork a nice quick char that tastes great with everything."

½ cup sugar or palm sugar
zest and juice of 4 limes
4 dashes fish sauce
1 tablespoon chili garlic sauce
2 pounds pork shoulder, trimmed and cut into thin strips
14- to 16-ounce package rice noodles, cooked according to package directions
    and cooled
2 cups shredded carrots

Hot and Cold Pork Noodles
PHOTO COURTESY OF YOSAKE DOWNTOWN SUSHI LOUNGE

2 cups shredded cabbage
crunchy salad greens (preferably romaine), chopped rough
1 cup chopped peanuts
8 sprigs cilantro
20 mint leaves

Mix sugar, lime zest and juice, fish sauce, and chili garlic sauce until dissolved. Pour ½ of this dressing over pork and marinate for 1 hour.

Preheat grill to high. Grill pork to desired doneness (an internal temperature of 160 degrees is recommended). Mix noodles, carrots, cabbage, and remaining dressing in a bowl.

PRESENTATION
Spread salad greens on 4 plates. Add noodles on top. Top plates with pork and garnish with peanuts, cilantro, and mint.

JOSEPH'S ITALIAN BISTRO

5003 O'Quinn Boulevard

Southport, N.C. 28461

910-454-4440

Josephsitalianbistro.com

Joe Borsuk
Photo courtesy of
Joseph's Italian Bistro

JOSEPH

The Chef

Joe Borsuk

When Joe Borsuk was finally able to open his own restaurant, he brought in a chef he had admired all his life to help run the kitchen: his mother. Rosemarie "Mama Rose" Orlando Borsuk was the youngest of 11 children in a traditional Italian family. "She was always cooking," Joe recalls.

Growing up in California, Joe loved motorcycles, minibikes, dirt bikes— anything he could ride that had an engine. But he needed money to feed his fantasy. His aunt and uncle owned an Italian restaurant in Orange County, where Joe started washing dishes at about age 14. He rode his bicycle to work, but his parents had to pick him up in the car when he finished after dark. The dish area was so hot that he would get sick. He would sneak away and stand inside the walk-in refrigerator several times during his shift in order to "just breathe." But he loved it. He has been working in restaurants ever since.

The family moved to the Finger Lakes region of Upstate New York when Joe was 17. He soon found a job in the town of Skaneateles at The Krebs, a landmark restaurant that served family-style. "It was in an old house," he says. "The waitresses wore white uniforms, and the hostess was always dressed in a white linen gown. The building had letters framed from early settlers and travelers as far back as the 18th century. You could not drink in the dining room. You had to go upstairs to the bar. It was only open during the summer resort season."

Joe's younger brother enrolled at UNC-Wilmington. "I have no idea how he heard about a school that far away," Joe remembers. "One winter, he brought some friends up for skiing. Then he invited me to come to Wilmington for a restaurant job. That was in 1982. I loaded my clothes in the back of my Camaro, drove to the South, and never went back."

He worked at the Bridge Tender in Wrightsville Beach for about 10 years. "They were a very desirable location, and they were able to require everybody to go through a system. You had to start by washing dishes or busing tables in order to work your way up to a waiter position."

He was successful enough to be offered a management position when owners Jim Wright and David Nye decided to open Margaux's in Greenville, North Carolina. In another expansion, he moved to Top of the Hill, in the original Kidd Brewer home overlooking Crabtree Valley Mall in Raleigh. But the Raleigh location did not do well, partly due to the financial drain of maintaining the building itself. Both the Greenville and Raleigh restaurants closed. Then a hurricane flooded the Bridge Tender, and large sections had to be rebuilt. The partners decided not to renew their lease, and the restaurant transferred to new ownership.

Joe and several partners opened Locals in Wilmington. Locals lasted several years, until a friend and customer told them about a large property on Oak Island that he was developing. He wanted a restaurant there. "It sounded like a great opportunity and a change of scenery" for both Joe and his wife, Deb. Deb was tiring of the corporate world, so she retired and established the Village Market & Deli. Meanwhile, Joe ran the Fish Factory. All three of Deb's children often worked in both places. Joe soon started making plans for his dream of a more upscale restaurant, which became Joseph's. It was a boom time in the area. They sold the deli, focused on Joseph's, and rode an economic wave, developing a strong following with area residents and tourists.

During the off-season, Joe and Deb go to other restaurants. "We like Rx (see pages 304-6) especially," Joe says. "James Doss used to work for me before he went to culinary school in Charleston. I like to go there because I get things I don't get anywhere else." They also enjoy sushi.

The Restaurant

Joseph's Italian Bistro

Joseph's is located at Dutchman Creek on the Intracoastal Waterway. Outdoor seating is available on a large covered deck overlooking South Harbour Village Marina. The look is upscale but casual.

Joe made the transition from the front of the house to the kitchen while he was running Locals. At Joseph's, he wanted to establish a style that focused on the kind of labor-intensive Italian cooking he had experienced growing up. "I do all the ordering, I make all the sauces, and I also cook on the line, with help. The money is in the kitchen. That's where you make it or lose it." Preparing the base that becomes several sauces takes days. "We roast veal bones, then simmer them with onions, celery, and carrots, constantly reducing the liquid. Then it is strained. We make a roux and add that to thicken the base just before serving, combining it with Marsala wine for Chicken Marsala, for example."

Until recently, his mother worked every day. "She did a lot of the prep work. She would pound veal, bread cutlets, and make meatballs. When we first opened, she insisted on searching the area until we found a type of tomato that worked properly in her sauces. She eventually wrote down her recipes, but she always just cooked from memory before that. Debra makes the meatballs now. She is the only person allowed. Mom taught her directly."

The restaurant has always been an extended-family function. Joe's father recently retired from his dishwashing position at age 79. Joe's son helps on the line. During the summer, the restaurant is open seven days per week. The family goes from Memorial Day to Labor Day without taking time off.

"I try to look for what people like," Joe says. "We serve real food. The plates look beautiful, but they are not designed to be fancy. Just fresh and homemade."

As many ingredients as possible come from local sources. "We use Haag & Sons Seafood. I ordered from John Haag for years at the Bridge Tender. Talked to him on the phone several times a week, knew him 20 years. I finally met him in person when we opened this place. The seafood comes in every afternoon. There's a pan-seared grouper dish that is very popular with our regular customers; it's so good because the fish is so fresh. John knows to make sure I get the reddest tuna, the best swordfish. We also get produce and dairy products from Carolina Farmin' in Wilmington."

In 2010, Joe was the only chef from Southport named to the *Wilmington Star-News'* "Top 10 Chefs" list. In the People's Choice Awards, area residents voted Joseph's "Most Romantic," "Best Italian," "Best Meatballs," and "Best Service" in 2013 and 2014. Joe and Deb attribute much of their success to their longtime employees. "We have several people that have been with us since the beginning, and most others average six to eight years. We are a family here," Joe says.

Chicken Parmigiana
PHOTO COURTESY OF JOSEPH'S ITALIAN BISTRO

The Recipes

Chicken Parmigiana
Serves 6

Marinara Sauce
4 28-ounce cans whole, peeled Roma tomatoes
¼ cup extra-virgin olive oil
½ large onion, diced
2 tablespoons chopped garlic
2 tablespoons oregano
½ tablespoon kosher salt
½ tablespoon crushed pepper
½ cup white wine (Chablis, Chardonnay, or similar)
handful of fresh basil, chopped

Prepare tomatoes by emulsifying or mashing by hand. If using an emulsifier, don't overdo. You want some bits of tomato in the sauce. Set aside. Add olive oil and onions to a medium saucepan. Over medium-high heat, sweat onions until translucent. Add garlic, oregano, salt, and pepper and sauté about 2 minutes longer. Deglaze with wine and continue cooking, stirring occasionally, until spoon splits onions when scraping. Add tomatoes and simmer for 2 hours and 15 minutes. Add basil to sauce when done.

Chicken

2 cups panko breadcrumbs
¼ cup shredded Parmesan cheese
1 teaspoon chopped fresh basil
1 teaspoon chopped fresh oregano
1 teaspoon coarsely ground pepper
1 teaspoon kosher salt
3 eggs
1¼ cups half-and-half or milk
6 6-ounce chicken breasts, sliced lengthwise so each person gets 2 pieces (if
    thick, they will need to be pounded with a meat mallet)
enough flour to dredge chicken
vegetable oil to coat bottom of pan
2 cups shredded Mozzarella cheese
chopped fresh parsley
2 16-ounce packages linguine or angel hair pasta

Preheat oven to 425 degrees. Mix first 6 ingredients and set aside in a container big enough to dredge chicken. Beat eggs and half-and-half together. Rinse chicken and pat dry. Dredge chicken in flour. Dip in egg wash. Dredge in breadcrumb mixture. Set aside. In a large saucepan, add vegetable oil and heat on medium until a dab of flour sizzles when it hits oil. Add chicken and brown on both sides. Remove to paper towels until ready to assemble. Spray a baking dish with nonstick spray, then spread a layer of Marinara Sauce on the bottom. Arrange chicken on top of Marinara. Cover with Marinara, then mozzarella. Sprinkle parsley on top. Bake for about 15 minutes until mozzarella is bubbly and lightly browned.

So that pasta and chicken can be served hot at the same time, bring water for pasta to almost boiling before you put chicken in preheated oven. Once chicken is in oven, bring water to a boil and add pasta. If using angel hair, wait until chicken is almost ready before cooking.

PRESENTATION

Put sides of pasta on plates and ladle heated Marinara over top. Ladle Marinara on bottom of plates and arrange chicken on top. You may substitute veal or eggplant for the chicken, using the same method as above.

Frutta de Mare

Serves 4 to 6

Frutta de Mare

linguine or angel hair pasta
oil to coat bottom of pan
1½ tablespoons crushed garlic
2 tablespoons diced shallot
2 tablespoons chopped green onion (optional)
1 pound mussels
12 to 18 clams
¼ to ½ cup white wine (Chablis or Chardonnay)
½ pound calamari
1½ pounds fish (grouper, swordfish, tuna, or salmon), cut into bite-sized chunks
1 pound shrimp, peeled and deveined
Marinara Sauce (recipe on previous page)

Start water for pasta ahead so pasta is cooking when you begin to cook Frutta. In a large saucepan, heat oil to medium temperature. Add garlic, shallots, green onions, mussels, and clams. Cook until shells start to open. Add wine and cook for 3 to 4 minutes to deglaze pan. Add calamari, fish, and shrimp and cook until tender. Ladle in Marinara Sauce and simmer until nice and hot.

PRESENTATION

Serve mixture over pasta.

LIVE OAK CAFÉ

614 North Howe Street

Southport, N.C. 28461

910-454-4360

liveoakcafenc.com

Sean Mundy
PHOTO BY JENNIFER CHARRON

The Chef

Sean Mundy

"I consider myself fortunate to be a part of people's memories, be it a first date, a wedding reception, or an anniversary dinner."

Sean Mundy grew up helping his mother in the kitchen. "We used to watch shows together on PBS, like *Yan Can Cook* and *The Frugal Gourmet*, as well as Justin Wilson and Julia Child."

He went to North Carolina State University to study engineering and worked as a chef to pay the bills. But "after graduating, I couldn't pull myself away from the kitchen, so I decided to make a career out of it. I had the benefit of learning on the job from several very talented chefs who remain close friends."

Sean spent summers at Topsail Island with family when he was young. His wife Jennifer Charron grew up on the coast of Maine. "Although we were happy living in Raleigh, both of us wanted to be closer to the ocean of our childhoods. We explored the North Carolina coast, and we were intrigued by the Southport area. When we moved to Southport in 2000, we could see that the small-town atmosphere and spirit would remain, despite growth in the surrounding areas."

Reflecting on a life in food service, he notes that "the kitchen is where family congregates at home. Even in a workplace kitchen, family-like relationships are formed. I've always been captivated by how food brings people together. Food is not just about sustenance; it is about experience; it is about art. The more I learned about how to combine ingredients to create something memorable, the more hooked I became. Now, cooking is more than a job for me. I cook at home on days off. I cook when I visit family. I just cook. It's what I do.

"I like to cook what I like to eat. This means that traditional dishes are modified to fit my tastes as well as my mood. At any given point, you will find a mix of classic French, island cuisine, Pacific Rim, or Low Country, just to name a few, on our menu. I like to find the freshest ingredients of the season and then think of creative spins on classics such as meat loaf, but with North Carolina bison and a homemade lamb demi-glace, for example.

"Cooking at home allows for even more creativity and experimentation. It gives me a chance to try out new ideas and combinations for future menus. My favorite meal starts with fish I caught that morning and vegetables my wife grew in our garden."

The Restaurant

Live Oak Café

Chef Mundy describes his vision: "Live Oak Café is a place where friends and family can come together for the food you expect in a fine-dining establishment, but in a casual environment. We strive to be a place where you can get a great meal while being comfortable wearing shorts and sneakers. We purposely renovated antique English oak pub tables so that no white tablecloths are needed. The restaurant is in a renovated turn-of-the-century home with nine tables divided among three small dining rooms and a screened-in porch. Three of our tables were handcrafted by a well-known local artist, Thom Seaman. We hope that guests feel the same comfort they would eating at a friend's house while still enjoying excellent cuisine. Our tag line, 'Creative cuisine in a cozy atmosphere,' sums it up nicely.

"My wife and I renovated the home with the help of family and friends over the course of nine months. We removed drop ceilings in favor of bead board and pulled up carpet to expose the original heart-pine floors. A book of photos in our lobby records the process."

Live Oak uses local produce whenever possible. "We currently order a number of seasonal items from Carolina Farmin' and source fish from North Carolina whenever we can get it. We also feature North Carolina–raised bison and rainbow trout."

Articles featuring Live Oak Café have appeared in the *Wilmington Star-News*, *Wilmington* magazine, *Focus on the Coast* magazine, and *North Carolina Boating*.

Chef Mundy is especially proud of the stability of the Live Oak staff. "We are lucky to have a server who has been with us since we opened in 2002 and a sous chef who has been with us since 2004."

The Recipes

Gorgonzola-Stuffed Portobello Mushrooms with Shrimp Velouté
Serves 6

CHEF'S NOTE "This recipe was born from a way to use leftover risotto, but it was so popular it became a crowd favorite with a permanent place on the menu."

Shrimp Velouté
¾ cup diced leeks, divided
1½ teaspoons minced garlic, divided
salt and pepper to taste
2 cups shrimp stock
¼ cup heavy cream
3 tablespoons unsalted butter
3 tablespoons all-purpose flour
¼ cup diced bacon
8 to 10 large shrimp, tails removed, chopped, and seasoned
2 to 3 tablespoons white wine
½ cup diced Roma tomato
½ teaspoon fresh thyme

Sprinkle ¼ cup of the leeks and ½ teaspoon of the garlic lightly with salt and pepper. In a medium-sized pot over medium-high heat,

Gorgonzola-Stuffed
Portobello Mushrooms
with Shrimp Velouté
PHOTO BY SEAN MUNDY

sauté leeks and garlic until translucent. Add stock and cream. Bring to a boil, then turn down heat and simmer for 10 minutes. While stock is simmering, make a roux. In a small sauté pan, melt butter over medium heat. Turn heat to low and whisk in flour a little at a time, avoiding lumps. Cook for 2 minutes, stirring constantly. Whisk roux into simmering stock; continue to whisk until smooth. Simmer for 10 to 15 minutes, stirring occasionally to make sure no lumps form.

In a large sauté pan over medium-high heat, cook bacon. When bacon just starts to crisp, add remainder of leeks and remainder of garlic and sauté for 1 minute. Add seasoned shrimp and cook for 2 minutes until about halfway done. Deglaze pan with wine and add stock mixture. Turn heat to low and simmer mixture another 2 minutes until shrimp are fully cooked. Mix tomatoes and thyme into mixture. Set aside and keep warm.

Stuffed Mushrooms
½ cup diced shallots
2 tablespoons unsalted butter
2 tablespoons olive oil
1 tablespoon minced garlic
1 cup Arborio rice
¼ cup white wine
3 cups chicken stock, warmed
salt and pepper to taste
½ cup crumbled Gorgonzola cheese
6 medium to large portobello mushrooms, stems and gills removed
shredded asiago cheese
fresh parsley

In a large, heavy-bottomed pot over high heat, sauté shallots in butter and olive oil until translucent. Add garlic and dry rice. Lightly toast rice for 1 to 2 minutes. Add wine and continue to simmer for 5 to 8 minutes until wine reduces by ½. Reduce heat to medium. Start adding warmed chicken stock 1 cup at a time, stirring occasionally. When almost all liquid has been absorbed, add another ½ cup stock. Continue to simmer and stir, adding stock until all liquid has been used and rice is fully cooked. Season with salt and pepper and stir in Gorgonzola.

Preheat oven to 350 degrees. Fill mushroom caps with ¼ to ½ cup risotto and place on a baking sheet. Bake mushrooms for 10 to 12 minutes.

PRESENTATION

Place 1 mushroom per plate and top with ½ cup Shrimp Velouté. Garnish with asiago and parsley.

Grilled Shrimp and Scallop Salad with Blood Orange Vinaigrette

Serves 4

Blood Orange Vinaigrette

½ cup blood orange juice
½ teaspoon minced garlic
1 teaspoon Dijon mustard
2 tablespoons local honey
¾ cup extra-virgin olive oil
salt and pepper to taste

Pour orange juice into a deep medium-sized bowl. Add garlic, Dijon, and honey. Using an immersion blender, start mixing ingredients. Slowly pour olive oil into bowl in a steady stream until all oil is incorporated. Season with salt and pepper and adjust to taste with more honey.

Grilled Shrimp and Scallop Salad

12 jumbo shrimp
12 jumbo scallops
¼ cup olive oil
1 tablespoon paprika
1 tablespoon minced garlic

Grilled Shrimp and Scallop Salad with Blood Orange Vinaigrette
PHOTO BY ANNE MCGOWAN

salt and pepper to taste
2 heads hydroponic Bibb lettuce
4 cups local mixed salad greens
1 pint local grape tomatoes
1 cup Bermuda sweet onion, sliced thin
1 cup hearts of palm, sliced into rounds
1½ cups canned artichoke hearts, quartered
1 cup crumbled feta cheese

Preheat grill to high. Coat shrimp and scallops with olive oil and toss with paprika, garlic, and salt and pepper. Place seafood on grill. Grill shrimp for 2 to 3 minutes per side and scallops for 4 to 5 minutes per side, rotating them 90 degrees halfway through. Scallops may take a little more time, depending on size and desired doneness. Remove from grill when finished and keep warm.

PRESENTATION

Portion out Bibb lettuce on plates. In a large bowl, toss mixed greens with Blood Orange Vinaigrette, then place on top of Bibb lettuce. Divide and place remaining ingredients around salads artfully. Drizzle more Blood Orange Vinaigrette around salads as desired. Arrange shrimp and scallops 3 each on top of finished salads.

MR. P'S BISTRO

309 North Howe Street

Southport, N.C. 28461

910-457-0801

mrpsbistro.com

Stephen Phipps
PHOTO BY CHRIS SMITH

The Chef

Stephen Phipps

Stephen Phipps describes himself as an outdoorsman. He has lived in Southport for 30 years. He enjoys hunting and fishing and feels connected to the land and the beaches. In particular, he likes the people and the food of the area.

Stephen started cooking professionally at age 16 in Southport. "I come from a restaurant family," he explains. His father's aunt owned Faircloth's Oyster Roast in Wrightsville Beach. His father, Norman Phipps, was a famous restaurant owner in the region who, with other family members, founded Mr. P's about 20 years ago. By the time Stephen finished his teens, he knew he wanted to be a chef. He went to culinary school at Johnson & Wales, graduating from the Charleston campus in 1986.

He spent some time cooking in several country clubs in South Carolina, then moved to Wilmington, where he worked at the Pilot House. He returned home to Southport in 1993 to take over the kitchen at Mr. P's. Other family members are involved as well.

His style, based on local ingredients, was influenced by his time in the South Carolina Low Country but is grounded in coastal North Carolina, with a little New Orleans showing up as well, especially in oyster preparations. Chef Phipps takes special delight in preparing things on a whim or by request. "If you don't see it on the menu, I'll fix it. We customize a lot for customers," he reports.

At home, he is devoted to Southern seafood, oysters being a particular passion. He considers duck "the best thing ever" when it is prepared well.

The Restaurant

Mr. P's Bistro

Mr. P's has always been a family operation. General management is provided by Chris Smith, Norman Phipps's son-in-law. Chris received a degree in restaurant management from Cape Fear Community College. He interned at Mr. P's and now oversees administrative and service responsibilities.

The restaurant lives by the motto, "Cuisine of the Lower Cape Fear." Weekly and daily specials are based on fresh seafood catches and connections with local farms.

Chef Phipps's seafood and prime rib have a devoted following. Seafood platters, broiled or blackened as well as fried, are popular. But his cooking is seasonal. Duck, veal, lamb, steaks, and other beef preparations are usually on the menu.

Most seafood comes from Haig & Sons on nearby Oak Island. "I've been dealing with John Haag way over 20 years. He has been in the fish business even longer than that," Chef Phipps says. He also works with Shelton Herb Farm; the Sheltons grow lettuces as well. Oysters are sourced locally in season, as are softshell crabs and shad roe. The restaurant's website provides updated information about what is fresh and local.

From 2008 to 2012, readers of *Brunswick Marketplace News* voted Mr. P's "Best Restaurant" in Brunswick County; in 2014, they named it "Best Bistro."

Oysters Bienville
Photo by Chris Smith

The Recipes

Oysters Bienville
Serves 6

1 cup unsalted butter
2 cups chopped shallots
½ cup chopped parsley
1 tablespoon chopped garlic
1 cup all-purpose flour
2 cups milk
2 cups half-and-half
1 pound shrimp, cooked and chopped
1 cup chopped mushrooms
2 teaspoons salt
2 teaspoons white pepper
½ teaspoon cayenne pepper
½ cup sherry
10 egg yolks
3 dozen medium oysters

In a pot over medium heat, melt butter, then add shallots, parsley, and garlic. Sauté until soft or translucent. Add flour a little at a time, stirring constantly. Cook with mixture slightly bubbling until it turns light brown. Add milk and half-and-half. Stir. Add shrimp and mushrooms and stir until thickened. Combine salt, white pepper, and cayenne. Mix sherry with egg yolks. Stir salt and pepper mixture into sherry mixture. Add to flour mixture and cook on stovetop until thick and bubbly. Pour into a shallow pan and chill for several hours.

PRESENTATION

Place a spoonful of topping on oysters on the half shell and broil until hot.

Lemon Blueberry Cheesecake

Yields 1 cheesecake

Crust
1 cup graham cracker crumbs
4 tablespoons butter, melted
½ cup sugar

Combine ingredients in a mixing bowl. Pack mixture into a 9-inch springform pan.

Cheesecake
4 8-ounce blocks cream cheese, room temperature
1½ cups sugar
5 eggs
juice of 2 lemons
1 pint blueberries
whipped cream

Using a heavy-duty mixer, combine cream cheese and sugar until creamy. Continue mixing while adding eggs 1 at a time. Add lemon juice. Gently stir in most of blueberries, saving a handful. Pour mixture over crust

Lemon Blueberry Cheesecake

and place remaining berries on top of cake for decoration.

Preheat oven to 325 degrees. Bake mixture in a water bath in oven for 1½ hours. Remove and let cool until it settles, then refrigerate for several hours. Remove pan after cheesecake is chilled.

PRESENTATION

Top with whipped cream and serve.

William "Billy" Wilkins
PHOTO BY JILL BROWN

YACHT BASIN EATERY

122 Yacht Basin Drive

Southport, N.C. 28461

910-363-4108

yachtbasineatery.us

The Chef

William "Billy" Wilkins

Billy Wilkins was hired as a busboy at the King's Ransom in Waldwick, New Jersey, when he was 13. "My busboy career was short-lived, though, because I was constantly in the kitchen watching the chef and asking a million questions," he reports. "After two weeks, the head waitress came into the kitchen and caught me hanging around the chef again. She pointed to the back door and yelled 'Get out!' Chef Ludwig jumped up from his stool and said in his thick German accent, 'Oh, no, he works for me now!' And that began my apprenticeship in the kitchen."

Although he is from Midland Park, New Jersey, Billy spent his childhood summers on the North Carolina coast. His grandmother was a native North Carolinian, and he often stayed with his grandparents on the Outer Banks or in

Wrightsville Beach. He began cooking as a child with his mother, grandmothers, great-grandmothers, and neighborhood grandmothers. "Anyone who would allow me to help them in the kitchen had my attention.

"I remained with Chef Ludwig through high school and two years beyond. Then I went to Alderson Broaddus College in West Virginia, where I studied business and ran a pizza delivery business out of the school commissary in the evenings. After graduation, I was hired by Gilbert and Robinson, a chain-restaurant company, as a kitchen assistant in Raleigh. After one month, they promoted me to kitchen manager and sent me to Kansas City to attend their corporate restaurant management school. After completing my training, I returned to Raleigh and was placed in charge of two Raleigh locations and one Durham location. While I became proficient at the corporate management side of the business, I also became disillusioned and frustrated with the lack of creative opportunity the role provided.

"So I put out my résumé and was hired by Chef Wes Smithe at the North Ridge Country Club in Raleigh. I studied under him for about a year. Chef Wes was a corporate chef with Club Management Resources, whose business was operating private clubs. The company promoted me to executive chef and sent me to Hickory, North Carolina, as an interim chef. After six months in Hickory, I was assigned to my own country club in Winchester, Virginia. I remained there as executive chef for two years.

"Then I returned to New Jersey and started my own landscaping business in the day, working evenings at Steaks and Stuff in Mahwah. I grew my landscaping business and expanded into excavating, and eventually into new home construction.

"About that time, I got married and left the restaurant industry. I spent some time in a situation that was focused on money and material possessions. A divorce and another marriage kept me away from the food industry for about 16 years. Then my father became very ill with cancer. On his deathbed, he told me to follow my passion in life and go back to being a chef. I decided that I had been away from what I truly loved for too long, so I got another divorce and returned to the restaurant business.

"I started working at Zocco's Italian Ristorante in Hillsdale, New Jersey, as sous chef. I stayed there for about a year and a half. In 2008, I reunited with my childhood love, Mia Rodriguez, whom my father always called the 'catty-cornered girl next door,' and through her I was reacquainted with another childhood friend, Jill Brown, who is now my business partner. Jilli was talking about relocating to North Carolina and opening a bar. I said, 'Hey, make it a bar/restaurant and I'll go with you.' What was born from a backyard barbecue conversation became a reality in 12 months' time. We opened the doors of the Yacht Basin Eatery in August 2011."

The Restaurant

Yacht Basin Eatery

As its name suggests, the Yacht Basin Eatery is located in the old yacht basin in Southport. The main dining area is a covered deck that sits over the water facing directly west, so the sunset views are breathtaking. Diners can see reflections from the water through the deck boards below their feet. The Cape Fear River, the entrance to the Intracoastal Waterway, and the channel inlet from the Atlantic Ocean converge within view of the restaurant. The Oak Island Lighthouse is directly across the water from the dining area. Dolphins, otters, eagles, and ospreys make frequent appearances.

"Our tag line says it all," Chef Wilkins says: " 'All Day Comfort Food.' Our menu is diverse. You could eat with us every day and have a different style of food at each meal. Our food is always fresh and prepared in-house. We make most everything from scratch.

"We wanted to introduce something different to Southport. We got a lot of flak from customers at the start. People said we should have opened a seafood restaurant, even though seafood restaurants surround us. We have plenty of seafood, but we provide other options as well—deli sandwiches, grill sandwiches, pizza, stromboli, pasta, veal, chicken sauté dishes, plus chops and steaks. We stayed our course, and our success demonstrates that our concept has been well received.

"I express my emotions through food. I cook and create in the kitchen to show my love for people. I thrive on giving people pleasure through the food that I create for them. I would describe my style as rustic European with an emphasis on Northern Italian. My philosophy is to use the best ingredients available and cross-utilize them into various creations. I will not serve anything that I would not eat myself."

The Yacht Basin Eatery is a member of Brunswick Catch. Almost all of the seafood served is caught by local fishermen. A majority of the produce comes from Southport's two fresh produce stands.

Grouper Florentine
PHOTO BY JILL BROWN

The Recipes

Grouper Florentine
Serves 2 to 4

2 cups all-purpose flour
1 teaspoon sea salt
1 teaspoon freshly ground pepper
1 teaspoon granulated garlic
6 eggs
1½ cups heavy cream, divided
2 cups penne pasta
1 cup extra-virgin olive oil
8 to 10 ounces grouper fillets
1 tablespoon minced garlic
1 tablespoon minced red onion
¼ pound lobster knuckles and claws
¼ pound bay scallops
¼ pound baby spinach
3 tablespoons unsalted butter, softened, divided
1 cup sherry

Mix flour, sea salt, pepper, and garlic with a dry fork. Set aside. Whisk together eggs and ½ cup of the cream. Set aside. Cook pasta according to package directions. Keep warm. Heat olive oil over high heat in a 12-inch sauté pan. Dredge fillets in flour mixture, coating all sides. Place fillets in egg mixture, rotating bowl to coat. Avoid touching with hands. Remove fillets using tongs and place directly in hot oil. Cook for 3 to 4 minutes until golden brown. Turn fillets and brown other side. Remove from pan and drain oil. Do not wash pan. Reduce heat to medium. Return fillets to pan. Add garlic, onions, lobster, scallops, spinach, and 1 tablespoon of the butter. Melt butter. Increase heat until sizzling. Add sherry, wait 20 seconds, and add remaining 1 cup cream and remainder of butter. Reduce heat to a gentle boil and allow sauce to reduce by approximately ½.

PRESENTATION

Place fillets in center of plates over pasta. Place lobster on top. Surround with other ingredients.

Zuppa Di Pesce

Serves 2 to 4

2 cups pasta (your choice)
2 tablespoons extra-virgin olive oil
2 tablespoons chopped garlic
1 tablespoon chopped red onion
8 ounces white fish (grouper recommended)
6 large shrimp, peeled and deveined
2 whole calamari, cut into ½-inch rounds, tentacles left whole
6 fresh clams in shells
6 fresh mussels in shells
1½ cups chopped clams in juice (canned or jarred)
½ cup white wine
12-ounce can plum tomatoes in juice
½ teaspoon dried oregano
½ teaspoon dried basil
3 fresh basil leaves

Cook pasta according to package directions. Keep warm. Heat olive oil in a 12-inch sauté pan over medium-high heat. Add garlic and onions and sauté until translucent. Add next 7 ingredients and bring to

Zuppa Di Pesce
PHOTO BY JILL BROWN

a simmer. Add tomatoes with juice and return to a simmer. Add oregano and dried basil. Simmer for 6 to 7 minutes until fish is tender and white and shells begin to open. Smash tomatoes. Add basil leaves. Continue simmering until basil wilts and clams have fully opened.

PRESENTATION

Serve immediately over pasta.

CALABASH

Calabash is a village in the southeastern corner of the North Carolina coast. Known in the 19th century as Pea Landing for its role in peanut shipping, it became Calabash when residents chose that name in applying for a post office. The name of the town comes from an Indian word meaning *gourd*, perhaps reflecting the shape of the Calabash River nearby.

Calabash has developed a huge following for its unique style of seafood preparation. That style originated when fishing boats returned with their catches. Friends and neighbors would gather on the docks, share some of what they had caught, and cook together. Over time, the tradition grew into what were called "fish camps"—small properties that served local seafood to both neighbors and visitors. Actual restaurants emerged during and after World War II.

By tradition, shrimp and flounder are the top seafood choices in Calabash. Oysters, deviled crab, and clams are popular as well. In the Calabash style, these are lightly coated with cornmeal and sometimes with a little extra pepper or spice to add kick. Some recipes call for soaking in buttermilk first. Frying is the only way traditional Calabash-style seafood is cooked. Coleslaw and French fries are the usual accompaniments. Abundant servings are one hallmark. Freshness is another. High value due to moderate prices rounds out the Calabash tradition.

Early Calabash restaurants were founded by local families and continue to be operated if not by the founders, then by their descendants or family members.

Beck's (1014 River Road; 910-579-6776; becksrestaurant.com), established in 1940, is considered the first actual restaurant in Calabash. Calabash Seafood Hut (1125 River Road; 910-579-6723) is reputed to be the second-oldest. Coleman's Original Calabash (9931 Nance Street; 910-579-6875) is a sister restaurant to Calabash Seafood Hut. Ruth Beck and Lucy Coleman, these restaurants' founders, were sisters. Local legend holds that when famous singer Jimmy Durante closed his shows with the sign-off, "Good night, Mrs. Calabash, wherever you are," he was paying homage to his meals in Calabash, where he called Lucy Coleman "Mrs. Calabash."

Ella's of Calabash (1148 River Road; 910-579-6776) was started by Ella and Lawrence High in 1950. The Price family opened The Dockside Seafood House (9955 Nance Street; 910-579-6775; thedocksideseafoodhouse.com) in 1955. Captain John Frink and his wife, Pearl, opened Captain John's Seafood House (9887 Oak Street; 910-579-6011) in 1976. He was captain of the *Thunderbird II* fishing boat. The owners of Captain Nance's (9939 Nance Street; 910-579-2574) are related to the Beck and Coleman families by marriage. Captain Nance's has been in operation for over 25 years.

A serious fire burned Coleman's in August 2014, but plans to rebuild were under way quickly. This was the most recent of several fires, bad storms, and hurricanes that have challenged the restaurants and residents of Calabash over the years.

This is by no means a comprehensive guide to all the restaurants in Calabash. In fact, several dozen restaurants are in the town. But these started the traditions. Some have websites, but most do not. As one owner told me, "the Internet is kind of new down here."

Note: Some of the above information came from a Steven Roberts travel article (nytimes.com/1983/08/28/travel/in-calabash-nc-it-s-seafood-aplenty.html), an article by Paul Stephen of the *Wilmington Star-News* (newsobserver.com/2014/10/02/4196539_calabash-restaurants-survive-changes.html?rh=1), and the Brunswick County travel website (ncbrunswick.com).

Index of Recipes

with Chablis Dill Sauce, 210-11
Charred Tuna, 34-35
Flounder Meunière, 148-49
Ginger-Seared Tuna with Lemon-Garlic
  Sautéed Purple Kale over Fruit Couscous
  and Quinoa, 252-53
Gingered Salmon, 7-8
Grilled Salmon over Wilted Kale with
  Roasted Sweet Potatoes and BBQ Peaches,
  40-41
Grilled Tuna Oscar, 131-32
Grouper Florentine, 340-41
Grouper Royale, 247-48
Mediterranean Flounder, 277-78
Mixed Seafood Grill with Cilantro-Lime
  Vinaigrette and Caribbean-Style Black
  Beans, 232-33
OBX Tuna, Tomato, Tomatillo, Grilled
  Okra, and Mojo de Ajo, 288-89
Pan-Blackened Red Drum with Black Bean
  and Corn Salsa, 110-11
Pan-Seared Grouper with Local Organic
  Ratatouille, 308-9
Pan-Seared Wahoo with Summer Succotash,
  111-12
Pecan Fish, 224-25
Red Snapper with Dijon Glaze and Heirloom
  Tomato, Corn, and Crab Relish, 189-90
Rockfish Ceviche, 51-52
Sambuca Grouper, 317-18
Seared Tuna Fillet over Jasmine Rice and
  Snow Peas, with Watermelon Salsa and
  Goat Cheese, 84-86
Tartare of Pepper-Crusted Yellowfin Tuna
  with Whole-Grain Mustard and Apple-
  wood Bacon Aioli, Chives, and Pumper-
  nickel Toast, 15-16
Teriyaki-Glazed Gulfstream Fish with Citrus
  Salsa, 76-78
Tuna Ceviche, 142-43
Tuna Sashimi, 59-60
Tuna Sashimi, 103-4

Fried Green Tomatoes:
Fried Green Tomato Tower with Fresh
  Mozzarella, Crispy Smoked Bacon, Green
  Tomato Chutney, Rosemary Honey, and
  Salted Pecans, 267-69

Pork:
Cider-Brined Pork Tenderloin with Vanilla
  Whipped Sweet Potatoes, 116-18
Grilled Heritage Pork Chop and Collards,
  296-97
Hot and Cold Pork Noodles, 318-19
JK's Baby Back Ribs, 70-71
Pepsi-Brined Heritage Pork Tenderloin with
  Bacon-Braised Collards and Sweet Potato

Purée, 163-65
Pork Belly Roulade with Ragout of Butter
  Beans, Corn, Padron Peppers, Smoked
  Paprika, and Sherry Vinaigrette, 290-91
Pork Tenderloin with Bourbon or Cognac
  Butter Sauce, 177-78

Risotto:
Collard Green–Parmesan Risotto, 190-91
Pea, Corn, and Bacon Risotto, 83
Risotto with Butter-Poached Lobster, Leeks,
  Pistachio Nuts, and Mascarpone, 302-3

Salads:
Aunt Marion's Apple and Onion Salad,
  176-77
Caprese Salad with Blueberry Basil Vinai-
  grette, 82-83
Crab Salad Caprese, 130-31
Fruit Couscous and Quinoa, 252
Grilled Shrimp and Scallop Salad with Blood
  Orange Vinaigrette, 330-31
Roasted Beet and Herbed Chèvre "Napo-
  leon," 182-83
Tabouelleh, 278

Sauces:
Apple Butter Sauce, 117-18
Beurre Blanc Sauce, 247
Ceviche Sauce, 142
Chablis Dill Sauce, 210-11
Chili Sauce, 231
Garlic Prawn Sauce, 190
Gruyère Sauce, 152
Lobster Cream Sauce, 159
Marinara Sauce, 323-24
Mushroom Curry Sauce, 199
Raspberry Sauce, 240
Red Wine–Caramel Sauce, 147
Roasted Red Bell Pepper Coulis, 28-29
Shrimp Velouté, 328-29
Tasso Gravy, 204-5
Teriyaki Sauce, 76

Scallops:
Bacon-Wrapped Scallops with Red Wine–
  Caramel Sauce, 147-48
Carteret Catch Grouper and Sea Scallops
  with Chablis Dill Sauce, 210-11
Chorizo Cheesecake with Shrimp and Scal-
  lops in Lobster Cream Sauce, 158-59
Icarus Pasta, 93-94
Pan-Seared Sea Scallops with Bacon Jalapeño
  Jam, 237-38
Scallops Casino, 33
Scalloped Scallops, 234
Seared Scallops over Pea, Corn, and Bacon

Risotto, 83-84
Seared Scallops with Balsamic Bacon Onion Jam, 313-14
Seared Sea Scallops in Penne Pasta, 183-84
Shrimp and Scallops with Collard Green–Parmesan Risotto and Garlic Prawn Sauce, 190-91

Shellfish:
Baked Oysters with Onion Bacon Jam and Creamed Collards, 196-97
Clams with Guajillo Chilies and Chorizo, 230-32
Frutta de Mare, 325
JK's Baked Oysters Rockefeller, 71-72
Mixed Seafood Grill with Cilantro-Lime Vinaigrette and Caribbean-Style Black Beans, 232-33
Oysters Bienville, 334-35
Oyster Stew, 136-37
Seafood Paella, 56-57
Thai Shellfish Hot Pot with Lo Mein Noodles, 42-43

Shrimp:
Buffalo Shrimp, 246
Chilled Poached Shrimp-Tomato Relish, 270
Chorizo Cheesecake with Shrimp and Scallops in Lobster Cream Sauce, 158-59
Herb-Grilled Shrimp with Black-Eyed Pea Succotash, 188-89
Herb Shrimp Tapenade, 254
Icarus Pasta, 93-94
Pecan Shrimp, 162-63
Shrimp and Chorizo Alfredo with Roasted Poblano and Sun-Dried Tomato Pesto, 97-99
Shrimp and Crab al Fresco, 156
Shrimp and Fried Grits Cake, 215
Shrimp and Grits, 105-6, 203-4
Shrimp and Grits with Andouille Sausage, 137-38
Shrimp and Orzo Gratin, 284-85
Shrimp and Prosciutto Pasta, 169-71
Shrimp and Scallops with Collard Green–Parmesan Risotto and Garlic Prawn Sauce, 190-91
Shrimp Curry, 58-59
Shrimp Scampi "Clean," 35-36
Shrimp with Andouille Sausage over Grits, 6-7

Soups, Stews, and Chowders:
Carolina Bouillabaisse, 124-25
Cioppino, 223-24
Conch Chowder, 222-23
Cream of Asparagus Soup with Hot Buttered Blue Crab, White Truffle Oil, and Garlic Breadcrumbs, 14-15
Frutta de Mare, 325
Lobster Bisque, 102-3
North Carolina Bouillabaisse, 274-77
Oyster Stew, 136-37
She Crab "A la Minute," 20-21
Spicy Saffron Cioppino with Wild Rice, 171-72
Watermelon Gazpacho with Carolina Peanuts, Feta Cheese, and Mint, 300-301
Zuppa Di Pesce, 341-42

Starches:
Grits, 6
Noodles, 60
Stone-Ground Cheese Grits, 106

Stocks, Bases:
Demi-Glace, 170
Fish Stock, 275

Vegetables:
Bacon-Braised Collards, 163-64
Butterbeans, 296
Butterbean Hummus, 307
Caribbean-Style Black Beans, 232
Celery Root Purée with Beets and Apples, 217
Collards, 297
Creamed Collards, 196
Green Beans, 206
Lemon-Garlic Sautéed Purple Kale, 253
Local Organic Ratatouille, 308-9
Mashed Potatoes, 206
Summer Succotash, 111
Vanilla Whipped Sweet Potatoes, 118

Vegetarian Entrees:
Gorgonzola Stuffed Portabella Mushroom with Shrimp Velouté, 328-30
Oven-Roasted Tomato Pie, 168-69
Thai Ginger-Peanut Zoodles with Crushed Peanuts and Chopped Cilantro, 42
Tomato Tartelette, 257-58
Tostones with Black Bean Purée, Goat Cheese, and Truffle Honey, 52-5

Index of Names

Grissom, K.J., 186
Groce, Edward and Tom, 101
Gruninger, Bud, 107-10

Haag, John, 322, 333
Haithcock, Troy, 306
Harris, Hunter, 19
Harris, Susan, 19
Hartman, Craig, 49
Hartmann, Stefan, 306
Herring, Dave, 305
High, Ella, 344
High, Lawrence, 344
Hogan, Patrick, 236
Holmes, Bob, xi
Homcy, John, 68-70
Homcy, Matt, 68-70
Hopper, Andy, 167
Hoveland, Carolyn, 155
Hoveland, Chris, 155
Hoveland, Shawn, 154-56
Howard, Hallock, 228-30
Howard, Sandy, 229
Howerin, Ken, 95
Humphries, Todd, 49
Hunt, Helen, 127
Hyman, Kenny, 44-46
Hyman, Melissa, 44-46

Ivey, Esther, 306
Ivey, Marlowe, 306

Jackson, B.J., 3
Janette, John, 244
Joyce, James, 63
Jurich, Todd, 18
Just, Charles, 192

Karole, Tommy, 26
King, Don, xii
Keller, Thomas, 48, 266
Kelly, Mike, 30, 74, 121-23
Kingery, William, 220-21
Kneasel, Ron, 110
Kristof, Matt, 12

Lachine, Johanna, 114-16
Lachine, Justin, 114-16
LaLaeut, Marc, 166-67
Landazuri, Alfredo R., 100-02
Lane, Jeff, 61-63
Lewis, Donnie and Beverly, 175
"Little Ann," 13
Long, Gene, 279, 294
Louchen, Michael, 298
Lozupone, Tom, 101
Ludwig, "Chef", 337-38

Maguire, Luke Daniel, 228-30

Mahoney, Mike, 236
Martin, Alison, 96
Maultsby, Laurel, xii
McAusland, Earl, 24
McClary, Dave, 49
McClelland, Scott, 229
McCullough, Fran, xi
McCune, Fred, 167-68
McCune, Joyce, 167-68
McClure, Joey, 167-68
McDonald, Heather, 12
McGann, Sam, 17-20, 49
McGregor, Jon, 200-204
McMillan, Michael, 244
Mackenzie, Christina, 80-81
Magruder, Mac, 69
Martin, Richard Aaron, 249-52
Martin, Steve, 155
Melvin, Colleen, 139
Merrell, Clarke, 212-14
Merrell, Liza, 212-13
Meurin, Marc, 167
Meyer, Scott, 81
Miller, Becky, 123
Miller, Bryan, 256
Miller, Lee, 122
Mills, Tom, 287
Mellon, William, 287-88
Mina, Michael, 48
Minnich, Jennifer, 44-46
Minnich, John, 44-46
Moity, Patricia, 255-57
Moity, Thierry, 255-57
Montaigne, Michel de, 146
Montero, Andy, 3-5
Montero, Anna, 4
Montero, Claire, 4
Montero, Emma, 4
Montero, Karin, 3-5
Montiel, Michael, 38-40, 87
Montiel, Tamara, 40
Moody, Shannon, 128
Moore, Bill, 294
Moore, Tina, 294
Morrell, John, 73
Mull, Jennifer, 186-87
Mundy, Sean, 326-28

Neal, Moreton, 299
Nelson, Steve, 141-142
Noble, Jim, 298, 305
Norfleet, J.K., 68-70
Novicki, Josh, 305
Nye, David, 321

O'Connell, Kevin, 287
O'Connell, Patrick, 116
Oaks, Charles, 186
Ortega, Abigail, 96